Citizens Defending America

Citizens Defending America

From Colonial Times to the Age of Terrorism

MARTIN ALAN GREENBERG

With a Foreword by John B. Wilt, Colonel (Retired), U.S. Air Force Reserve

UNIVERSITY OF PITTSBURGH PRESS

Published by the University of Pittsburgh Press,
Pittsburgh, PA 15260

Copyright © 2005, University of Pittsburgh Press

Manufactured in the United States of America

Printed on acid-free paper

10 9 8 7 6 5 4 3 2 1

Library of Congress Cataloging-in-Publication Data
Greenberg, Martin Alan.
  Citizens defending America : from colonial times to the age of ter-
rorism / Martin Alan Greenberg ; with a foreword by John B. Wilt.
      p. cm.
  Includes bibliographical references and index.
  ISBN 0-8229-4264-X (hardcover : alk. paper)
  1. Volunteer workers in law enforcement—United States—History.
2. Crime prevention—United States—Citizen participation—His-
tory. 3. National security—United States—Citizen participation—
History. 4. Community policing—United States—History. I. Title.
  HV8135.G74 2005
  363.2—dc22
                        2005004965

*This book is dedicated to
the memory of my friend Gary Morgan.*

CONTENTS

FOREWORD

In *Citizens Defending America,* Martin Greenberg presents a history of the important role citizens have played in defending America as volunteers in state militias, as well as in federal- and municipal-level security forces. He describes and analyzes America's long history of volunteer participation in enforcement of the criminal law, and in some cases military defense, through a wide variety of institutions with greatly varying objectives, organizational structures, tactics, and results. Detailing how most volunteer police have operated within the legal boundaries of their communities, Greenberg offers a very useful definition of *volunteer police,* along with a fourfold typology of such forces (proactive, reactive, general, and special purpose) that serves to guide the reader through an interesting maze of "legally sanctioned" volunteer police examples.

Citizens Defending America is an excellent contribution to the literature on community policing and justice studies. The author has compiled several hundred years of criminal justice history, organizing volunteer police events into several eras: the "lay justice" era, the "vigilant" era, the "spy" era, the "transformation" era, and the "assimilation" era. While these eras are useful for thinking about the history of volunteer policing, it must be emphasized that they have only approximately defined termini, with some degree of overlap. Of equal significance are Greenberg's numerous examples of how volunteer policing has played a crucial role in preserving U.S. democratic ideals during periods of insecurity, natural disaster, declared war, or the day-to-day fight against crime. Greenberg chronicles the key building blocks of modern-day "community policing": the Citizens Home Defense League, junior police, Explorer programs, citizen patrol groups, riverkeeper organizations, Volunteers-in-Parks, and many other groups. Greenberg also revisits the contributions of many well-known justice system pioneers (e.g.,

Chief August Vollmer of Berkeley, California) but acknowledges lesser-known but nonetheless important volunteer justice system figures such as Lewis Rodman Wanamaker, who helped oversee the work of the New York Reserve Police.

This work sends a forceful message that strengthening volunteer police efforts at all levels limits opportunities for neighborhood vigilantism, as well as secrecy in law-enforcement circles. Government decision makers, community activists, and civic leaders will be well served by *Citizens Defending America,* which offers cost-effective solutions to a society working to harness the efforts of public-safety-minded citizens in their continuing support for existing volunteer police organizations (e.g., airport watch programs, reserve and auxiliary police) or in their creation of new volunteer police efforts directed at a resolution of the challenging and complex issues surrounding what is now referred to as homeland security. Clearly, Greenberg's work is a significant contribution to justice studies and law enforcement literature, extolling the virtues of "grassroots" volunteer efforts, without which the American justice system—police, courts, and corrections—might fall apart.

JOHN B. WILT, Colonel (Retired),
U.S. Air Force Reserve

ACKNOWLEDGMENTS

I joined the auxiliary police force of New York City in 1965. At the time, I had no way of knowing that I was embarking on a journey that would involve twelve years of service in that organization, as well as the eventual publication of two books and numerous articles and the completion of a doctoral dissertation concerning the history and deployment of America's volunteer police. Along the way, I have had the opportunity to learn from hundreds of volunteer and regular police, as well as many others, about the field of public safety. I have also had contacts with numerous members of the academic community who have dedicated their lives to researching and teaching about the criminal justice system. My own teaching career, which drew upon my earlier contacts with professionals and volunteers, began in Hawaii in 1977.

Public safety, I am convinced, is and must always be a joint enterprise between the people and the police. While this conclusion and the others in this book are my responsibility, they have certainly been informed by my contacts with dedicated volunteers and professionals. I will always be indebted to my John Jay College of Criminal Justice professors and mentors, including Warren Benton, John Kleinig, James Levine, and Larry Sullivan. A very large debt of gratitude is also pleasantly owed to Christina Czechowicz, the former associate director of the Ph.D. Program in Criminal Justice at John Jay College.

I am also grateful to an anonymous reviewer for the University of Pittsburgh Press who indicated that the present book "makes an important contribution to the literature on police" since its publication may help to overcome "an inherent academic bias toward studying only the paid professionals. This bias persists despite the fact that volunteers are an important component of America's national, state, and municipal level defense."

I am extremely thankful for the pioneering achievements and sage advice of Eliot H. Lumbard, a major shaper of criminal justice policy during the 1960s. The present work also owes deep intellectual gratitude to the following scholars: Sally Hadden, David Rothman, Raphael Semmes, Barry Stentiford, John A. Tilley, Samuel Walker, and Howard Zinn. I am especially grateful to Dennis Rousey, who pointed out various historical omissions prior to publication, and to Richard B. Weinblatt, who has substantially contributed to the literature in the field of reserve policing. In recent months, I have significantly benefited from the support of my closest colleagues at Point Park University, especially Robert Alexander, Kim Bell, Judy Bolsinger, Gwen Elliott, John Gobble, Greg Rogers, and Grant Snider. I have also been heartened by the wisdom, courage, and example of Bill Cosby, who has taken a personal interest in helping combat crime in our nation's cities.

In addition, I wish to thank Col. John B. Wilt, author of the book's foreword, who recently retired from the U.S. Air Force Reserve after thirty years of active and reserve duty in the Security Police (now the Security Forces) and the Office of Special Investigations. Colonel Wilt heads the administration of justice program at Danville Community College, in Virginia, having held a similar position for over twenty years at Maui Community College. Colonel Wilt received the Hung Wo and Elizabeth Ching Foundation Faculty Service to the Community Award for his wide-ranging volunteer efforts in Hawaii, having done reserve officer work with the Maui Police Department and having volunteered for Maui Crime Stoppers. He was also a Volunteer Guardian Ad Litem and the cofounder of the Neighborhood Justice Center (now Mediation Services of Maui), where he served as a volunteer mediator for nearly twenty years.

The events of September 11, 2001, necessitated the addition of a new final chapter to the present publication. I wish to extend to the publisher of the *Journal of Security Administration* my appreciation for permission to use materials from its June 2003 issue; chapter 8 of *Citizens Defending America* relies heavily on my previously published work in this journal (see M. A. Greenberg 2003).

I would also like to take this opportunity to express my deep appreciation to the editors at the University of Pittsburgh Press for their expert advice and assistance throughout all phases of the book's preparation. I shall always owe a great debt of gratitude to them and to Carol Sickman-Garner for her extraordinary care in copyediting this book.

Finally, without the love and sacrifice of my wife and son, this book would never have been written. My wife, Ellen Wertlieb, has consistently encouraged my enthusiasm for this project and assisted in all aspects of the book's creation. My son, Edward, is a far better writer and he is bound to become a well-known author.

INTRODUCTION

We learned about an enemy who . . . makes no distinction between military and civilian targets.

The 9/11 Commission Report

On September 11, 2001, thousands of Americans perished as four commercial aircraft plunged into the towers of the World Trade Center in New York City; the Pentagon in Washington, D.C.; and the ground at Shanksville, Pennsylvania. Millions watched as the horrible events of the day unfolded, but many Americans were subsequently heartened when Mayor Rudolph Giuliani declared that the city of New York and the United States of America were much stronger than any group of barbaric terrorists—"that our democracy, . . . our rule of law, . . . [and] our strength and willingness to defend ourselves will ultimately prevail" (qtd. in Miller, Stone, and Mitchell 2002, 26). Americans also took heart when they learned that a group of passengers aboard Flight 93, which crashed in Pennsylvania, had apparently decided to fight the terrorists when they realized the plane had been hijacked. The final report of the National Commission on Terrorist Attacks upon the United States concludes that the terrorists intended to crash "into symbols of the American Republic, the Capitol or the White House," but were "defeated by the alerted, unarmed passengers of United 93" (9/11 Commission 2004, 14).

It is important to note that these passengers were not law enforcement or military personnel but ordinary citizens who made a valiant attempt to save the lives of their fellow Americans. While professional law enforcement groups today remain on alert in anticipation of future attacks by Islamic extremists linked to the al-Qaida terrorist network, little attention is paid to the role the average citizen can play in homeland security. This is surprising, since historically the general public has always held a very prominent role in the detection of crime. Police agencies have traditionally been reactive organizations responsible for detecting only a small proportion of crimes; their investigative and related services generally commence only after the more proactive citizenry has called them to report an incident (see Mitchell 1984, 459, 466). Indeed, under the community policing concept, the police are the public, and the public are the police! Police officers are merely those paid to give full-time attention to the duties of every citizen.

Furthermore, there currently exists a network of officially recognized volunteer groups that specialize in community safety and the overall protection of the homeland. Their contributions have been largely unheralded throughout American history, although numerous famous Americans have been active members of such groups, including Benjamin Franklin, Abraham Lincoln, Babe Ruth, Jimmy Carter, Humphrey Bogart, Col. Frank Borman, Harrison Ford, James Woods, Chuck Norris, Robert F. Kennedy Jr., Shaquille O'Neal, and Bobby Sherman. Franklin basically invented the idea of voluntary associations, establishing the first volunteer fire department in the city of Philadelphia. Seven other signers of the Declaration of Independence, including Samuel Adams and John Hancock, were volunteer firefighters. Lincoln served as the captain of his militia unit during the Black Hawk War. Ruth was a New York Reserve Police lieutenant during the 1920s. As a youth, President Carter was a devoted member of his local American Automobile Association (AAA) school safety patrol in Plains, Georgia. Bogart volunteered his services and yacht as part of the U.S. Coast Guard Temporary Reserve in 1944. Air Force colonel Frank Borman, the pioneering astronaut who acted as the command-module pilot on *Apollo VIII*, the mission that paved the way for Neil Armstrong's historic lunar landing, was a Civil Air Patrol cadet in his youth. Harrison Ford, who starred as the movie hero Indiana Jones, acts as a real-life hero in his work with several county sheriff rescue units in Wyoming, regularly volunteering his flying skills and Bell helicopter for rescue missions. James Woods, who has appeared in over seventy-five feature films, is a reserve Los Angeles police officer. Chuck Norris, a well-known actor, athlete, and producer, is also a reserve police officer for the city of Terrell, Texas (about twenty-five miles east of Dallas). Robert F. Kennedy Jr. is the president of the Riverkeeper Alliance and has been very active as the chief prosecuting attorney for the Hudson Riverkeeper organization, an environmental neighborhood watch program. Since the 1980s, he has been credited with leading the fight to protect New York City's water supply by helping to prosecute Hudson River and New York City watershed polluters. Shaquille O'Neal, the great basketball center, undertook about one thousand hours of training in order to become a Los Angeles Port Police reserve officer. In 1984, Bobby Sherman, a popular 1960s teen recording artist, established a volunteer paramedic squad that has worked at hundreds of events throughout southern California. In the following decade, he was recruited to teach first aid to reserve police officers (Pool 1993).

Volunteer policing, in fact, is and has been ubiquitous in the United States—a fact of which few people are aware. This book is the only one to date that considers the full history of volunteer police in America—a history that parallels that of the regular police but has been virtually hidden until now. Through exploring the activities and organization of various types of volunteer police units, this book provides a roadmap for those contemplating the contemporary citizen's role in homeland security and community safety.

Before beginning the full story of volunteer policing in the United States, it might be useful to contrast its history with that of regular policing. The history of regular policing in America can be roughly divided into four periods, each based on the dominance of a particular strategy of policing. In 1805, New Orleans inaugurated a distinctive paramilitary model of policing that was duplicated in "Deep South cities with large slave concentrations" (Rousey 1996, 4). During the first few decades of the nineteenth century, such military-style policing was in vogue in New Orleans, Richmond, Mobile, Savannah, and Charleston (see Rousey 1996, 11–39). This southern military model represents the first era of modern policing, used in the South because "policemen who looked like soldiers probably helped ameliorate the deep anxieties many whites harbored about the dangers of slave crime and revolt" (Rousey 1996, 39). The second period saw the end of the Deep South's military model and the beginning of the adoption of a civil style of urban policing during the 1840s, which continued throughout the Progressive period and ended after the first third of the twentieth century. The third period lasted from the 1930s through the late 1970s, while the years since comprise the fourth era. The second, third, and fourth periods have been referred to, respectively, as (1) the political era, (2) the reform era, and (3) the community problem-solving or community policing era (Kelling and Moore 1988). The political era is so named because of the close ties that existed between police and politics. The reform era, a reaction to the political era, has now given way to a period emphasizing community policing strategies (Hartmann 1988).[1]

The history of volunteer policing, however, may be divided into a slightly more diverse set of periods, with some degree of overlap. These epochs include (1) the lay justice era, marked by Native American military societies, the militia (including slave patrols), and the constable and watch systems of the colonial settlements, used until the establishment of unified day and night watches in the 1840s; (2) the vigilant era, featuring the detective societies and posses (including slave patrols) of the nineteenth century, as well as the rise of a score of antivice societies during the last quarter of the nineteenth century; (3) the spy era of the Progressive Era and World War I, with operatives including individuals from the Anti-Saloon League and the American Protective League, as well as charity workers; (4) the transformation era, which lasted from 1920 to 1941, during which special-purpose units evolved into general-purpose police reserves; and finally (5) the assimilation era, when civil defense workers and other kinds of volunteer police became an integrated part of the community policing strategy of many police departments.

These time frames shape the discussion that follows, which uses the generic term *volunteer police* to refer to the overall history of both involuntary and voluntary citizen police. While this study indicates that the existence of volunteer police (especially since the Civil War) has generally contributed to the growth of democratic institutions in the United States, it is important to keep in mind that during most of American history the police have been used to maintain a political order that has promoted slavery, segregation, and discrimination. This work, however, is interested not only in the history of volunteer policing but also in its present and future potential—in current community practices and in recommendations for the future deployment of citizens as keepers of the public safety.

The overwhelming majority of volunteer police groups were legally sanctioned to perform one or more police functions (e.g., law enforcement, peacekeeping, crime prevention, the delivery of services) in an overt manner. Such organizations—anti-horse-thief societies, southern slave patrols, "friendly visitors" (early charity workers), National Guard and state guard units, police reserves, the junior police—tended to be permanent in nature unless mobilized in response to a wartime emergency. Many of the anti-horse-thief or law-and-order societies of the nineteenth century, for example, had the support of local law enforcement authorities, their existence eventually authorized by statutes. Reserve/auxiliary units began to appear in the pre-Depression era of the twentieth century in some of America's largest cities, but some of these "volunteers" rarely performed law enforcement functions, their appointments sometimes made merely as a political favor and/or to provide a constituent with an added credential for employment purposes.

Nevertheless, in the late 1940s, one prominent police expert, Bruce Smith, proclaimed that the establishment of volunteer law enforcement units was one of the most practical ideas that he had heard of in his thirty-eight years of work as a police consultant and researcher (B. Smith 1949). Since then, his sentiments have been echoed by many other police scholars and practitioners. In 1960, Lt. Everett King of the Alameda County, California, sheriff's department wrote that the hundreds of "auxiliary law enforcement components throughout the country . . . are proving, in practice, that the concept is both valid and practical" (E. M. King 1960, 15). Don Blankenship of the Maricopa County, Arizona, sheriff's department was referring to the Sun City volunteer deputies when he stated, "It's an idea that's gaining rapid and widespread acceptance, an idea that's here to stay" (qtd. in Mehren 1981). Maj. Donald Woodruff of the Duluth, Georgia, police department states that the volunteer police reserves are made up of "serious, dedicated individuals, who want to make this city a better place to live" (personal communication, September 29, 2000). Police chief James G. Jackson of Columbus, Ohio, declares that the police reserve is "a valuable part of the Division's effort to combat crime and to make Columbus a better place to live" (Columbus Police Reserve 2000). In Arizona, Sheriff Joe Arpaio of Maricopa County, with a population of about three million, has assembled a volunteer posse of over twenty-five hundred men and women to supplement his regular full-time deputies. The volunteer force outnumbers the regulars five to one. Arpaio believes that "you can't get more into volunteerism than this . . . to help protect the neighborhoods and protect the people. . . . I have faith in my posse, and that's the way it's going to be as long as I'm the sheriff" (Arpaio and Sherman 1996, 96).

This study centers on organizations such as those described above—organizations (private or public) that have directly assumed or been empowered to undertake law enforcement functions (e.g., criminal investigations, arrest, and prosecution) and/or the related tasks of peacekeeping. Such organizations are generally associated with governmental authorities and tend to operate under some real or pretended "color of authority" (e.g., to wear police uniforms and insignias or display badges). Of course, membership in authorized or official volunteer police organizations is not the only way for private citizens to contribute to community safety and homeland security. Individuals or groups may supplement the role of the government in crime control and public safety by, for example, engaging in efforts to improve neighborhood security, hiring private security guards, or patrolling themselves. They can contribute time or funds to nonprofit organizations that provide drug-rehabilitation services or special care for juvenile offenders. There are literally thousands of such worthwhile local groups throughout the nation—Mothers against Drunk Driving, neighborhood watches, Court Watch, and so on—though they are not the focus here.

In general, volunteer policing in America has moved from the general-purpose policing of the early night watches, to the special-purpose volunteers of the vigilant and spying eras, and then back again to the general-purpose activities of reserve and auxiliary units. The events of September 11, however, may trigger a return to the former spy era unless careful attention is paid to the civil liberties and rights of the American public by all sectors of society. Fortunately, current indications are that modern units of volunteer police are being trained to respect individual civil rights and liberties. In addition, some federal units (e.g., the Civil Air Patrol) have been assigned highly important and visible roles in the war on terror, particularly homeland defense.

Citizens Defending America

1

Unraveling the Concept of Volunteer Policing

The strength of a democracy is not in bureaucracy; it is in the people and their communities. In everything we do, let us unleash the potential of our most precious resource—our citizens.

PRESIDENT GEORGE H. W. BUSH, State of the Union Message, January 29, 1991

In the thirteenth century, Henry III mandated that all his male subjects (between the ages of fifteen and fifty) own a weapon other than a knife so that they could stand guard in order to preserve the peace of the realm: "In the event of a crime, every man had to join in the 'hue and cry'—summoning aid and joining the pursuit of anyone who resisted arrest or escaped from custody" (Levy 1999, 136). Today, while most American states still require private citizens to come to the aid of a law enforcement officer if called upon, they are not asked to carry a weapon or routinely serve as a constable or member of the watch in either England or the United States. Nevertheless, tens of thousands of citizens in both nations currently routinely serve as volunteer police officers, and it is not uncommon for these volunteers to have paid for their own training, uniforms, and other equipment.

The use of generally uncompensated voluntary and involuntary police in the Western world dates back at least a thousand years or more. At that time, England was divided into ten family units called "tithings" and ten tithings called "hundreds." All of the men over the age of fifteen in these units formed a *posse comitatus,* required upon being alerted to pursue any fleeing felons (Roberg, Crank, and Kuykendall 2000, 34). In the thirteenth century, town constables were empowered to draft citizens for a night watch (Travis 1995, 117), and in colonial America, local militia units and town watches composed of all free adult white males provided the most visible means for the maintenance of social control. Thus, in earlier times, ordinary citizens occupied the most conspicuous and responsible positions for order maintenance.

The History of Volunteer Police from Colonial Times to 1941

Although the most dramatic advances in volunteer policing have taken place in recent times, the beginnings of the journey no doubt predate the arrival of the first colonists to the New World. Native American societies, for example, maintained order through clearly defined customs "enforced by public opinion and religious sanctions" (Hagan 1966, 16). Nearly everyone knew and respected tribal customs and beliefs, such conformity made possible because the "tribes were homogeneous units—linguistically, religiously, economically, and politically" (Deloria and Lytle 1983, xi). By the time of the arrival of the European settlers, many tribes had founded numerous societies and cults to preserve order in camp and "to foster a military spirit among themselves and the rest of the tribe, since war was a matter of survival" (Mails 1973, 46). The Plains Indians instituted honorary military societies to police their annual reunion ceremonies and buffalo hunts. Similar societies were operated year-round by the Cheyenne and the Teton Sioux (Hagan 1966).

On the other hand, justice in the colonies, prior to America's independence, was administered by lay judges, community residents, militia and watch members, foreign soldiers, clergymen, constables, various administrative officers (e.g., governors, sheriffs), and legislative assemblies. One of the earliest uses of an organized militia came in 1636 when companies were formed in the Massachusetts Bay Colony to protect against attacks by Native Americans: "Colonial militiamen defended the colonies and participated in expeditions against Indians and the French until the War of Independence" (Stentiford 2002, 6). During the Revolutionary War, "militia augmented Washington's Continental Army, as well as enforced revolutionary discipline among the populace, clearly demonstrating the dual roles of militia during wartime of fighting the enemy and . . . stabilizing the homefront" (Stentiford 2002, 6).

Most eastern American port cities abandoned the informal system of "watch and ward" (a system involving separate organizations for evening and day patrols) during the two or three decades just prior to the Civil War.

A wave of urban riots took place in this period that caused many persons to fear that America's experiment with democratic institutions was threatened. While the establishment of the London Metropolitan Police Force in 1829 served as a convenient model for reform (S. S. Walker 1976), the organization of paid, unified, day and night police departments and the abandonment of the older model did not serve as a guarantee that democratic traditions and the rule of law would be respected, especially with regard to the protection of minority citizens and their rights. These new police forces, in fact, excluded minority-group members. Moreover, between 1882 and 1969, more than forty-seven hundred people, mostly black, were lynched in the United States (Perloff 2000). A Census Bureau study conducted in 1973 found that in America's five largest cities, "blacks were much more likely than whites to be the victims of robbery and burglary, in some cases by a ratio of nearly two to one" (Wilson 1975, 34). In the United States, the high point of this crisis was reached in the late 1960s when civil protests and riots erupted in over one hundred American cities (Travis 1995). Lawsuits were eventually filed in many regions of the country to spur integration in housing and the schools and to create public employment opportunities.

Clearly, the establishment of public police agencies did not do away with any existing threats to America's democratic institutions. The earliest of these public police agencies are only about 175 years old. In England, prior to 1829, law enforcement had slowly evolved from the basic concept of preserving the King's Peace by mutual responsibility (during the Anglo-Saxon era, from 550 to 1066) to the use of various constables and the keeping of a "watch and ward." The two latter developments were officially set forth in the Statute of Winchester of 1285 (Seth 1961). In the late 1600s, local justices of the peace were empowered to appoint additional or "special" parish constables (Critchley 1967; Leon 1991). Before the nineteenth century, citizens generally considered it their unpaid compulsory obligation to serve as tithingmen, constables, and members of the "watch and ward" (Prassel 1972).[1]

In New England, during colonial times, "watch and ward committees" were also established, representing an early version of citizen patrols. The Dutch settlement of New Amsterdam, later New York, "created a burgher watch in 1643, one year after it was founded, but did not pay them until 1712" (Bayley 1985, 32). The governor of New Amsterdam, Peter Stuyvesant, also created the first volunteer fire department in America in 1648. Eventually, constables (elected or appointed), marshals, and watches were established in every settlement in the colonies (Bayley 1985, 32). Initially, constable work was the communal responsibility of all adult males, and fines could be levied for refusing to assume this obligation (S. S. Walker 1998, 27). The South took community policing even further during the colonial and antebellum periods, adopting slave-patrol laws that led to the recruitment of militia members to maintain the institution of slavery. The western "posse," on the other hand, was a somewhat later phenomenon (Garry 1980). Belonging to a posse was a form of "obligatory avocational policing" (Klockars 1985, 22): an individual was liable to be arrested for failure to serve when called upon. During the nineteenth century, some northeastern and midwestern states passed laws authorizing the establishment of various protective, detective, or anti-horse-thief associations. Today, most states still have laws that require the average citizen to come to the aid of a police officer when requested.

The existence of a militia is referred to in the U.S. Constitution (see Articles I and II and the Second Amendment), and the Militia Act of 1792 required most free white males between the ages of eighteen and forty-five to arm themselves and attend regular drills. However, "neither the federal government nor the states enforced the law, . . . [and] in the years following the War of 1812, the militia as an institution fell into disuse. Few Americans, including Congressmen, saw any need for citizens to waste time drilling when no danger threatened and more profitable pursuits beckoned" (Stentiford 2002, 7).[2] Still, the militia tradition developed over time into today's well-known concept of the "citizen soldier," who serves the nation in peacetime and in war as a volunteer member of the National Guard. Members of the New York Army National Guard, for example, were called to active duty after September 11, 2001, to provide security at airports, bridges, and train stations (Debnam 2003).

A new institution arose in 1806, supplanting the use of the militia during wartime, known simply as "the Volunteers"—usually companies and regiments recruited at the local level: "The men from each company elected their officers; the governor of the state appointed the regimental officers; and the regiment was then mustered into federal service for an agreed-upon period" (Stentiford 2002, 7–8). Significantly, such voluntary military organizations existed throughout the nineteenth century, assisting state governments in strike breaking, riot control, and disaster relief, their existence obviating the need to enforce the Militia Act of 1792. In essence, they represented a body of self-selected men derived from the unorganized militia who "formed or joined companies out of patriotism, from fear of slave uprisings . . . or as a way of establishing social and political contacts, . . . not out of legal obligation" (Stentiford 2002, 8). Abraham Lincoln served in such a company during the Black Hawk War, and Theodore Roosevelt led his Volunteer "Rough Riders" during the Spanish-American War.

As early as the 1830s, Alexis de Tocqueville, the noted French aristocrat who visited the United States to study its people and institutions, discerned a trend in American society toward the establishment of a variety of such voluntary associations. Many of these were not solely of the amateur soldier variety but were concerned with the welfare of diverse immigrant groups: "In Philadelphia alone, in 1878, there were some 800 such groups of one kind or another in existence" (Trattner 1989, 85). The growth in their number created a need for the establishment of umbrella associations known as charity organization societies. These societies did not directly dispense relief but instead served as clearinghouses, registering, screening, and referring applicants in need of charity. The largest such organization existed in New York City. Initially, the New York Charity Organization Society relied on a corps of volunteer "friendly visitors" to perform home visits: "Friendly Visitors helped worthy families negotiate the maze of relief and social services and learn to make do with what they had" (M. B. Katz 1996, 165). In counseling families, however, these volunteers were also in a position to see that laws were obeyed. Other groups were mainly concerned with the morals of the tide of immigrants arriving daily from Europe during the latter part of the nineteenth century and the first two decades of the twentieth. The pioneer organization in this regard was the New York Society for the Suppression of Vice. The agents of this society identified and prosecuted vendors of pornography and birth control for more than forty years (Hovey 1998).

In the United States, various types of vigilante organizations were also common in the nineteenth century. Vigilantism has been defined as "organized, extralegal movements, the members of which take the law into their own hands" (R. M. Brown 1975, 95–96). Vigilantes, of course, "don't 'take' the law; they break the law. They don't act in self-defense, which is legal; they react aggressively, which is illegal" (Karmen 1990, 357). Two of the most infamous vigilante organizations arose after the Civil War—the Ku Klux Klan (KKK) and the White Caps. The KKK was founded to resist any efforts by southern blacks to achieve racial equality, while the White Caps were concerned with the control of morality (e.g., wife beating, prostitution, drunkards, poor providers, etc.). Members of both groups wore masks, but while the KKK was known for lynching, the White Caps relied on whipping to fulfill their goals (R. M. Brown 1971; Friedman 1993).

The advent of extralegal vigilante groups in many ways represents the antithesis of the role of modern-day volunteer police. Vigilante groups deviated from the traditional and contemporary democratic hallmarks of voluntary community service, going about their business without regard for individual rights and liberties. Furthermore, these groups lacked any statutory authority when they engaged in punitive activities. In contrast, the evolving role of volunteer policing appears to be deeply rooted in the democratic spirit of America, which is best characterized by its concern for free speech; religious tolerance; universal suffrage; and other egalitarian concepts, such as hiring and promotion based on merit.

On the other hand, the evolution of volunteer policing has also had its undemocratic side, especially when it has been linked to branches of government that have abused the rights of citizens. This occurred, of course, when slave patrols were used in the South and also later, during World War I, when the federal government condoned the use of thousands of volunteer citizen spies for the purpose of identifying draft evaders and suspected anarchists. These volunteer spies were part of a giant civic organization entitled the American Protective League (APL).

World War I also saw the beginning of the recruitment of the youth of America in a volunteer police role. In the second decade of the twentieth century, various articles about "junior police" appeared in such popular national periodicals as the *Literary Digest*, the *Survey*, and the *Outlook*. However, by the mid-1920s, some of these groups had been either transformed or replaced by school safety patrols. The growth of such patrols was triggered in the 1920s when the automobile's newfound popularity led to a rise in traffic fatalities among children aged five to fourteen. In 1926, the city fathers of Newark, New Jersey, took stock of their nine-year-old safety patrol program, finding that no serious injuries had taken place since its implementation (Rosseland 1926). The Honolulu sheriff swore in thirty-three members of the Boy Scouts of America as "junior traffic police officers" in 1923 (Honolulu Police Department 2000b). By 1932, there were approximately ten thousand safety patrol units involving two hundred thousand boys in eighteen hundred cities and towns ("Guarding Five Million Children" 1932; "Schoolboy Patrols Approved" 1933).

Volunteer Policing from 1941 to the Present

On December 7, 1941, the United States entered World War II with the bombing of Pearl Harbor. On the same day, the governor of the territory of Hawaii signed a proclamation turning the government of Hawaii over to the U.S. military, and the entire area was declared to be under martial law (Honolulu Police Department 2000a). Throughout World War II and during the Korean War, personnel shortages, coupled with the need for increased civil defense services, led to the growth of various types of auxiliary citizen police units and the reactivation of the state guard.

From the territory of Hawaii to the eastern seaboard, Americans volunteered to protect the home front by enlisting in volunteer police organizations. For example, a reserve police unit of 124 individuals had been appointed by the Honolulu police chief just five months prior to the bombing of Pearl Harbor, the Federal Bureau of Investigation (FBI) helping to screen each of the initial applicants. For the duration of the war, each volunteer police officer was issued the same seven-pointed star badge, with the word "emergency" stamped on top, as was worn by regular Honolulu police (Honolulu Police Department 2000b). In addition, citizens throughout Hawaii formed militia units. The city of Honolulu had several different militia units organized along ethnic lines: the Businessmen's Military Training Corps, for example, contained white men and men of mixed white and Native Hawaiian ancestry, while the Hawaii Defense Volunteers included mostly men of Chinese descent but also Filipinos, Hawaiians, Puerto Ricans, Koreans, and whites. In addition, in October 1942, 1,500 men formed the Hawaii Air Depot Volunteer Corps to assist in any emergency at Hickam Field: "This was probably the only volunteer militia in the nation to get antiaircraft machine guns in World War II" (Stentiford 2002, 150–51). Such groups, of course, did not form only in Hawaii. Less than one year after the bombing of Pearl Harbor by a Japanese naval task force, in September 1942, 1,063 auxiliary police officers in Wichita, Kansas, were sworn in and given armbands (Wichita Police Department 2000). By the end of 1943 there were 4,499 New York City Patrol Corps volunteers guarding strategic locations in America's largest city (New York City Police Department 1943, 21).

In addition, within months of American entry into World War II, forty thousand volunteers had been recruited for a new organization known as the Civil Air Patrol (CAP). CAP was officially born on December 1, 1941, just days before the Japanese attacked Pearl Harbor. The program was "conceived in the late 1930s by legendary New Jersey aviation advocate Gill Robb Wilson, who foresaw aviation's role in war and general aviation's potential to supplement America's unprepared military" ("Civil Air Patrol Story" 2003). Like other stateside groups, CAP actively recruited women; by war's end, women made up about 20 percent of its membership.

Throughout World War II, concern about the shortage of police personnel also led to the recruitment of junior police. For example, in November 1941, a Boys' Police Force was established in Blacksburg, Virginia, consisting of eighteen high school students who were assigned to patrol public gatherings on school grounds, patrol school buildings, and direct traffic at the school (Blacksburg Police Department 1949). In Hawaii, after Pearl Harbor, the territorial governor organized a territorial guard that included many high school boys from the local Junior Reserve Officer Training Corps (JROTC) program. Initially, they were posted at strategic locations to guard against sabotage after dark (Stentiford 2002, 147–48).

As a consequence of the Korean conflict, in New York City, former police commissioner Arthur Wallender was appointed to head the civil defense effort. His plans called for the organization of an auxiliary police corps consisting of forty thousand men and women, twice the size of the city's regular police force. The mass media was called upon to aid in recruitment to the force, which would be patterned after the regular police system, although members would have military titles. Although only about twenty thousand auxiliaries were actually recruited, the number substantially declining in later years, this initial cadre was later drawn upon for the establishment of routine street crime patrols. The current structure of auxiliary police precinct units within New York City, in fact, is directly traceable to the Korean War–era approach of these civil defense auxiliary police.

In the late 1950s and throughout the turbulent 1960s, many cities re-vamped their old-style civil defense volunteers in order to cope with urban unrest and the need for increased and visible police strength (Garry 1980). Columbus, Ohio, for example, originally created an auxiliary police organi-zation in 1951 for civil defense purposes, but by 1955 these police had been assigned on an emergency basis to assist regular police engaged in anti-crime patrols and had been authorized to make arrests (Columbus Police Reserve 2000).

In the 1970s, following a decade of civil protests over the second-class status of African Americans and the nation's involvement in the war in Viet-nam, calls for reform resulted in new efforts to bridge the gap between the people and the police. New federal crime control initiatives were under-taken. For example, in order to help restore public confidence in the police, significant projects for organizing community residents through start-up grants were funded by the Law Enforcement Assistance Administration, a division of the U.S. Department of Justice. Citizens in hundreds of cities were organized to patrol their own neighborhoods, keep watch on neigh-bors' homes, report suspicious activities, and learn how to strengthen the security of their homes and businesses. Increased concern about the care of the elderly also led to the establishment of a volunteer nursing home om-budsman program. A widespread understanding grew, within police de-partments and other agencies concerned with the administration of justice, that the available professional resources marshaled on behalf of social con-trol were inadequate. In truth, municipal treasuries were limited in their ability to meet growing demands for more police. Such cities as New York and Detroit were compelled to lay off hundreds of police and other public servants in order to maintain fiscal integrity.

By the 1980s, it was estimated that as many as two hundred thousand adult auxiliary and reserve police officers were working as part-time volun-teers in local law enforcement agencies in the United States (Burden 1988).[3] In Denver, Colorado, for example, members of the police reserve must per-form a five-hour shift each week and work for eight hours every third week-end (Gill and Mawby 1990, 67). Some volunteer police regularly perform peacekeeping patrols in urban neighborhoods, while others are only called upon to assist in traffic control at special events. In recent years, a rather special group of experienced volunteer deputies has been active in Precinct

6 of Houston, Texas. Their commitment to law-enforcement work has resulted in the arrest of over two thousand parole violators. Houston's volunteer deputies also help reduce truancy rates by initiating family visits (Claiborne 1994). There are, of course, volunteer police units in many other cities and in nations around the world (Berkley 1969).

Other new initiatives in the field of community policing have not only spurred the growth of many new citizen-police projects but have led to the implementation of expanded opportunities for youth. In 2002, for example, the American Automobile Association (AAA) reported that nationwide there were more than one half million school safety patrol members serving in fifty thousand schools in every state (Melton 2002). There were over four thousand safety patrollers from 128 schools just in the city and county of Honolulu in the year 2000 (Honolulu Police Department 2000b).

The Boy Scouts of America (BSA) has also been active in engaging youth in such community activities. The BSA undertook the establishment of various career-exploration posts in the 1970s, perhaps as a way of integrating young women into their programs. Currently thousands of young people between the ages of fourteen and twenty are enrolled in law-enforcement-sponsored "Explorer" posts. Innovations like this benefit not only youth but the community as a whole: "Law Enforcement Exploring has two primary benefits: it provides personnel in community support areas that would otherwise go begging, and helps develop police/youth relationships while building awareness of law enforcement tasks and an understanding of the related problems and objectives" (Runyon and Falzarano 1983, 18). One of the most interesting features of these programs is the opportunity they provide for permitting Explorers to accompany police officers on patrol ("ride-along programs"). In 1979, a national certification program for ride-along participation was designed jointly by the National Law Enforcement Exploring Committee and the International Association of Chiefs of Police (Runyon and Falzarano 1983).

In addition, the BSA has also established junior police academies and special "youth courts." In Edinburg, Texas, for example, a coeducational Explorer program was established by the local school district to provide young adults (ages fourteen through twenty-one) with the opportunity to engage in community service and receive training in the field of law enforcement (Edinburg C.I.S.D. Police Department 2000). In Boston, the police department conducts a junior police academy during the summer months for children ages nine to twelve who may be at risk of dropping out of school (Boston Police Department 2004).

Older Americans are also very much involved in volunteer programs. One such program involves seniors serving as nursing home ombudsmen to resolve resident-facility disputes and help ensure the safety and well-being of residents. Begun in 1972 as a demonstration program and run by the Administration on Aging (AoA), a division of the Department of Health and Human Services, it is now established in all fifty states and has a staff that includes fourteen thousand volunteers and one thousand paid employees who investigate over 260,000 complaints each year ("Elder Rights" 2004).

The routine use of volunteer police personnel has not been without controversy, however. Volunteer police may appear to challenge the idea of policing as a "profession" and undermine the political clout of police unions. In both the United States and the United Kingdom, the most vocal critics of volunteer police maintain that policing requires the services of full-time, professionally trained personnel. Various police union members have even categorized volunteers as scabs, social misfits, or misguided do-gooders (Garry 1980). Police union leaders are in fact unlikely to support any type of policing strategy that empowers citizens to act in their place. Even "the practice of using retired cops as volunteers may be viewed by the police union as 'scab labor': uncompensated labor that would otherwise be performed by regular hires" (Champion and Rush 1997, 363–64). In September 1987, the *New York Times* reported that the auxiliary police unit in Quincy, Massachusetts, had ceased to patrol as a result of pressure exerted by regular police officers who felt that their jobs were in peril. Overall, however, "most primary and secondary sources at our disposal imply that reserves have managed to gain acceptance in police departments, even if some police officers remained skeptical" (Gill and Mawby 1990, 73).

Definitions of Volunteer Police

In America, the history of citizen participation in policing has been long and varied. This history, however, has been relatively unstudied and thus has lacked any generally accepted definition or typology. Clearly the topic is broad and needs to be narrowed for the sake of better understanding.

What might be a good working definition of the term *volunteer police*? The variety of current and past community policing initiatives has blurred the meaning of the concept, while the lack of any history that traces the origins of direct citizen participation in policing has doubtless contributed to this confusion and imprecision in terminology. A working definition would enable more consistent and meaningful work by future researchers, students, and policy makers and give the general population a better idea of whether this kind of public service is worthy of support. Although the subject has become more widely known since September 11, 2001, the title "Volunteers in Police Service" (VIPS), officially sanctioned by the U.S. government, can be confusing.

A variety of agencies in fact exist that have law enforcement responsibilities (e.g., the U.S. Coast Guard, the U. S. Customs Service) but are not typically thought of as police agencies, and it is not uncommon for such organizations to rely on volunteer personnel to help implement their missions. The U.S. Coast Guard, for example, supervises and trains thousands of volunteers in its auxiliary branch. In addition, there also exist various private groups and individuals engaged in certain aspects of policing or law enforcement (e.g., private detectives and security guards, community watches). Thus, to enable an effective study and concrete statements about volunteer police, the words *volunteer* and *police* need, in combination, to be defined.

Police agencies have been defined as "those agencies that stand ready to employ force upon the citizenry on the basis of situationally determined exigencies" (Manning 1977, 40). Similarly, police themselves have been defined as "people authorized by a group to regulate interpersonal relations within the group through the application of physical force" (Bayley 1985, 7). Police, according to this definition, "are not self-created; they are tied to the social units from which they derive authority" (8). This conceptualization of police has been generally adopted throughout this book with some key adjustments: police are here defined as "people authorized by a group to regulate interpersonal *or intragroup* relations through the application of physical *and/or moral* persuasion." Linking *volunteer* to *police*, of course, adds a further dimension. The word *volunteer*, broadly used, encompasses both participation that is freely given and participation that is considered involuntary, given as a requirement of the law (e.g., militia or juror duty). It is sometimes hard to distinguish the latter from the former, since some persons "volunteer" before they are called for duty. In addition, some civic obligations may have compensatory features, as well as penalties for nonperformance.

The following typology of volunteer police (table 1) is designed to help clarify both the various types of volunteer organizations encountered throughout American history and their impact on democratic institutions.[4] Through this typology's use, for example, one can readily discern the extent to which volunteer police units have either contributed to or detracted from the rule of law and other democratic values (e.g., interpersonal trust, concern for human rights).

It will be useful to briefly examine here the basic features of the typology in some detail. Type I volunteer police units perform a variety of policing functions and are defensive in nature, seldom undertaking overt or aggressive actions. Since World War I, most auxiliary/reserve units have fallen into this category, their members contributing countless hours of public service and thereby helping to preserve American institutions. Type II units also perform a variety of policing tasks but are more aggressive or proactive in their crime prevention activities. This kind of volunteer policing is more prevalent in the western parts of the United States. Reserve police units are most closely identified with this category, receiving better training and screening than their Type I counterparts. Their more rigorous qualifications often in fact equal those of the regular police. Thus, while their services may be more useful in citizen protection, they also entail more risk for both the volunteers and the persons whom they encounter. Type III organizations have only one or two specific functions and carry them out with restraint. Examples of such organizations include charity agents such as the "friendly visitors," anti-horse-thief and detective societies, and various junior police groups. Their work directly involves specific activities (e.g., the prevention and recovery of stolen property, financial aid, traffic safety). While such services can sometimes be rendered inappropriately, they contribute to the overall welfare of society and play an important role in the maintenance of stable communities. Type IV organizations also exist for specific purposes but are aggressive in their approach. Slave patrollers, special agents of the New York Society for the Prevention of Vice, APL operatives, and detectives and attorneys of the Anti-Saloon League (ASL) readily fall into this category.

Type IV organizations clearly had the most adverse consequences for America's democratic institutions and the cause of personal freedom. Their legacy is a reminder of the inherent dangers of overzealous police and civic conduct. On the other hand, some Type IV organizations provided their members with lessons in democracy. For example, the militia companies from which the earliest slave patrols were drawn "demanded the right to elect their officers and insisted on the enfranchisement of all soldiers, whether or not they met age and property qualifications" (Foner 1998, 17). Members of the ASL learned how to effectively lobby in a representative democracy.

All these types of volunteer police, however, share some common characteristics that, taken together, lead to the following working definition: volunteer police are members of a permanent organization (or one established during wartime mobilization) authorized by either governmental or societal action for the purpose of performing one or more functions of policing in an overt manner (i.e., functions that go beyond surveillance or communications work) for minimal or no salary. This initial, general definition is sufficiently robust to include or account for the varieties of community policing organizations encountered throughout American history: the Native American military societies, the colonial militias, the night watch, constables, slave patrollers, posses, anti-horse-thief and detective societies, charity workers, and so on.[5]

Until now, attempts to arrive at a working definition of *volunteer police* have made no mention of early Native American, colonial, nineteenth-, or early twentieth-century groups, primarily centering instead on post-1950 organizations. The National Advisory Commission on Criminal Justice

Table 1 A Typology of Volunteer Police

	Reactive	Proactive
General purpose	I	II
Special purpose	III	IV

Standards and Goals (1973), for example, researched just two modern varieties of volunteer police in the United States, auxiliary and reserve, concluding that "auxiliary police" are unpaid, wear police uniforms, do not possess peace officer powers, and usually are assigned to perform routine civil defense activities. "Reserve officers," on the other hand, may be salaried, wear police uniforms, carry firearms, possess full peace officer powers, and are assigned to a wide range of regular police duties. Reserve units, according to a different definition, are "under statutory provision, operate within the police station, involve officers wearing uniforms similar to those of regulars, and place volunteers under police control" (Gill and Mawby 1990, 73). The Commission on Criminal Justice Standards and Goals, however, points out that unfortunately the words *auxiliary* and *reserve* are often used interchangeably, thus causing the distinctions enumerated above to be applied unevenly in some jurisdictions. In other words, a particular program may be officially called an "auxiliary police program" even though it resembles a "reserve unit," or vice versa. Nevertheless, in either case, such units are authorized to perform their services in the name of the community, an essential element in any definition of *police* (Bayley 1985). Moreover, members of all varieties of volunteer police programs are deployed on a part-time basis.

At least one contemporary definition of *volunteer police* is available. In New York State, a definition of *auxiliary police officer* may be found in the *Auxiliary Police Guidance Manual* (New York State Disaster Preparedness Commission 1991). Today, many local New York State volunteer police officers are currently designated "auxiliary police officers," fitting a definition derived by the commission from the relevant sections of the New York State Defense Emergency Act. This law was enacted in 1951, establishing state and local civil defense offices and delineating specific roles for volunteers recruited by these offices. Sections 22 and 23D of the act require counties and cities to recruit and train civil-defense volunteers, including auxiliary police. The act's definition states:

> *Auxiliary Police Officer:* Originally authorized under the *Defense Emergency Act* to maintain order and control traffic and to perform such other police and emergency civil defense functions as required. Auxiliary police are volunteers and may be utilized for civil defense or Article 2-B emergen-

cies or during official drills authorized by the local emergency management office. They have limited peace officer powers during drills which consist of those powers needed to direct and control traffic. (Their peace officer powers during Article 2B and National Defense Emergencies are not limited.) Section 2.20 of the *New York State Criminal Procedure Law* reveals that the peace officer powers connected with directing and controlling traffic will probably only relate to the issuance of appearance tickets. Auxiliary police are commonly used for traffic control during parades or other routine community events such as athletic events and fairs. They also can perform a variety of other non-essential police functions, while also being the "eyes and ears" of the police in the community.

The need for a better understanding of the phenomenon of volunteer police is especially important in view of the recent emergence of new varieties of volunteer self-defense groups, from various self-styled underground "militia" groups to the more visible activities of the Guardian Angels. A recent review of U.S. volunteer groups divides volunteer police efforts into the categories of (1) self-defense and (2) organized auxiliary (Garry 1980). Groups of the former variety, like the Guardian Angels, involve citizens who are dissatisfied with governmental police services and undertake relatively independent activities (e.g., training, patrols). Groups of the other variety, "organized auxiliary," exemplify the 1973 National Advisory Commission descriptions of both uniformed auxiliary and reserve volunteer police. A key distinction between the two varieties appears to be the nature of the organization's association with the regular police. The closer the association is, the more likely the group is to be characterized as an "organized auxiliary" of either the peace officer (reserve) or non-peace officer (auxiliary) variety. In the United States, the importance of peace officer status may be somewhat overrated: at least one big-city volunteer police organization has been advised to resist making arrests unless absolutely necessary (M. A. Greenberg 1984). Furthermore, even without "peace officer" authority, volunteer police may make a citizen's arrest as provided by statute in most states.

Currently, not only do state statutes specifically provide their citizens the power to make such arrests, but under the principles of common law, all persons still possess wide authority to protect themselves, their family, "and to some degree the general peace of the land" (Prassel 1972, 126). Thus, the line between peace officer and private citizen is a relative and rather thin one: "while the concept is today increasingly ignored, every citizen is a policeman" (Prassel 1972, 126).

In recent decades, new types of nonregular and volunteer police personnel have arisen: part-time police officers, seasonal police officers, special police officers, Police Explorers, police interns, and police cadets. Until the practice was ended in 2003, some agencies in various rural parts of New York State temporarily deputized individuals for the sole purpose of attending a regionally approved academy. This practice was terminated when Governor George E. Pataki approved a provision to permit preservice basic-training programs at local colleges. The often fine distinctions among all these categories require any discussion of community-based policing to provide an explicit definition of the kind of volunteer or nonregular police being studied—a definition like the one given here, based on lengthy research into the practices of numerous organizations.

The Need for a Citizen Role in Community Safety

The Gulf War, at the start of the 1990s, braced the United States and Europe for acts of terrorism. Security forces at government offices, airports, airline offices, and train and bus stations were strengthened. On the U.S. home front, many municipal and county police departments had their ranks thinned as more and more military and naval reservists were called into active duty. The events of September 11, 2001, further underscored the importance of having qualified and trained volunteer police during a period of national emergency. Later, the invasions of Afghanistan and Iraq also thinned the ranks of the National Guard and the reserve branches of the armed forces. These events all raise an essential question. What types of volunteer police, if any, are needed to protect and police the home front? Recent events have left Americans feeling susceptible, and "research suggests that the vivid nature of these events is likely to add to people's sense of vulnerability. Clearly, the vast on-going media coverage of terrorism-related events makes it exceedingly easy for all of us to imagine scenarios in which we are the victims of terrorism" (Pyszczynski, Solomon, and Greenberg 2003, 113). We can all feel a little less vulnerable, however, by learning what to do in an emergency, and we can gain confidence in our skills by becoming members of official volunteer police organizations.[6]

The trade-off between public "professional" protection and part-time citizen "volunteer" protection is, of course, a topic of contemporary importance, especially given the economic dimensions of security. In any society where essential public service functions are in high demand but short supply (e.g., police), there exists an ongoing need for officials to make informed public policy decisions about the use of available resources.

During the 1980s, town, city, county, state, and federal agency heads were all told to accomplish more with fewer resources. Such downsizing became common nationwide. The improved economy during the 1990s, however, along with an aggressive national agenda to increase the number of police officers by one hundred thousand, substantially increased police numbers. While it might thus be argued that the need for volunteer police has been substantially diminished, the costs of adding more police have been high. The increased presence and better deployment of police have led to more arrests, which have increased the need for more prisons and courtrooms and more staff to run them. The added monetary demands have often been met by cutting expenditures in other public programs such as education and delinquency prevention. Such a policy approach seems to favor the idea that it is better to have personnel ready to arrest troubled youth and incarcerate them than to invest in programs designed to keep them out of trouble in the first place (Fisher 1999). Volunteer police programs could be particularly helpful in the prevention of juvenile delinquency and substance abuse, therefore decreasing the need for cash-starved communities to engage in a triage approach with respect to the services of municipal human service workers.

The recruitment and deployment of volunteers may also help address real needs that have received little attention from government agencies. For many years, for example, the field of criminal justice has been subjected to criticism for failing to meet the needs of crime victims. Currently, much of the credit for present laws regarding the control of intoxicated drivers is owed to the citizen-based organization Mothers against Drunk Driving (MADD) (Weed 1987). Volunteers, in fact, have many potential roles to play in delinquency prevention, narcotics control, and other types of crime control.

The need for a citizen role in community safety can also be illustrated by considering less tangible matters. The public's contribution to a civic enterprise, for example, can be of value for its own sake: active citizen participation in community affairs is one of the hallmarks of a stable democracy. In addition, citizens who become involved in public affairs often gain a better sense of purpose in life, as well as the opportunity to develop new competencies. Volunteer police learn not only about street survival in their training but also about how the various branches of government serve to check each other and how the existence of law is dependent on the consent of the governed. Near the close of the twentieth century, there was a general need for higher levels of civic engagement by Americans. The period from 1973 to 1994, for example, saw a 40 percent decline in the ranks of those who had served as an officer or committee member of any local club or organization (Putnam 2000, 42). Fortunately, this trend may soon be reversed, since "young Americans in the 1990s displayed a commitment to volunteerism without parallel among their immediate predecessors" (Putnam 2000, 133). This spirit of volunteerism, however, must persist into adulthood and "expand beyond individual care giving to broader engagement with social and political issues" (Putnam 2000, 133).

Volunteer policing is also relevant to the problem of race relations in America. After the Civil War and the passage of the Civil Rights Amendments to the Constitution, the U.S. Army, during Reconstruction, helped protect the rights of former slaves living in the South. Reconstruction, however, came to an abrupt end when federal troops were withdrawn toward the end of the 1870s. By 1890, racial injustice in the form of "Jim Crow" laws (the poll tax, segregated public accommodations, etc.) had become part of the fabric of American life, especially in the South. Even by the time of World War II, racism was still in full force in America. In 1940, for example, African Americans were permitted to serve only in segregated army units, and all blacks were barred from the army's air corps and the marines (Abrahamson 1983, 163). By the end of the twentieth century, observers in the field of American justice had learned about a new form of racial injustice: racial profiling. As police patrols searched for drug traffickers, it became standard practice to include a subject's race as part of his or her profile in order to decide which persons and cars to stop on the nation's highways ("Sweeping Ruling Cites" 1999). In fact, according to a recent survey conducted by the Siena College Research Institute, most blacks and Hispanics believe that the American justice system is flawed. In particular, 74 percent of blacks and 85 percent of Hispanics believe that police actively use racial profiling (Siena Research Institute 2000). Moreover, while the percentage of minorities in local police departments has risen steadily since 1987, there is still room for improvement (Bureau of Justice Statistics 1999). Efforts to re-cruit minorities directly into the ranks of the regular police, however, have not always met with success. Perhaps the recruitment of more minority vol-unteer police could lead to a solution: the number of full-time minority po-lice could be increased after volunteers have served for awhile and had a chance to become familiar with police work. In recent years, indeed, this trend has emerged in general, certain volunteer police becoming regular police. Thus, an increase in the number of minorities serving in volunteer police units might very well lead to a corresponding increase in the number of regular minority police officers.[7]

In the United States, as well as in many other parts of the world, there ex-ists an ongoing need for emergency public services, in large part because paid professional human resources have not always been affordable or available. Many communities have opted to meet their needs through the recruitment and training of volunteers. While the activities of volunteer firemen, ambulance squads, and hospital volunteers are fairly well-known, volunteer policing remains a mystery to many Americans, its contributions only recently publicized.

In the late 1980s, President George H. W. Bush announced a national campaign to recruit volunteers for social work and other similar occupa-tions, stating, "Just imagine an America where service to others is a fact of life, part of everyone's everyday thinking" (Bush 1989). Yet we still "know practically nothing about the ecology of neighborhood or city self-defense" (Kelling and Stewart 1989, 5). Research into the history, organization, and activities of volunteer police should ultimately help shed some new light on the citizen's role in public safety and homeland security.

2

The Lay Justice Era   From 1607 to 1800

The only thing necessary for the triumph of evil is for good men to do nothing.
EDMUND BURKE, 1770

The settlements of the early colonists, who depended on boats for their transportation to the New World, were usually close to deep water. For example, in 1607, the first permanent English settlement was established at Jamestown, at the mouth of the James River (Carnes, Garraty, and Williams 1996). The first white settlement in New York—originally controlled by the Dutch East India Company and known as Fort Amsterdam, later renamed by the English in honor of the Duke of York—took place at the southern end of the island of Manhattan. During the 1620s, English immigrants settled along the banks of the James and York Rivers and the Chesapeake Bay. The English Puritans founded Plymouth Colony in 1620 and Massachusetts Bay Colony in 1630 along the Massachusetts Bay. Roger Williams established Rhode Island in 1636 on the shores of Narragansett Bay after being forced out of Massachusetts for advocating religious toleration.

More than a hundred years before Benjamin Franklin organized the first volunteer fire company in Philadelphia, the early settlers of Jamestown, New Amsterdam, and Plymouth, vast sections of their settlements having been destroyed by disastrous fires, recognized the need for organized fire-prevention activities. Their earliest efforts at fire prevention included the patrols of a night watch, inspection of chimneys, and the provision of water resources (Hashagan 1998).[1]

The special conditions of the New World also required colonists to modify some of their Old World customs regarding law and order. Initially, since the colonists lived in small settlements, most individuals knew one another. Thus, evading detection was rare—especially since "every colonist was a policeman" (H. A. Johnson and Wolfe 1996, 79)—and the constant need for workers reduced the number of executions. However, as settlements later grew in size, especially in the seaports, the notion that social control merely required neighborly vigilance faded, and colonists, during times of public disorder, began to call upon units of the colonial militias.

The Maintenance of Social Order

Every American colony except Pennsylvania organized a militia system during the seventeenth century. Militia companies generally consisted of all free adult white males, and members were required to provide their own weapons, to keep them in good working order, and to attend regular drills. The power to muster militia units was given to local militia officers, since "the threat of surprise attack and the isolation of many localities made that power essential" (Cress 1982, 4). These officers were either elected—by militia members, local assemblies, or officials—or appointed by the colonial governor. By the middle of the eighteenth century, however, militias no longer acted as a viable citizen army that could be mustered for frontier defense or other military requirements: "Instead of a citizen army, colonists relied on special fighting forces manned by draftees and volunteers and officered by British regulars or American colonists holding commissions outside the militia establishment" (Cress 1982, 7).

The changing role of the militia, away from the provision of external defense, coincided with the need to provide internal protection for America's centers of commerce, especially its growing and crowded seaports, with their transient populations (H. A. Johnson and Wolfe 1996). In New York and other parts of New England, the militia was directly connected with the provision of police services as a result of the formation of night watches. By statute, militias were used "as the organizational base for distributing night-watch duty among the citizenry" (Cress 1982, 7). In times of emergency, the militia could also be called upon to restore order in conjunction with the *posse comitatus*. The *posse comitatus*, or "power of the county," refers to an ancient British common-law right empowering sheriffs to summon the assistance of any citizen in times of civil disorder. In America, this right was put into statutory form and extended to other types of peace officers and most magistrates (Prassel 1972).

In both the North and the South, militias were used to maintain the institution of slavery. In the North, the New York City militia subdued a slave revolt in 1741 (Cress 1982). In 1739, southern militia groups suppressed the Stono Rebellion, a significant slave revolt that resulted in the loss of more than sixty lives. The rebellion began near the western branch of the Stono River, about twenty miles from Charleston, South Carolina, eventually leading to an amendment to the law requiring at least one white for every ten blacks on any plantation. The amendment also raised the fines for violations and dictated that any monies collected be earmarked for the support of slave patrols (see Wood 1974, 308–25).

The formal system of social control in colonial America also included local courts or justices of the peace, legislative bodies, town constables, and local sheriffs (H. A. Johnson and Wolfe 1996). Initially, sheriffs were appointed by colonial governors, but since persons of means were sometimes able to influence such decisions, over time the office of sheriff became an elected one, as it still is. Sheriffs typically derived their income from local fees paid for serving court papers and housing prisoners. On the other hand, male adults were most often obligated to serve as members of the watch and as constables. In 1712, a law was passed in Philadelphia that imposed a fine on anyone who refused such a role. Constables were later able to derive income from fees collected from local courts and from individuals for services rendered, thus making the position less onerous. Eventually, in 1800, the office of constable in New York City became an elected one (S. S. Walker 1998, 25–27).

Constables acted "as the line peace officers in every jurisdiction" (Chapin 1983, 96). New England towns elected these officers of the peace for a one-year term, following the English pattern, while constables were appointed by the governors of Virginia and Maryland (Chapin 1983, 96). The responsibilities of colonial constables included apprehending minor offenders and suspicious persons, executing warrants and other court orders, initiating and pursuing the hue and cry, inspecting taverns to see that all patrons were orderly, establishing and supervising the town watch, collecting local taxes, supervising the sealing of weights and measures, maintaining custody of all lost goods, identifying and arresting runaway servants, ensuring family cohesion, serving as town coroner, acting as the chief election official, escorting offenders to court and presenting the charges, recommending that certain persons secure a bond (recognizance) for the peace or for good behavior, and placing accused or convicted persons in the stocks or in jail (Chapin 1983, 28, 31, 52, 96–97). The "recognizance system" was an early form of community crime prevention that involved warnings, the posting of bonds for good behavior, and monitoring whether or not persons met the conditions of a bond. The system was effective because pre-1660 communities were small (Chapin 1983, 28).

A guard group was used to protect the port town of Charleston, South Carolina, toward the end of the seventeenth century. A local ordinance provided for the establishment of a night watch, which consisted of regular constables and groups of six citizens who served on a rotating basis. Heads of households, both men and women, were required to serve on the watch, and a fine of fifteen pence was charged for each missed rotation unless a substitute was provided. The watch, authorized to arrest any wrongdoer, served from ten in the evening until sunrise (Hadden 1993, 23).

Slavery in North America probably began with the arrival of twenty black slaves at Jamestown in 1619; with slavery "developed that special racial feeling—whether hatred, or contempt, or pity, or patronization—that accompanied the inferior position of blacks in America for the next 350 years—that combination of inferior status and derogatory thought we call racism" (Zinn 1990, 23). These first slaves were used by Virginia's corn and tobacco growers, who sold their corn crop locally and exported their tobacco. By the time slaves arrived in Jamestown, a million had already been forced to labor in the Portuguese and Spanish colonies of the Caribbean and South America (Zinn 1990, 25).

America's earliest criminal justice systems—established in Virginia, Plymouth, Massachusetts Bay, Maryland, Rhode Island, Connecticut, and New Haven prior to 1660, and aided by demographic patterns, small populations, and relatively short distances—were the most efficient the nation has ever had: "Courts met regularly, normally every month, and usually cleared their dockets in each session" (Chapin 1983, 97). These early courts were also rigid. Those convicted of the crime of fornication in the Massachusetts Bay colony, for example, frequently met with such punishments as being whipped, being fined, being put in the stocks, or being forced to marry (W. Friedman 1998, 187). Such strict views were also held and enforced regarding Sabbath observance. In colonial Maryland, Sabbath violations (swearing, drinking, or working) could lead to a fine and public repentance; a third violation might incur a whipping. Sorcery was a capital offense. Maryland's punishment for adultery or fornication included anything deemed appropriate, short of taking a "life or member" (Semmes 1966, 174). No doubt, such harsh punishments, along with judicial efficiency, helped account for the very low rate of recidivism in most colonial settlements.

Regulations regarding servants and slavery were also of special concern to colonists. The early settlers of Maryland had been encouraged to bring servants with them, and it was considered essential for any "gentleman" to have at least one.[2] Servants helped build houses, clear fields, plant and harvest crops, and take care of livestock. The services of boatwrights, brickmakers, coopers, and other skilled workers were especially needed (Semmes 1966).

Most servants in early Maryland were indentured, although many worked for wages (sometimes in the form of tobacco, clothing, or land). An indenture was a contract that pledged a servant to work for a master for a number of years in exchange for food, clothing, shelter, and the cost of transportation to the New World. The average period of indenture was five years, although skilled workers could bargain for smaller periods and other favorable terms. A servant's work was hard and long, and indentured servants could be sold or assigned to new masters during their period of indenture. Typically, however, masters were at least obligated at the end of servants' indenture to provide them with some goods and even land so that they could become self-supporting (Semmes 1966).

Maidservants who were mistreated by their masters could be freed or sold to another master. Masters who brutalized their servants might receive a light fine to be paid with tobacco, but some were not required to pay anything (Semmes 1966, 100). Runaway servants were often recaptured. The "hue and cry" would be raised, and a reward of two hundred pounds of tobacco might be paid for their return. This bounty doubled for the return of a servant who had fled to some other colony, Indians being promised "a matchcoat as a reward" for returning a runaway (Semmes 1966, 110). Any person who helped transport or protect a runaway servant "had to pay the servant's master all damages he had sustained by the loss of the servant's services" (Semmes 1966, 112). Colonists were nonetheless frequently accused of aiding servants, and by 1666, a law had been passed that punished such activity by imposing a progressive fine.

Recaptured servants faced such penalties as two extra days of service for each day of absence, as well as an additional seven years of servitude, although whippings could be substituted for additional service. By 1662, a pass had to be carried by a servant traveling more than ten miles from his or her master's house, and all colonists were empowered to stop strangers and inquire about their identity (Semmes 1966, 116–17).

The institution of slavery in North America was not officially regularized or legalized before the latter half of the seventeenth century. Still, from slavery's North American inception, various invidious forms of discrimination were based on the skin color of servants and slaves. In 1640, for example, a Virginia court ordered that a black woman servant be whipped for having a white man's child, while the white man was sentenced to attend church and perform a penance. Maryland adopted slave-control statutes in the 1660s. By 1750, slaves made up about a third of Maryland's population. It is also possible that by the end of the first decade of the eighteenth century, 10 percent of New York's population consisted of slaves, while slaves comprised nearly half of Virginia's population by the mid-1700s (Zinn 1990, 30–34). Slavery developed in America as a result of the following factors: "the desperation of starving settlers, the special helplessness of the displaced African, the powerful incentive of profit for slave trader and planter, the temptation of superior status for poor whites, the elaborate controls against escape and rebellion, the legal and social punishments of black and white collaboration" (Zinn 1990, 37).

In order for colonists to maintain strict control over slaves, various slave codes were adopted. The laws that southern colonists used to regulate slaves derived from either their own creative thinking or from laws already adopted in the Caribbean slave-holding colonies: "It has long been accepted that South Carolina relied heavily on the slave code formulated in Barbados, England's West Indian sugar producing colony" (Hadden 1993, 4). Such early island slave codes established curfews and included restrictions regarding holding meetings, the use of passes for travel, possession of weapons, riding horses, and selling goods without permission (Hadden 1993, 5). In the South, slave overseers were empowered to use severe punishments for rebellious slaves—whipping, burning, mutilation, and death (Zinn 1990, 35). The Virginia slave code contained the following provision regarding the treatment of runaway slaves: "if the slave does not immediately return, anyone whatsoever may kill or destroy such slaves by such ways and means as he . . . shall think fit" (qtd. in Zinn 1990, 34). Even after the American Revolution, the plight of both free blacks and slaves in the South did not improve. All blacks lived in constant fear of white violence.

Although colonial courts and other official agencies of the criminal justice system played a large role in regulating servitude and slavery and otherwise maintaining order, as in modern times, this role was secondary to that of the family. Then as now, family values and mores were the most important factors in society's quest for social order. In early colonial times, some localized portions of society had strong communitarian bonds and near cultural homogeneity. The Puritans, for example, maintained a distinctive set of traits that have come to be known as "the Puritan ideal," centered on the patriarchal family and other values common to the seventeenth-century Puritan settlers. The essential features of the Puritan patriarchal model required "the father to become the minister of his dependents, disciplining them, catechizing them, praying with them, reading the Bible to them, generally putting the fear of God into them" (Thompson 1986, xvi).

Such fundamentalist religious practices clearly dominated the overall maintenance of social control during the early years of the colonial era, even though the Puritan lifestyle eventually failed, probably because grown-up children were not converted in sufficient numbers. Still, several aspects of the Puritan way of life stand out as illustrations of how the earliest American communities maintained social order. Single persons, for example, were required to find patriarchal families to live with. Selectmen were dispatched to make sure families were attending to the educational needs of their children. Tithingmen were selected to generally oversee the good order of groups made up of ten to twelve families (Morgan 1966, 145–49). These tithingmen, along with members of night watches and constables, were among America's first volunteer police. Tithingmen were appointed by governmental action and did not receive a salary.

Early New Yorkers, like most southerners, were concerned about controlling their slave population. Slave conspiracies were discovered in 1712 and 1741. In 1712, eighteen slaves and nine white coconspirators were executed; in 1741, thirty-one slaves and five white coconspirators were executed (Bailey and Green 1999, 8).

Despite these convictions, however, in colonial New York during the eighteenth century, 37 percent of about fifty-three hundred court cases resulted in neither conviction nor acquittal. Courts were unable to carry cases to final judgment because of the lack of an effective criminal justice system in most regions of the colony. For example, in some instances, appointed constables refused to take their oath of office or perform required duties. New York's system of jurisprudence suffered overall from the poor quality of its constabulary, jails, local judges, and juries (D. Greenberg 1976, 66, 71, 217).

In Philadelphia, from colonial times through the middle of the nineteenth century, private prosecution of crime—"one citizen taking another to court without the intervention of the police" (Steinberg 1989, 1)—was the basis of law enforcement. The democratic and egalitarian aspects of this system helped account for its longevity, private prosecutions providing a stake in the legal and political system for relatively powerless classes and groups. For example, battered wives could avail themselves of this method of justice, which often resulted in prison sentences for their husbands (Steinberg 1989, 231, 69).

In many other jurisdictions, however, the phrase "civilly dead" aptly summarizes the legal status of women before the early part of the twentieth century. During the early colonial period, women seem to have suffered physical punishment more than men. For example, in cases of adultery or fornication, some men might be fined, but women were often whipped. The penalty of whipping was more likely to be imposed if a woman had no means to pay a fine or no friends to help her pay it (Semmes 1966, 176–83). Although women in America had to endure a subordinate role until the latter half of the twentieth century, their situation perhaps first began to change in August 1775, when Thomas Paine, editor of the *Pennsylvania Magazine*, featured a landmark essay on their underprivileged position. Later, in 1776, his publication of the pamphlet *Common Sense* helped convert thousands of colonists to the cause of independence.

The more localized nature of colonial society permitted greater reliance on the church, the family, and the community for the maintenance of social control. In general, the colonists' concern focused primarily on the need to return an offender to the community as soon as possible. Thus, sentencing was aimed at producing public shame and humiliation. This proved effective in preventing future wrongdoing not only by the particular offender but also in the community at large. When most towns had fewer than a thousand residents, most residents attended the same church, and when only a few persons could afford to travel, the threat of public embarrassment was a strong deterrent. Obviously, the stranger or newcomer was not as easily subjected to shame, and most colonial towns were quite wary of such persons. Special ordinances were adopted to cope with strangers who had no visible means of support, the majority of the laws designed to encourage strangers to return to their place of origin or risk corporal punishment, such as whipping. In 1663, for example, a Connecticut law empowered constables to detain any person who seemed out of place and could not reasonably account for his or her actions (S. S. Walker 1998, 26). A practice known as "outlawing" was even more forbidding. Outlawing meant that an individual could legally be hunted and killed and their property sold at auction, with proceeds going to the government. In 1770, a provision for outlawing was included in a North Carolina antiriot statute (Kars 2002, 187).

Legal rights and duties did exist in the midst of all the formal and informal colonial institutions of social control. These included the right to trial by jury, the prohibition of search or seizure without a warrant, the right to reasonable bail, grand-jury indictments in capital cases, and the right to know the charges being pressed against one, along with other rights well-known to twenty-first-century Americans. These rights, however, were more representative of a set of attitudes than of reality, and even a brief examination of the colonial criminal justice period should quickly dispel "any notion that the rights of defendants embodied modern definitions in anything other than embryonic form" (Bodenhamer 1992, 20). Significantly, while the language of colonial rights resembles language common in modern America, the substance of these rights was different. Thus, during the colonial period, general procedural fairness was important, "but the good order of society took precedence over the liberty of the individual" (Bodenhamer 1992, 28). Moreover, because of the scarcity of law books and legal training, "many constables and justices of the peace simply did not know the law" (S. S. Walker 1998, 26). It was also not uncommon for bribes to be offered and accepted and for constables to enforce the law in an arbitrary manner.

Volunteer Police Organizations

In a variety of ways, the formal or official agencies of social control during the colonial era were, in fact, volunteer police organizations. The volunteer police of this period included militia members, Native American military societies, slave patrollers (necessary because of the peculiar institution of slavery in the South and its expansion after independence), members of the night watch, and constables. In addition, members of the general citizenry could be summoned immediately in times of emergency through the "hue and cry" or the *posse comitatus*. Generally, colonial citizens were expected to work, raise families, and respond to calls for assistance from one another. They were also obligated to serve as constables when called upon. The idea that everyone held police responsibility was generally accepted.

Not only did militia members help fill the ranks of the night watch and slave patrols, but membership provided individuals with a sense of identification with their settlement, town, or county. This feeling of affiliation was critical not only for general peacekeeping but for survival. Militias alone, however, were not always sufficient. In the most rural parts of the colony of South Carolina, for example, the lack of sufficient means of mobilization or even a court system contributed to the rise of a vigilante organization of self-appointed citizens known as "regulators." Regulators were "law-abiding citizens who organized patrols and tried members of criminal bands and others deemed to have committed crimes" (H. A. Johnson and Wolfe 1996, 121). Back-country conditions in South Carolina were summarized in a petition for assistance sent to the British government in 1764 by the Reverend Charles Woodmason: "Our large stocks of cattle are either stolen or destroyed, our cow pens are broken up, and all our valuable horses carried off. Houses have been burned by these rogues, and families stripped and turned naked into the wood. . . . No responsible persons and traders dare keep cash or any valuable articles by them. Nor can women stir abroad but with a guard, or in terror" (qtd. in Albanese 1999, 152). Woodmason's petition also included requests for the establishment of a court system and local jails, a printed criminal code, requiring public officials to carry out their duty under penalty of law, the founding of public schools, and the establishment of parishes with ministers (Albanese 1999, 153).[3] There was also a significant regulator movement in North Carolina ten years before the outbreak of the American Revolution. Now known as the Regulator Rebellion of 1766–71, it involved thousands of backcountry farmers who hoped to overturn repressive structural economic conditions in order to attain "a reasonable chance to earn and retain economic independence" (Kars 2002, 216). These farmers "advocated laws that gave those who improved the land first right to obtain title, . . . a secret ballot, so they could vote their political interests without fear of reprisals, . . . fair debt collection laws and small-claims courts" (Kars 2002, 216).

Native American military societies were grounded in the traditions of a communal people. Long ago, a hardy band of Mongolian hunters and gatherers crossed the vast land bridge between North American and Asia and traveled south and east (Jennings 1974; Thornton 1987). As they moved over the North and South American continents, they developed diverse languages and other separate cultural traits, though details of their early customs and traditions are unknown, "since most . . . subscribed to a non-literate, oral tradition" (Driver 1975; French 1982, 2). Still, legal anthropologists have studied the history of the Great Plains Indian tribes, discovering that when community norms were violated, sanctions were imposed, including mutilation, execution, and banishment (Hoebel 1954; Roberts 1979). The rendering of justice, however, was honed through an overriding interest in the restoration of social equilibrium (Deloria and Lytle 1983). Thus, restitution (e.g., forced labor for the tribe or the victim) and public scorn (e.g., public ridicule, group pressure) were common punishments for even relatively serious crimes (M. L. Barker 1994).

Generally, disputes between Native Americans were most often settled privately, with restitution a frequent option, its amount dependent on the victim's importance (Hagan 1966). For example, "a horse and blanket might satisfy the widow of a murdered warrior who had been unproductive and of low status" (M. L. Barker 1994, 34). However, when private bargaining failed, the help of a third party, such as the tribal chief or another respected individual, might be sought (Hoebel 1968). In a variation on this practice, the Sioux and Cherokee both enforced communal punishment by members of volunteer tribal police forces when restitution was deemed inappropriate.

The Sioux maintained an organized system of volunteer police known as the *akicitas*. (Such police forces are also called "warrior societies," "policing societies," or "whip-bearers" by various authors [see, e.g., Humphrey 1942;

Hoxie 1986; Hassrick 1964].) The *akicitas* lived in their own separate tents when the band was on the move and were supported by tribal contributions. Each band usually had several such societies that a young warrior could join. The *akicita* societies served as an enforcement arm of the tribal council, used as a last resort to ensure law and order and selected at the spring gathering of the various bands of the Sioux by the tribal leader or a council of leaders. Since their authority was derived from tribal leaders, the *akicitas* were accountable to them. Their assignments could last just for the duration of the summer hunts or throughout the year. During communal hunting activities, *akicitas* kept noise levels down, performed scouting missions to ensure security, repressed the tendency of some hunters to behave too anxiously, helped prevent others from falling behind, and questioned tribe members to learn the identity of individuals who violated community rules (M. L. Barker 1994, 37–39). *Akicitas* could also be called upon to carry out various types of punishment—such as the destruction of property (shelters, rifles, etc.), corporal punishment, and banishment—but only as a last resort (M. L. Barker 1994, 39). Where several such warrior societies were active, the responsibilities of each group would be rotated to ensure that as many young warriors as possible could have a chance to perform the most important duties (M. L. Barker 1994, 37).

The Cherokee lived in an area that is today the state of Georgia. Perhaps because of their location, they adopted many of the customs of their white neighbors. In 1808, the Cherokee (one of the "Five Civilized Tribes"), "admired and respected by the settlers because of their apparent willingness to acculturate" (M. L. Barker 1994, 40), instituted a system of appointed sheriffs and a group of quasi-police they called the "lighthorse." These men enforced the first written legal code adopted by a native tribe (Hagan 1966). The lighthorse consisted of small companies, each including four privates and two officers who patrolled on horseback, one company assigned to each district of the Cherokee nation. Their main responsibility was to apprehend criminals and deliver them to tribal courts. In 1825, the Cherokee National Council replaced the lighthorse companies with marshals, sheriffs, and constables. Cherokee sheriffs and constables were elected at the district level, while marshals were tribal-level officers required to enforce tribal laws, such as the prohibition of alcohol. The Cherokee were also the first tribe to establish a central legislature and a system of tribal courts. All such arrangements, however, lasted only until about 1838, when the Cherokee were disbanded as a result of their forced removal from Georgia to Oklahoma (M. L. Barker 1994, 41–42).

The experience of the Cherokee was typical. The "harmony model of justice" remained relatively consistent in the Indian territories of North America until the destruction of traditional ways through forced segregation onto reservations and the abolition of communal land ownership. The Dawes Act of 1887 and the Curtis Act of 1898 marked the end of most traditional tribal governmental practices. These acts "required Natives to abide by the laws of the non-Indian governments operating in their area—state or territorial"—and prohibited the communal ownership of most reservation land (M. L. Barker 1994, 44).

The military or warrior societies of the Plains Indians carried out overt police functions—preserving order in the camp, during moves, and during hunts; punishing offenders who violated the public welfare—on a permanent basis (Mails 1973, 370). Indeed, the Cherokee lighthorsemen and the Sioux *akicitas* might be thought of as "the first 'police departments' in America" (M. L. Barker 1994, 36). Warrior societies also served as "the war force of the tribe. Every man whose age made him eligible for the responsibility of being a defender of his tribe and land was expected to make his choice among the available orders in the non-graded tribal scheme or to start up the ladder at the appropriate point in the age-graded complex" (Mails 1973, 46). The societies had tremendous secular and religious significance:

> They: preserved order in the camp; preserved order during camp moves; preserved order during hunts; punished offenders against the public welfare; guarded the camp against possible attacks by an enemy, both at the camp and while moving; kept the camp informed at all times as to the movements of the buffalo herds; fostered intersociety rivalry to cultivate bravery and a military spirit among themselves, and among boys who needed a living example of their future responsibilities; took the commanding and most dangerous places in battle; ministered to the desires of members for recreation through feasts and dances; served as keepers and reminders of the tribe's heritage and traditions; played a unique role in government by serving as the active but temporary dispensers of author-

ity; and served as creative display centers where recognition was given for honors earned by warriors and women's guild workers for tasks well done on behalf of the tribe. (Mails 1973, 370)

By now many of these functions have been forgotten, certainly by the whites who took over Native American lands and forced Native Americans onto reservations, but members of warrior societies played powerful community roles, worthy of admiration.

In contrast, a rather different type of volunteer policing emerged as a result of the slaveholding practices of colonial Americans, who held a quarter of a million people as slaves by the mid-1700s and double that number by the time the Declaration of Independence was signed. By 1790, the slave population numbered nearly seven hundred thousand. The invention of the cotton gin in 1793 decreased the cost of cotton and increased demand for cotton goods, making the South even more dependent on slave labor (W. L. Katz 1990, 19, 21). America's justice system, throughout this period, treated both African Americans and Native Americans in accordance with the dictates of a racist society (S. S. Walker 1998, 23).

During much of the seventeenth century, slave patrols did not exist.[4] The control and discipline of slaves were considered the responsibility of any free and responsible citizen. The slave population was small, and large-scale cotton plantations, made possible by the invention of the cotton gin, did not yet exist, so a truly voluntary system of policing was adequate (Yanochik 1997, 179). Eventually, however, the slave owners' need for a more organized system to protect their "assets" became clear.

The need for law enforcement in the coastline city of Charleston, South Carolina, was more urgent, and organization took place early. Local laws provided for the establishment of a night watch that was mainly concerned with slave activities. In more rural areas of South Carolina, where the slave population was growing quickly, special slave patrols were established by the end of the seventeenth century. Members of these patrols, both slave owners and nonowners, were selected by captains of the regular militia companies and were obligated to stay behind when the regular militia was needed to contend with possible invasion on the coast or possible Indian attack. Typically, slave patrols were organized when the number of slaves increased to a level that made it impractical for individual slave owners to supervise them. Their most routine activities were checking suspicious persons and limiting nighttime movement on country lanes, as well as searching for missing slaves hiding on local plantations. The patrols and the militia formally merged in South Carolina after 1721, and for a period of three years, beginning in 1734, a yearly stipend was paid to patrollers, patrol captains receiving fifty pounds each and other patrol members allotted twenty-five pounds (Hadden 1993, x–xi, 30–38).

While South Carolina's slave-patrol system provided a model for Georgia, the colonies of Virginia and North Carolina developed a different system. These colonies took longer to begin patrols in part since they had fewer slaves. Their systems, like South Carolina's, were modeled on laws designed for controlling indentured servants, fleeing debtors, and Indians. Procedures for the recovery of servants and slaves included responding to the "hue and cry" and posting rewards. The latter practice encouraged the growth of a new trade: that of the independent slave catcher. In 1727, the slave patrol system in Virginia became yet more organized when members became formally excused from militia drills and received exemptions from various county or parish taxes (Hadden 1993, 41–47, 58).

Slave patrols regulated the conduct of slaves who journeyed to and from plantations, traveling on their masters' errands. Slaves were also permitted time away from their duties as an incentive to increase their productivity. Thus, "slaves were frequently granted permission by their owners to travel unescorted to nearby towns for recreation" (Yanochik 1997, 171).

While courts could mandate punishment after trial for serious crimes, slave patrols were used by southerners to contend with more common disorderly activities. Patrols, then, not only limited opportunities for slaves to gather for the purpose of planning a revolt but also could help limit recreation that might make them less fit for work on the following day. Patrols could monitor all slaves in transit by checking their passes, which were written by slave masters or their family members and served as orders permitting slaves to travel during specified periods of time. In the early nineteenth century, a South Carolina law provided that any person who forged a pass could receive a maximum fine of one thousand dollars and twelve months' imprisonment (M. A. Henry 1968, 28–30).

However, a regular system of patrols was not immediately perceived as an efficient way to check passes. At first, colonists adopted laws that merely permitted any person to apprehend, summarily punish, and send back to the plantation any slave without a proper pass. Such a law was adopted in South Carolina, for example, in 1686. In 1690, this statute was strengthened by the establishment of a fine of forty shillings for anyone who failed to carry out these responsibilities. Although the first patrols were officially sanctioned in 1704, their members were to be drawn from existing militia companies and, moreover, were only to patrol in time of general public danger or alarm. Thirty years later, patrols were regularized by a new statute that provided annual compensation for each member. The South Carolina slave patrol laws remained consistent from 1740 through 1819, with the duty of working on a slave patrol restricted to slave owners and overseers (M. A. Henry 1968, 31–35). The Georgia Colonial Assembly enacted its first formal patrol law in 1757, requiring justices of the peace and constables to monitor slaves in towns and assigning control of slaves in rural areas to sheriffs (Yanochik 1997, 182–83).

Most slave patrollers were essentially drafted for such work, and the existence of exemptions for various groups "created a feeling of animosity between the men forced to serve and the fortunate enough to avoid service" (Yanochik 1997, 206). Involuntary slave patrols thus had much to do with diminishing the growth of democratic institutions, especially in the South. This was especially true for free blacks, for controlling them was considered to be of the utmost importance in securing the safety of the white population: it was feared that free blacks might encourage slave uprisings. The fate of free blacks, therefore, was often directly linked to the treatment afforded slaves in a given community (Yanochik 1997, 188–90). Most participatory democratic options for both free blacks and slaves were severely repressed in colonial America and for many years thereafter. In South Carolina, the repression of African Americans was codified between 1690 and 1740 through codes restricting almost all aspects of life, including freedom of movement, religious worship, and work habits. These codes were enforced by sheriffs, constables, and slave patrols (W. C. Henderson 1976, 34–35). As the colonial era unfolded and gave way to the antebellum period that preceded the Civil War, laws pertaining to slave patrols were revised and adjusted according to such factors as geography, population density, the slave population, and the occurrence and severity of slave revolts. The transformation of the colonists' approach to slave control—from a generally shared civic duty to one involving more specialized roles—became inevitable as a consequence of economic development: increased productivity, greater investment, capital accumulation, technological improvements, and corresponding changes in the division of labor. The colonists, in other words, began to rely on specialists, "individuals with comparative advantages to other members of the community . . . (e.g., individuals with proper equipment, training, attitudes, etc., for police work)" (Yanochik 1997, 182).

While the South relied primarily on a system of slave patrols for the maintenance of social order, the key instrument of volunteer policing in the emerging industrial regions of the North was the watch system. The watch system required that all adult males provide service on a rotating basis. Tours usually began at either nine or ten p.m. and lasted until the early morning hours. The watch was authorized by governmental action for the purpose of permanently and overtly performing one or more police functions. During the colonial era, the most common emergencies that watch members encountered included fires, Indian attacks, wild animals, runaway slaves, thieves, and grave robbers. They were expected to cope with such incidents by suppressing disorder, arresting drunks, and enforcing the curfew (National Advisory Commission 1976, 30). Watch members received little or no compensation and no training, and in time, those individuals who could hire substitutes did so.

Social forces other than economic ones, however, also contributed to a gradual shift away from reliance on informal methods of social control during the colonial period. The declining influence of the clergy, as well as a more rapidly growing and diverse population, also led to the rise of specialists in law enforcement. Nevertheless, the importance of economic factors in the history of law enforcement cannot be overestimated. These economic factors, in fact, particularly regarding servitude, have persisted through time. Even today, various forms of servitude are still in existence in the United States. Thomas Perez, a former U.S. deputy assistant attorney general, indicates that more than one hundred cases involving victims of involuntary servitude are processed yearly. The U.S. Department of Justice currently defines involuntary servitude as "using physical force, threats of force or legal coercion (such as threats of arrest or incarceration) to keep someone working" (Gordy 2000, 4). Currently, many countries, including the United States, express deep concern about human rights violations.

Perhaps such violations may sufficiently outrage public opinion that new varieties of volunteer and/or professional police units will be established.

While those in a position of servitude, then as now, suffered a variety of abuses during the colonial era, white community members fared better, and there were some positive developments regarding their civil rights. In New York, by the middle of the eighteenth century, "public officials were surprisingly accessible and responsive to petitioners, often pardoning convicted defendants when the interests of justice seemed to be served" (D. Greenberg 1976, 216).

Although the end of America's colonial experience marked the beginning of a new nation, most colonial criminal justice institutions continued, with one notable exception: the new, specialized institution of the prison took the place of America's earlier reliance on public shame and embarrassment. Still, such humiliations as whipping, the use of stocks and pillories, branding, and the rituals associated with public execution were not necessarily replaced by the prison; rather, they were moved into a closed setting— inside prison walls. Moreover, while branding and the wearing of scarlet letters have faded away as forms of punishment, many might argue that more insidious criminal sanctions have taken their place. For example, in 1998, Delaware adopted a law requiring that the driver's licenses of convicted sex offenders be issued with the letter Y on the reverse side. The law was justified on the grounds that the "Y" designation would alert authorities regarding the status of the offender, especially when he or she moved to another state and applied for a new driver's license (Janofsky 1998, 16).

Whatever one may think of the effectiveness of such modern-day practices, they are grounded in the various colonial systems of law enforcement, which were mostly voluntary. Native American military societies, slave patrollers, watch members, and constables were all volunteer police: all members of a permanent organization or one established during wartime mobilization by governmental or societal action for the purpose of performing one or more police functions in an overt manner for minimal or no salary. Early constables and watch members were looked upon as members of permanent organizations established for the purpose of maintaining the order and safety of a city's inhabitants. Individuals were selected through governmental procedures (initially from the ranks of the local militia) and eventually were rewarded by receiving fees or a minimal salary for their services.

Similarly, southern slave patrollers were selected and provided small stipends. Native American military societies were permanent organizations until required to disband by congressional mandates, their members sharing in the communal ownership of property and sometimes receiving extra gifts for their services.

The volunteer police of the colonial era can also be categorized according to the special or general nature of their purpose and whether or not they acted in an aggressive (proactive) or defensive (reactive) manner (see table 1). The watchmen and constables of colonial America appear to represent Type I volunteer police (general purpose/reactive). Their duties were numerous, and in the absence of any other frontline support groups, they were the primary law enforcers of their era. As towns grew and crime became a more frequent concern, their duties expanded and became more difficult, leading many to evade them whenever possible (Peak 1997, 7). Native American military societies, on the other hand, were Type II (general purpose/proactive), their members performing a wide range of peacekeeping and tribal functions. Since they could also punish individuals for violating tribal customs, they performed a necessary role using proactive enforcement methods. Slave patrollers clearly demonstrated Type IV traits (special-purpose/proactive). Since patrollers had a central focus, their service was for a special purpose (i.e., slave control) rather than a general one. Moreover, slave patrollers were quite aggressive in their activities, never hesitating to use punitive means to carry out their duties.

While such general distinctions are helpful in developing a classification of volunteer police in American history, slave patrollers, as we have seen, were merely one variety of a growing band of "specialists," such as salaried sheriffs and constables. What is important is not so much the nature of the "specific" duties performed but the fact that the population at large was no longer being looked to for the maintenance of their own order (Yanochik 1997). The differentiation in roles between the ordinary citizen and officers of the law had begun.

3

The Vigilant Era From 1800 to the 1880s

If there is no struggle, there is no progress. Those who profess to favor freedom, and yet deprecate agitation, are men who want crops without plowing up the ground. They want the ocean without the awful roar of its many waters.

FREDERICK DOUGLASS, "The Significance of Emancipation in the West Indies"

By the middle of the eighteenth century, some American colonists had become discontented with British rule from across the Atlantic Ocean for both economic and political reasons. Politically, enlightened Americans wanted all the rights of the English; they wanted to be governed by Parliament, rather than by the Privy Council. Economically, they wanted to be permitted to engage in unfettered trade with other countries. These beliefs about the need for local autonomy were gradually manifested in actions. In Philadelphia, the first Continental Congress met on September 5, 1774, and conflicts took place in Massachusetts, Virginia, and North Carolina well before the signing of the Declaration of Independence on July 4, 1776 (H. A. Johnson and Wolfe 1996, 111, 119–20). On April 19, 1775, colonists fought in the battles at Lexington and Concord, marking the beginning of America's War for Independence. Less than two months later, George Washington was officially appointed commander in chief of the Continental Army. One year later, Richard Henry Lee, chairman of the Virginia delegation to the Second Continental Congress, offered the resolution that "these United Colonies are and of right ought to be free and independent states" and that a plan of confederation should be submitted to the several colonies. Congress adopted Lee's resolution declaring independence on July 2, 1776, and the draft of the formal Declaration of Independence, prepared by a committee chaired by Thomas Jefferson, on July 4, 1776. Underpinning the revolution was the fact that "America now embodied a mature and powerful

English-speaking community with a mind of its own and a future that it considered peculiarly its own" (Gibson 1954, 232). Cornwallis surrendered at Yorktown on October 19, 1781, but it took another two years for the end of the war to be officially proclaimed by Congress.

The founding fathers of the United States were some of the most learned men of their day, aware of the importance of representative institutions and of the value of written charters as guarantees of their freedoms. Far removed from the mother country of England, charters granted to trading companies and other entities were highly regarded (Nevins and Commager 1976, 19). The philosophical and political writings of the French intellectuals of the eighteenth century also had a profound effect on the course of U.S. history. Montesquieu, one of the most important of these intellectuals, published a treatise in 1748 entitled *L'esprit des lois* (The Spirit of the Laws). The section of this work that had the most impact on American government concerns the separation of governmental powers into three branches: the legislative, the executive, and the judicial. In the summer of 1787, at the Constitutional Convention in Philadelphia, James Madison cited Montesquieu's treatise as his authority for a system of separation of powers, as well as for the need to engage in compromise in order to complete the work of the Convention (Wernick 1989).

As previously noted, prior to America's independence, justice was administered along the coastline colonies by lay judges, community residents, militia members (some as slave patrollers), soldiers (English or Dutch), clergymen, various administrative officers (e.g., governors appointed by the English king), and legislative assemblies. On a broader scale, the Constitution of the United States, drafted in 1787, sets forth the structure of the legal system of the federal government. Former chief justice of the United States Warren Burger has declared that the "Constitution has had as great an impact on humanity as the splitting of the atom" (qtd. in Bowen 1986, x). Alexander Hamilton, "the most potent single influence toward calling the Convention of '87" (Bowen 1986, 5–6), acted as Washington's aide-de-camp during the war, but James Madison's total commitment to the actual work of the Convention has earned him the title of "Father of the Constitution." The central government established by the Constitution is one of limited powers, with most common police powers reserved for the states. After the adoption of the Constitution, during an extended period that lasted until

1873, state legislatures eliminated the earlier common practices of public whippings and hangings. At the same time, local courts shaped laws to meet the needs of America's rural settlements and agricultural areas (Pound 1930).

The basic, familiar machinery of the current justice system, including the courts and substantive and criminal procedural law, was introduced during the nineteenth century, a time of relatively "simple problems and straightforward tasks to lawmaker, prosecutor, judge, and jurist" (Pound 1930, 141). Most members of the legal profession were trained through the apprentice method of law office practice, a system marked by lack of organization, decentralized responsibility, and little cooperation that produced for the practice of criminal law a "type of politician lawyer, of little standing at the bar, or of the lowest stratum of the profession" (Pound 1930, 159). At the beginning of the twentieth century, much of this system had become a burden for the progressive development of America's urban industrial centers (Pound 1930, 155).

Thus, when the twentieth century dawned, America's legal and law enforcement establishments were far from perfect. In addition, the nation's experience with slavery until fairly late in the nineteenth century contributed to racial and class divisions that have persisted into the twenty-first century and have left a substantial mark on America's legal institutions. For one thing, slave patrol duty was a citizen obligation, much like duty on the night watch. The organization of such patrols played a major role not only in the ultimate development of police agencies but also in the evolving role of volunteer police in the United States.

The impact of slavery on the nation's institutions, however, was not limited to the legacy of the patrols. At the time of the American Revolution, British governors and generals issued various proclamations concerning slaves, promising freedom to slaves in exchange for either their services or their loyalty. Near the end of the war, in fact, the British recruited several black companies: "the choice of Loyalism permitted legal revenge against an American population that not only enslaved blacks but also terrorized them with a patrol system legally enforced by constables, justices of the peace, and minutemen, and a judicial system that employed quick execution for minor crimes" (Hodges 1998, 69). In 1776, when the Second Continental Congress formally declared in the Declaration of Independence that "all men are created equal" and possessed of the God-given right to "liberty," every one of the thirteen original colonies, soon to become independent states, contained many slaves of African descent. Only near the very end of the Revolutionary War did the states begin their slow journey toward the emancipation of all the new nation's slaves. The New England states and Pennsylvania led the way in 1784 by providing that the children of slaves born thereafter were to be freed upon reaching maturity. At the beginning of the nineteenth century, New York and New Jersey adopted the same position. Initially, only Massachusetts decided to emancipate existing slaves. Slave trading in the District of Columbia did not end until 1850. The Emancipation Proclamation, issued by President Abraham Lincoln during the Civil War, applied only to those areas still in rebellion. Slavery was finally banned throughout the entire nation, including its territories, by virtue of the ratification of the Thirteenth Amendment in 1865. It is important to keep in mind that the northern states engaged in the Civil War primarily to save the Union. The destruction of the institution of slavery served only as a means toward this end (Carnes, Garraty, and Williams 1996, 104–6).

Throughout the slavery era itself, runaways were pursued vigorously, and when caught they were severely punished.[1] While southern slave owners resented the assistance given to runaways by northern abolitionists, "the number of slaves who managed to get from the cotton belt to any free state was tiny, and was confined to blacks with special skills or circumstances" (Carnes, Garraty, and Williams 1996, 106). Indeed, it has been estimated that during the 1850s only about a thousand slaves each year were able to make successful escapes into the North, Canada, and Mexico (Zinn 1990, 171). Nevertheless, in general, running away was a more realistic solution than engaging in armed conflict with slaveholders, slave overseers, the militia, and slave patrollers.

In the early 1850s, a former slave from Georgia, renamed John Brown, dictated his memoirs to Louis Alexis Chamerovzow, secretary of the British and Foreign Anti-Slavery Society. Brown, who had lived in bondage for more than thirty years, had escaped to Canada and eventually settled in England, "where he worked at his slave-learned trade of carpentry and served the abolition cause as a lecturer and author" (Boney 1972, vii). Brown describes various types of punishment inflicted on runaway or disobedient slaves. In one instance, for example, he witnessed a ·practice known as "bucking," and on another occasion Brown himself was punished by being severely whipped and having to wear an iron device of bells and horns for three months. Bucking involved whipping a naked and defenseless slave for hours with willow switches and cowhide, placing the person in a sitting position with the hands tied over the knees. The knees were doubled up under the chin, and a stout stake was then placed under the part of the legs behind the knees: "In this position he [the slave] was turned first on one side and then on the other, and flogged . . . until the blood ran down in streams and settled under him in puddles" (Boney 1972, 35). The bells and horns were affixed in the following manner: "A circle of iron, having a hinge behind, with a staple and padlock before, which hangs under the chin, is fastened round the neck. Another circle of iron fits quite close around the crown of the head. The two are held together in this position by three rods of iron, which are fixed in each circle. These rods, or horns, stick out three feet above the head, and have a bell attached to each. The bells and horns do not weigh less than twelve to fourteen pounds" (Boney 1972, 76).

The U.S. Constitution, adopted in 1787, had not abolished slavery but only declared that the slave trade could end in 1808 if Congress so chose (Article I, Section 9). In fact, demand for slaves actually increased in the South during the last decade of the eighteenth century and the early part of the nineteenth because of the expansion of the cotton industry after the invention of the cotton gin, which resulted in increased domestic and overseas demand for cotton goods. By 1794, while all the states had banned the importation of slaves, enforcement was limited. In late 1803, South Carolina went so far as to repeal its ban, "bowing to economic pressure and the difficulty of enforcing its law" (D. F. Henderson 1985, 163). In 1808, however, Congress did finally prohibit the slave trade.

Congress adopted various compromises between 1820 and 1850, trying to contend with the problem of whether to permit slavery in the new federal territories and attempting also to balance representation in the U.S. Senate between slave and free states. Representation in the House was not in dispute: the free states of the North had almost twice the population of the slave states of the South. The compromise that resulted in the Fugitive Slave Act of 1850 was probably the most contentious. In exchange for the admission of California into the Union as a nonslave state, slaveholders were granted the right to special procedures and the aid of federal officials in securing the return of runaway slaves. By 1860, there were four million slaves in the United States, owned by approximately 350,000 white families. In the South, "African Americans raised 90 percent of all cotton, an even larger percentage of Virginia's tobacco, and almost all of Kentucky's hemp, Louisiana's sugar, and Carolina's rice" (W. L. Katz 1990, 20). The states of the South, in other words, were highly dependent on the labor of their slaves and were unrelenting in their pursuit of any who tried to escape, most often through the use of slave patrols.

In North Carolina, the first slave patrollers were known simply as "searchers." In 1757, these searchers were selected by county judges and empowered to enter slave dwellings to seize weapons. Each searcher was excused from jury duty and service in the militia and also exempted from local taxes (Hadden 1993, 64–65). The responsibility for establishing patrols in North Carolina originally rested in the county courts instead of with militia captains (as in Virginia and South Carolina). The patrols were so organized because militia companies might not regularly meet, whereas "the county court would always convene, and hence the court would be a more responsible agent for this delegated duty" (Hadden 1993, 65). Nonetheless, it was not until after the American Revolution that patrollers in North Carolina were authorized to detain slaves who were traveling between plantations and to enter the homes of whites in search of runaway slaves. In 1830, North Carolina's approach to establishing slave patrols changed: committees composed of three prominent men from each district of a county were appointed for the purpose of selecting and supervising patrol members. The use of such committees permitted county courts to focus on their increasing caseloads (Hadden 1993, 65–66, 83).

In South Carolina, slave owners sought to evade patrol responsibilities in several ways: "One way was to confuse officials as to their true residence. Claiming residence at different plantations allowed slave owners to move back and forth without fulfilling any patrol service" (Green 1997, 115). Slaveholders might also employ substitutes "to perform their duties in exchange for money, foodstuffs, or use of their slaves" (Green 1997, 115). A new and elaborate patrol law, adopted in South Carolina in 1819, sought to remedy such problems as the evasion of patrol duty, the disorderly behavior of patrol members, and interference with carrying out patrol duties. Persons failing to patrol could be fined two dollars as well as a sum equal to 10 percent of their last tax levy. Moreover, for each instance of disobedience of orders or other disorderly conduct, patrol captains could be fined five dollars and their subordinates two dollars. Individuals unjustly punishing a slave could be fined five dollars. In order to reduce the likelihood of interference with patrol work, individuals who unsuccessfully sued a patrol would be subject to pay three times the costs of the legal proceeding. In addition, captains had to report at stated times to their militia superiors about the performance of their patrol unit or be fined twenty dollars. In 1840, the South Carolina Court of Appeals determined that enforcement of this latter penalty could be by a court martial (M. A. Henry 1968, 36–37).

The organization of slave patrols differed in urban settings. Growing communities and towns created their own patrols in order to protect their properties and families from any threats posed by revenge-seeking slaves. Their recruitment of patrollers was also spurred by the fact that county-appointed patrollers might have to be deployed away from home. Irrespective of their method of appointment, however, patrol members who failed to report for duty posed a consistent problem. Heavy penalties were assessed to ensure sufficient attendance, but wealthier citizens evaded patrol work by simply paying these fines. Eventually, the largest communities adopted the practice of hiring patrol members in order to maintain regular protection through either direct payment or a combination of tax and service exemptions (Hadden 1993, 90–91, 96–97, 119–20).

In Charleston, South Carolina, a guardhouse was established to which slaves and free blacks were sent for running away or violating curfew or for other offenses (e.g., gambling, loitering, traveling without a proper pass, visiting a saloon, congregating on the street during public occasions). For a fee, slave owners could have their disobedient slaves whipped or placed in chains within such a facility, also known as a workhouse, where slaves could be required to cut stones. An alternative system was thus created for those slave owners who preferred others to punish their slaves (M. A. Henry 1968, 46–49).

Throughout most of the South, the slave patrol system was based on legislation, but there were a variety of community-based groups. In South Carolina, unofficial associations formed in Branchville and in St. Matthews Parish, each member receiving an indemnification with respect to the legal costs of any lawsuit brought by an association member for causing injury to another's slave. In 1823, the members of the Edisto Island Auxiliary Association sought official recognition from the state legislature of South Carolina. They were worried about a possible slave attack, since the ratio of whites to slaves on the island was two hundred to three thousand, or about one to fifteen (Hadden 1993, 126–28). In addition, just before the outbreak of the Civil War, at least one South Carolina district (the 96th) established a separate body known as the "Military Vigilance Poliece" [*sic*]. Their distinctive purpose was to organize juries to quickly try any slave suspected of sedition (Hadden 1993, 303–4). During the course of the Civil War, fewer and fewer southern adults were available for slave patrol work, all their time and resources absorbed by the Confederate Army. Eventually, patrol groups' selective and structured nature gave way to more informal arrangements involving the use of children, aging adults, and injured soldiers (Hadden 1993, 312, 328–30, 342).

In North Carolina, the legislature adopted a requirement in 1794 that all patrols have at least two members and that two members be present when a slave was punished. The activities of patrollers, as well as the precise nature of who belonged within a patrol group, were the subject of *Richardson v. Salter*, a lawsuit brought to the Supreme Court of North Carolina in 1816. Salter, a patroller, had visited the plantation of Major Owen with three of his friends (none of whom was enrolled as a member of a slave patrol). At Owen's farm, the four men encountered a slave belonging to a nearby farmer. The men demanded to see the slave's pass, and when an invalid document was produced, they inflicted a severe beating on the slave. The slave's owner (Richardson) sued the men for causing injury to his property without justification. While the trial court acquitted the four men, the Supreme Court of North Carolina remanded the case for a retrial on the grounds that none of the men with Salter were patrollers and Salter could not inflict punishment alone (Hadden 1993, 148).

Slave patrollers of this period had some things in common with town constables, their duties also involving various aspects of law enforcement. Both constables and patrollers were required to disperse gatherings, to search and seize fugitives, and to confiscate contraband. However, the functions of slave patrollers, of course, differed from those of constables in that patrol activities had to relate to slave control. Constables, unlike patrollers, for example, carried out duties relating to court procedures (e.g., escorting prisoners to court or serving judicial summonses for witnesses to appear in court), while patrol members rarely had reason to appear in court (Hadden 1993, 159). The case of *Richardson v. Salter* also helps differentiate the role of patrollers from that of unaffiliated, private southern citizens: a private citizen who sought to discipline or otherwise control a slave was presumed to be engaged in an unlawful act unless seeking a posted reward or acting under the authority of other existing statutes. In order to identify themselves, patrollers carried with them their appointment documents or notices. Hundreds of these documents (creased from having been carried on patrols) have survived and are in the collection of the North Carolina Department of Archives and History. They were originally preserved because patrollers had to return them to county courts in order to receive compensation. Proper identification was needed whenever patrollers were called upon to exercise their special functions (e.g., punishing slaves through the use of whips and ropes) (Hadden 1993, 146–47). Significantly, slave patrollers did not wear any distinctive badges. During the period before the end of the Civil War, the persons most likely to wear a metal badge or tag for identification purposes were slaves.

Case law relating to the activities of slave patrols, especially regarding their powers of arrest, set useful legal precedents in cases involving regular police for several decades following the Civil War (Hadden 1993, 401). As an illustration, in the eighteenth century, slave patrol service was required only from slaveholders and overseers. In South Carolina, by virtue of a 1740 statute, patrol group membership was also restricted to persons who either owned a minimum of fifty acres or paid at least forty shillings in taxes. It has been speculated that such membership restrictions may have resulted from a distrust of nonslaveholders or a belief that it was unfair to impose such a burden on individuals with no direct interest in the maintenance of slavery. In any case, such limitations discouraged the services of strictly voluntary patrol members. Membership requirements did begin to change after two unsuccessful slave revolts in 1815 and an 1819 revision to the law. The new law made all white males over eighteen eligible for patrol duty until the age of forty-five. After age forty-five, nonslaveholders could be excused from service. Patrol members were no longer required to own any land, nor were they to be compensated for their services (M. A. Henry 1968, 33–38). During the Civil War, most such restrictions were abandoned because of the shortage of eligible males. Later, when additional personnel were needed during the wars of the twentieth century to supplement the delivery of police services in American cities, the use of strictly voluntary aid would again become the norm.

For several decades prior to the Civil War, the debate about slavery was continuously fueled by the speeches and writings of the abolitionists. Some held moderate views that advocated the gradual elimination of slavery, while others called for immediate abolition. The publication of Harriet Beecher Stowe's novel *Uncle Tom's Cabin* (1852), which depicted the harsh realities of plantation living, and various decisions by the U.S. Supreme Court added to the discord of the times. In its 1842 decision in the *Prigg* case, for example, the Court ruled that in every state of the Union, slaveholders were entitled to recapture their slaves so long as no unnecessary violence was used. However, the case was also interpreted to mean that state authorities were not obligated to assist slave catchers. Subsequently, Vermont, Pennsylvania, and Rhode Island adopted new laws that specifically prohibited state authorities from assisting slave catchers (Buckmaster 1941, 124). In the case of *Dred Scott v. Sanford* (1857), slaves were forbidden to sue for their freedom on the grounds that they were merely the property of their masters. The Court held in the *Scott* case that since slaves were property, and since under the Fifth Amendment the federal government could not deprive anyone of life, liberty, or property, slave owners could not be prevented from bringing their slaves into any of the new territories. In spite of these decisions, after Lincoln was elected president, the southern states, led by South Carolina, voted in special state conventions to secede from the Union (Stich, Pingel, and Farrell 1988, 43–45).

Most of the three million combatants in the Civil War were under the age of twenty-five and could read and write. Before the war, they had worked as farmers or as skilled and unskilled laborers. Their recruitment was dependent on such local efforts as parades and patriotic speeches. Once a regiment was formed—consisting of one thousand men organized from ten companies—its members elected their own officers (Browne and Kreiser 2003, 4–7). Regimental soldiers came from all over the country. For example, nearly three quarters of the Union troops "came from the eleven Midwest and Middle Atlantic states. The remainder of Union soldiers came from eleven New England and border states, with a sprinkling of soldiers from both the West Coast and various Confederate states. In the Confederate army, three-quarters of soldiers came from the nine states of the Upper South and the Lower South. The remaining one-quarter of Confederate soldiers came from the five Trans-Mississippi and border states" (Browne and Kreiser 2003, 7).

Despite growing abolitionist concern for the freedom of African Americans, the causes of the Civil War had more to do with the interests of the decision makers (i.e., the elite classes) of the North and South: "The northern elite wanted economic expansion—free land, free labor, a free market, a high protective tariff for manufacturers, a bank of the United States. The slave interests opposed all that; they saw Lincoln and the Republicans as making continuation of their pleasant and prosperous way of life impossible in the future" (Zinn 1990, 184).

Throughout the Civil War, President Lincoln consistently stated that the war was being fought to restore the Union, even though he personally found slavery morally repugnant. Eventually, however, the continuing failure of the Union Army to achieve victories contributed to the formulation of a strategic plan incorporating the possibility of emancipation. Strategists hoped that many newly emancipated slaves would be motivated to fight for the Union because unless the Union was victorious emancipation would become null and void. On September 22, 1862, President Lincoln issued the Preliminary Emancipation Proclamation, declaring that all slaves in states still in rebellion on January 1, 1863, "shall be then, thenceforward, and forever free." When the appointed date arrived and the South was still in full rebellion, Lincoln issued his final Emancipation Proclamation, declaring that "all persons held as slaves. . . shall be free." By attacking the institutional bedrock of the Confederacy, the proclamation made the war seem less like a rebellion and more like a war of liberation. Moreover, it stimulated the enlistment of nearly two hundred thousand black men into the Union's army and its naval forces (Archibold 2000), numbers representing "about 9 percent of the total Union manpower organized during the war" (Browne and Kreiser 2003, 8).

For a short period following the Civil War, southern states were able to maintain control of their former slave populations through the adoption of "Black Codes," laws that severely restricted the ability of blacks to improve their status. For example, in Virginia, a law was passed that permitted any idle person to be sent to a workhouse and required to work for three months for the highest bidder. The new laws could be enforced by "county or voluntary militia units much like the former slave patrols" (Hadden 1993, 368). After such laws were voided, a new form of economic and social dependency developed in the South, especially in cotton-producing regions: sharecropping. Under this system, many former slaves became tenants, and their former slave masters became their landlords. Individual farm lots were cultivated and farmed, landlords providing stock, tools, and other provisions to sustain the tenant families. The produce was then divided between the tenant family and the landlord in a system that held little profit for black families (Carnes, Garraty, and Williams 1996, 124): "the resignation of the black sharecroppers, the vicissitudes of climate, and the venality of the plantation owners usually meant that the sharecropper received little reward when all the accounts were settled at harvest time" (Cagin and Dray 1991, 181). It was not uncommon for landlords to claim that the produce did not fully pay for what credit they had already extended, so sharecroppers were constantly in debt. Moreover, when such credit was extended, it was often only valid for goods purchased at unreasonable prices at the plantation store. In this way, landlords were able to control many of the daily routines of former slaves (Cagin and Dray 1991, 181–82), and African Americans "who refused to live up to a sharecropping contract could be arrested and punished" (Green 1997, 119).

Coalitions of northern and southern capitalists, as well as political forces, combined to diminish the limited gains of blacks after the Civil War. In particular, "the southern white oligarchy used its economic power to organize the Ku Klux Klan and other terrorist groups" (Zinn 1990, 198). The Klan was formed in 1867, after the Civil War, by ex-Confederate generals (Green 1997, 117). The nature of slave patrols may be usefully contrasted with those patrols conducted by the Ku Klux Klan. Both organizations operated mostly at night, inspected the travel passes of blacks in rural areas, disciplined or brutalized blacks, and consisted of members from all levels of white society (Hadden 1993). The chief distinction between the two groups, of course, was that the slave patrols possessed legal authority for their actions, while the Klan did not. Consequently, Klan members adopted the white sheet and mask to disguise themselves and thus reduce their risk (however slight) of being convicted for any illegal conduct (Hadden 1993,

392–96). The Klan engaged in many brutal tactics against blacks: Klan members "would burn the homes of African Americans, especially those that were perceived as advocating black rights, as well as kill livestock, trample crops, and even kill individuals" (Green 1997, 118).

The issue of segregation was another post–Civil War battleground. The Supreme Court in 1883 and 1894 refused to declare segregation in the use of various public facilities and schools unconstitutional: "By 1900, all the southern states, in new constitutions and new statutes, had written into law the disfranchisement and segregation of Negroes" (Zinn 1990, 203). These laws effectually denied basic political rights and economic opportunities to most southern blacks. Lawmakers were oblivious to the early studies of such groups as the Massachusetts Anti-Slavery Society, which noted the existence of segregation in Boston's public schools in 1847 and declared, "The prejudice of color can never be eradicated from the general mind, as long as it is permitted to poison the mind of our youth at its very springs" (Massachusetts Anti-Slavery Society 1970, 70).

After the Civil War, the United States not only still remained racially divided but was also faced with a titanic struggle between labor and management. In the 1870s and again in the 1890s, Americans experienced severe economic depressions. In each of these decades, unprecedented episodes of labor violence took place (Carnes, Garraty, and Williams 1996). Significantly, racial and class divisions would continue to influence the domestic policies of the United States throughout the twentieth century.

The development of volunteer policing also continued to influence U.S. domestic policy. While slave patrols were prominent in the South until the end of the Civil War, in other parts of the nation a variety of other organizations constituted the ranks of volunteer police, especially in the second half of the nineteenth century. The most well-known were vice-suppression leagues, anti-horse-thief and detective societies, and charity-organization caseworkers. A New Yorker named Anthony Comstock, for example, nearly single-handedly policed the U.S. mails as a volunteer postal inspector. In a brief span of time, during the mid-1870s, Comstock made nearly three hundred arrests as the leader of the New York Society for the Suppression of Vice (D. R. Bennett 1971, 1083). The members of these organizations generally fit the generic definition of "volunteer police" provided earlier: they performed one or more police functions in an overt manner and were paid either a minimal wage or received no salary, and their organizations were either endorsed or created by legislative enactment or recognized by governmental bodies.

Vigilantism at times took a different turn. Vigilantism has been defined as "an organized movement that seeks to impose law and order, independent of the existing legal authorities . . . [or] at times . . . simultaneously with legal institutions of law enforcement" (H. A. Johnson and Wolfe 1996,170). In the nineteenth century, both frontier midwestern communities and rural eastern regions developed their own brand of volunteer law enforcement, creating private organizations to restrain violence and protect property rights through private acts of incorporation, incorporation under the general laws of the state, or general enabling statutes. Such legalized vigilantism should be distinguished from the kinds of extralegal vigilantism that existed in other regions of the country. In the 1850s, for example, when California began to experience rapid growth, especially in the San Francisco Bay area, citizens established an extralegal vigilante movement to control lawlessness. Beginning with the events in San Francisco, until the end of the nineteenth century, there were about 210 vigilante organizations west of the Mississippi River, their activities primarily of the extralegal variety. On the other hand, a variety of legalized vigilantism was also practiced in the twentieth century, when the activities of the American Protective League reached their peak. During and just after World War I, the APL consisted of "250,000 private citizens who rounded up draft dodgers and looked for spies with more enthusiasm than due process" (Schrecker 1998, 53).

An important distinction regarding America's experience with vigilantism is that some movements were of relatively short duration and without legal authorization, while other volunteer crime control groups (e.g., slave patrols, anti-horse-thief detective associations) "were frequently authorized by state statute and functioned for long periods of time as a sort of independent, private agency of law enforcement" (Nolan 1987, 35). The latter type of organization is the variety under investigation here.

After the Civil War, there was a significant growth in the northeastern part of the nation in the formation of local detective societies and anti-horse-thief or protective associations. Although the name "anti-horse-thief detective society" is most often used to designate these groups, their actual titles varied. Such societies first came into existence in the 1790s and became

most numerous between 1870 and 1890: "Organized as volunteer law enforcement agencies, these societies existed as a parallel structure to the official institutions of the county or the state" (Nolan 1987, 35). The explanation
for their development is rooted in the lack of competent law enforcement
agencies and in the "breakdown of rural and small-town communities under the impact of social and economic change . . . as well as the impact of social dislocation caused by wars and the extensive and endemic violence of
American life" (Nolan 1987, 32). These legalized protective associations were
primarily created for the identification and arrest of criminals.

Until the establishment of the New Jersey State Police in 1921, there were
more than eighty different vigilant and detective societies in New Jersey
(Nicolosi 1968), including "The Bergen County Vigilance Association," "The
Englishtown Pursuing and Detecting Company," and "The Paramus Society
for the Detection of Horse Thieves." "The Grand Consolidated Vigilant Society of New Jersey and Pennsylvania for the Recovery of Stolen Property and
the Detection of Thieves," as its lengthy name implies, included members
from two states. Elsewhere, one could find "The Newton (Pennsylvania) Reliance Company for Detecting and Apprehending Horse Thieves and Other
Villains," "The Worcester (Massachusetts) Association of Mutual Aid in Detecting Thieves," and "The Waseca County (Minnesota) Horse Thief Detective Society," among many others (Nolan 1987).

During the latter half of the nineteenth century, various other societies
for the protection of horses and other property were specifically authorized
by statute in several midwestern and eastern states. State laws were passed
declaring that such organizations could be established. In some cases, laws
were amended to grant the power of arrest to organization members (see
table 2).

In states such as Massachusetts, Rhode Island, and Delaware, as well as
in the West, similar societies were prevalent, but no authorizing statutes
were enacted. Possibly, many western states did not enact such laws because of their late arrival to statehood and their greater reliance on military
forces for domestic security. Most societies for the protection of private
property were established under the general incorporation laws of the particular state where they were located (Nolan 1987, 49). December 21, 1795,
for example, saw the Massachusetts inception of the Society for Detecting
Horse Thieves in the Towns of Mendon, Bellingham, and Millford. The

Table 2 The Adoption of Anti-Horse-Thief Association Laws

State	Year Authorized	Arrest Power Granted
New Jersey	1851	1878
Vermont	1851	
Indiana	1852	1852
New York	1859	1878
Michigan	1859	1859
Wisconsin	1861	1861
Kansas	1868	
Iowa	1870	
Missouri	1874	1874
Ohio	1885	1887
Nebraska	1885	1885
Illinois	1887	1887
Minnesota	1893	

Nolan 1987

American Antiquarian Society in Worcester, Massachusetts, has a collection of this society's constitution and bylaws, along with those of the following societies: the Dorchester Association for the Detention and Prosecution of Trespassers on Gardens, Fields, and Orchards; the Norton Detecting Society; the Dedham Society for Apprehending Horse Thieves; and the Society in the Towns of Wrentham, Franklin, Medway, Medfield, Walpole, Foxborough, Mansfield, and Attenborough, for Detecting Horse Thieves (hereafter the Wrentham Association).

According to constitutional article VII of the Society for Detecting Horse Thieves in the Towns of Mendon, Bellingham, and Millford, it was the duty of the "Pursuing Committee" to try to find stolen horses and horse thieves. Each of the three towns had its own pursuing committee consisting of five members, who were expected to join in a pursuit up to a range of seventy-five miles. If they possessed more specific information, they could continue as long as there was reasonable probability of recovering the horse or arresting the thief. Only one member of the committee could travel a particular route, unless there was specific information available about the horse's or the thief's whereabouts. In that case, another pursuer could be added at the discretion of the society's president. Committee members were required to keep records of the route traveled, the time spent in pursuit, the distance covered, and the nature of all expenses. Article X provided that any costs or damages incurred through the detection of any horse thief, or any other criminal, would be the responsibility of the association; likewise, any rewards received or any other property recovered would revert to the association. Dues were one dollar (article XII). Although the society's sole purpose was to recover horses stolen from its members, assistance was provided only if the theft occurred within thirty miles of the member's home, unless at the time of theft the owner, his wife, or his child had direct custody of the animal (article XVI). In 1860, the society had an active membership of 291, and its treasury totaled $1,733.64.

The Dorchester Association required an initial payment of one dollar in dues, and members had to be approved by a majority of the board of directors (article VIII). The directors were authorized to hire and suitably reward agents who could detect trespassers on its members' premises. The association appears to have been organized after the Massachusetts legislature adopted a law in 1828 that made it a crime to trespass "upon any grass land, orchard, [or] garden . . . with intent to cut, destroy, take or convey away, any grass, hay, fruit, or vegetables, with the intent to injure or defraud such owner . . . or with intent to injure, cut or destroy any fruit tree, or shrub" (Dorchester Association 1829, 9–10). The penalties for trespassing were doubled if the offense took place on Sunday or any evening (from sunset to sunrise).

The constitution of the Norton Detecting Society specifically listed certain members who were designated as "riders," additionally providing that members who suffered a horse theft could become riders to pursue any horse thieves or appoint others for this purpose (article V). All riders were required to keep account of their expenses (article VIII). Interestingly, descriptions of members' horses must have been previously submitted to an official of the society (article XVIII), possibly to avoid any lost time in organizing pursuit of a horse thief. In 1859, the Norton Detecting Society had over two hundred members, twenty-six of whom were designated as riders.

Other such organizations also included designated riders. The 1872 constitution of the Waseca County, Minnesota, Horse Thief Detectives, for example, provided for the annual election of fifteen men to serve as riders. These riders, in turn, selected a leader from their ranks to serve as their captain. The riders pursued thieves who had taken from any member of the society any kind of property valued at more than fifty dollars; in cases of emergency, all members of the society could be called into service by the captain. The organization was most active in the 1860s and 1870s, when horse thieves were prevalent in southern Minnesota and northern Iowa (Du Priest 1932).

In general, anti-horse-thief societies in Massachusetts and elsewhere maintained modest sliding membership-fee schedules. In 1837, for example, the Wrentham Association charged initial dues of one dollar, plus seventy-five cents for a second horse, fifty cents for a third horse, and twenty-five cents for each additional horse. Membership was open to inhabitants of specifically defined communities, and protection of members' property was limited to particular geographic zones. Annual meetings were usually held in either September or October. Advertised rewards for the recovery of both horses and thieves were encouraged but limited to specific amounts.

In the northeastern United States, horse stealing steadily declined after the Civil War. In post–Civil War New Jersey, for example, vigilance associations placed more emphasis on the crimes of "robbery, marauding, vagrancy and trespassing" (Nicolosi 1968, 36). Furthermore, some of the new societies established after 1860 provided protection for all persons residing in their community, not just their members. For example, New Jersey's Flemington Mutual Protection Society, established in 1873, instituted night patrols, was instrumental in securing street lighting, and afforded protection to all residents of the town. In various states, including New Jersey, all society members were authorized to make arrests. All members of the Westfield, Cranford, Passaic, and Scotch Plains societies, for example, performed in a police capacity and could arrest lawbreakers (Nicolosi 1968, 38). Some of these early vigilant societies have continued to hold annual meetings that today serve as social gatherings. The New Jersey vigilance associations declined after 1900; they "were not equipped to handle the new and enlarged problems of crime engendered by the advent of the automobile and the phenomenal rise in the rural population. . . . The coup de grace . . . came in the form of the state police force which was established in 1921" (Nicolosi 1968, 44).

While slave patrols help account for later developments in professional law enforcement in the South, anti-horse-thief societies in rural areas of the Midwest and the East also served as important precursors for changes in law enforcement. Organizers of such rural vigilant and detective associations considered their need for self-protection their major justification for existence. Meanwhile, in more urban areas, various aid societies had been established for the provision of specific health and welfare services by the last quarter of the nineteenth century. In New York City, the work of such private welfare agencies appeared to encompass a multitude of activities, in one sense making "every member of these societies a special policeman . . . by reason of the pride he takes in the work of his society" (Andrews 1904, 284).

In late nineteenth-century America, the "Progressive movement" accounted for the establishment of many additional charitable organizations, as well as urban police reforms. Significant incidents of labor unrest, economic declines between 1893 and 1897, and popular-media depictions of degrading conditions among the urban poor contributed to uneasiness among the middle and wealthier classes. These emotions helped stimulate the progressive impulses of some of the more secure members of American society. For example, in New York City, the New York Society for the Prevention of Cruelty to Children, modeled on a related British organization, was established in the 1870s. The New York society was empowered by the state legislature to investigate and prosecute all cases of child abuse and by 1904 had secured 53,620 convictions. New York's Legal Aid Society was established in 1876. Its primary purpose was to aid poor persons in recovering losses through civil court procedures (Andrews 1904, 281). The Medical Society of the County of New York employed its own agents to identify and prosecute medical charlatans throughout the nineteenth century.

Women played a significant role in the work of many private enforcement societies. In 1882, for example, Josephine Shaw Lowell, a commissioner of the New York State Board of Charities, organized direct charitable aid or relief, establishing the New York Charity Organization Society (COS) to coordinate the delivery of charity. The COS recruited hundreds of "society women" to help screen candidates for assistance and to serve as role models for the poorer classes (Burrows and Wallace 1999). Lowell believed that "no able-bodied man who refused a labor test—chopping wood or breaking stone—should get a cent" (M. B. Katz 1996, 74).

A unique exception to the pattern of the establishment of such urban charitable institutions was the founding of the Women's Christian Temperance Union (WCTU). The WCTU was concerned with the effect of hard liquor on the lives of families, but it also engaged in other moral pursuits, including the creation of a Department for the Suppression of Impure Literature. In 1892, it had about 150,000 members nationwide, its followers rallying under the banner of "Home Protection" (Foner 1998, 110–11). Members of both the WCTU and the New York Committee for the Prevention of State Regulation of Vice also led the higher-age-of-consent campaign: "By 1920 nearly every state in the country had raised the age at which a woman could legally consent to sexual relations to either sixteen or eighteen years" (Odem 1995, 37).

The establishment of the national WCTU also contributed to the presence of women in criminal justice work, in large part due to the leadership of Frances E. Willard. Willard began her role in the WCTU in 1874 and became its president five years later, holding that office until her death in 1898. At that time, she was one of the most well-known persons of her day (Asbury 1968, 86–87). Under Willard's leadership, the WCTU became involved in a series of matters related to improving the treatment of women prisoners. In the 1870s, for example, the WCTU pushed for the first significant use of "police matrons." In Portland, Maine, in 1877, the full salaries of these matrons were contributed by the local chapter of the WCTU, the city only gradually agreeing to assume the full cost of such personnel. In the 1880s, largely through WCTU efforts, police matrons were appointed in many major cities (e.g., Buffalo, Chicago, Philadelphia, Boston, Baltimore, St. Louis, Milwaukee), and by the next decade, matrons had become commonplace in most urban areas.

Reformers' concerns about not only confined women prisoners but what they perceived as breeding grounds of delinquency and vice led to the appointment of the first policewomen during the Progressive Era (S. S.

Walker 1977, 85–86). One of these pioneer policewomen was Alice Stebbins Wells. In order to gain entry into police work, she gathered the support of more than one hundred of the leading citizens of Los Angeles. When Wells joined the Los Angeles police force, it consisted of 350 members. All officers worked every day of the year, except for fifteen days of vacation. In 1911, one year after she was appointed a member of the police department, the WCTU arranged a speaking tour for Wells that took her to thirty-one different cities within a thirty-day period. She became the president of the International Association of Policewomen in 1915 (S. S. Walker 1977, 85–86; Schulz 1995, 23, 29).

The WCTU also focused attention on the need for improving worker safety in the mining and timber industries, rescuing prostitutes, and suffrage campaigns (Blocker 1989). Frances Willard made considerable efforts to control prostitution out of fear for the welfare of the family due to the consequences of venereal disease. It was one thing for men to drink up their wages and abuse their wives, but it was even more callous for men to trans-

Frances E. Willard (1839–98), leader of the Women's
Christian Temperance Union, c. 1889

mit prostitutes' venereal diseases to their wives and children. In one New York study, it was discovered that nearly one third of infected women were married and had been infected by their husbands (Rosen 1982, 52–53). The WCTU also worked to have laws passed in every state and territory (except Arizona) requiring temperance teaching in the public schools, as well as specialized teacher training for the delivery of temperance instruction (Blocker 1989, 82; Sinclair 1964, 43). The curriculum endorsed by the WCTU consistently referred to alcohol as a poison; by constant repetition of the word *poison,* and "by similar exaggerations, the WCTU-approved textbooks seemed calculated to frighten children into total abstinence" (Timberlake 1963, 49).[2]

The WCTU, the Society for the Prevention of Cruelty to Children, and other public aid societies were not the only crusading organizations of the period. For nearly forty years, American morals were policed by Anthony Comstock (1844–1915), the chief special agent and secretary of the New York Society for the Suppression of Vice. After brief careers as a shipping clerk and a dry-goods salesman, he spent the remainder of his life crusading against nudity, pornography, contraception, prostitution, and abortion. Comstock's career as America's chief censor of sex began when he obtained a donation of 650 dollars from the wealthy president of the New York branch of the Young Men's Christian Association (YMCA). The YMCA also formed its own Committee for the Suppression of Vice and appointed Comstock to be its field operative, paying him 100 dollars a year as partial compensation for lost commissions on dry-goods sales (Andrist 1973, 84, 86).

In 1873, Comstock instigated prosecution of the publishers of a weekly newspaper that dealt with such topics as "women's rights, the spirit world, free love, and other unorthodox subjects" (Andrist 1973, 85). A federal district court, however, dismissed the case on the grounds that the existing federal law only prohibited the mailing of obscene books, pamphlets, and pictures. In order to remedy the omission of newspapers from the law, and to strengthen some of its other aspects, Comstock traveled to Washington, D.C. Once there, he was able to convince the members of Congress to fix what he saw as existing loopholes. The new law banned the mailing of any obscene, lewd, lascivious, or filthy materials. The revised statute has widely become known as the Comstock Law, in honor of its author. Comstock was eventually appointed a special federal agent of the U.S. Postal Service in order to enforce "his" law: "He asked that he be paid no salary, so that the office would not become a political plum" (Andrist 1973, 86). A few months later, the YMCA ended its affiliation with Comstock, and he created a separate organization, the New York Society for the Suppression of Vice.

Comstock became the new organization's chief special agent and secretary and was paid a moderate salary that enabled him to devote himself full-time to the elimination of obscene materials. After his first year as a volunteer postal inspector, a private report indicated that he had caused to be seized approximately 134,000 pounds of obscene books; 194,000 lewd pictures and photographs; 14,200 pounds of stereotype plates; 60,300 articles made of rubber; 5,500 sets of playing cards; and 31,150 boxes of pills and powders intended for use as aphrodisiacs (Andrist 1973, 86). In 1883, Comstock's *Traps for the Young* appeared, trumpeting his belief that "vile books and papers are branding-irons heated in the fires of hell" (qtd. in L. M. Friedman 1993, 132). During the 1870s, organizations similar to Comstock's became active in some cities. One of the most well-known was the Watch and Ward Society of Boston, whose patrons included such upper-class families as the Cabots and the Lodges (L. M. Friedman 1993, 135).

Comstock himself died of pneumonia in 1915, shortly after traveling to the International Purity Congress, held in San Francisco, as an American delegate. By the time of his death, Comstock had become somewhat of an anachronism, the general public having become tired of his highly narrow and censored view of the world. One of his most publicized attempts at censorship involved an unsuccessful effort to suppress the exhibition of an award-winning French painting entitled *September Morn,* a print copy of which had been placed in an art dealer's window. As a direct consequence of Comstock's demand that it be taken out of the window, the public's interest was stimulated, and copies of the print "sold in quantities far beyond its value as art or any slight ability to titillate" (Andrist 1973, 88).

Comstock's successor as secretary of the society was John Saxton Sumner (1876–1971). When Sumner joined the staff of the Society for the Suppression of Vice in 1913, he was a lawyer and a member of a prestigious banking firm. He was also a Son of the American Revolution, a member of the Founders and Patriots of America, an Episcopalian, and a Republican. He was duly deputized as a police agent to investigate obscenity violations in New York State, and "during the interwar years, his successes in prosecuting booksellers and publishers under federal and state Comstock Laws made him a chief spokesman for anti-obscenity advocates, and a touchstone against which proponents of freedom of expression articulated their demands" (Gertzman 1994, 41). Sumner served in this capacity for thirty-five years.

In 1931, however, the tide began to shift when the American Civil Liberties Union organized the National Council on Freedom from Censorship. Its main goal was to repeal the special police powers of the agents of the Society for the Suppression of Vice. In support of this effort, the council criticized in particular the society's reliance on entrapment tactics (P. Boyer 1968). The expertise of such attorneys as Morris Ernst in defense of free expression was also highly effective. Consequently, by the mid-1930s, the work of the society was much less influential than it had been (Gertzman 1994).

Public aid societies were often led by educated and devoted middle-class women, Comstock and his successor Sumner representing notable exceptions to this pattern of female leadership. In the more rural and frontier regions of America, however, a rather male-dominated form of volunteer law enforcement was routinely used: the posse.

Today, members of sheriffs' posses are "unpaid volunteers organized by official action" (Bayley 1985, 23), but in the past, posse work was compulsory, though likely to be only temporary. Posses were initially needed to render assistance in the capture of serious criminal offenders when regular law enforcement officials were in short supply. The word *posse* is itself a shortened version of the Latin *posse comitatus* (Bayley 1985, 24). Under early principles of English common law, sheriffs were empowered to summon the *posse comitatus,* or the "power of the county." Over time, various parts of the United States, especially the West, adopted numerous statutes that extended the authority to muster a posse to a variety of local officials. For example, in 1885, Montana adopted a statute giving livestock inspectors the power to summon a posse (Prassel 1972, 98, 145).

Sheriffs today have all the powers of peace officers and are generally considered to be the chief law enforcement officers of their counties. In general, their main tasks include preserving the peace, serving court papers, running the county jail, and making both civil and criminal arrests. Significantly, "during the later part of the nineteenth century the sheriff occupied the foremost position in law enforcement throughout most of the West" (Prassel 1972, 101). Since the office of sheriff was and still is an elected one, incumbents have often benefited from campaign contributions. Thus, successful businessmen and other persons or groups with either financial or organizational resources have wielded a great deal of influence on their initial selection and ultimate election. In return for political support, sheriffs, like other elected officials, have often been inclined to extend the traditional courtesies (i.e., a system of patronage is in place). Consequently, depending on the particular era and jurisdiction involved, sheriffs have routinely "allied themselves with particular classes, ethnic minorities, companies, economic blocs, or even vigilante movements" (Prassel 1972, 112). The collection of various fees for executing routine law enforcement duties (e.g., serving a summons, subpoena, or writ; levying execution on foreclosed property) meant that the office of sheriff could also be economically advantageous (Prassel 1972, 114, 264–65).

Some sheriffs have also used the practice of issuing "special deputy" commissions to attract supporters. Although these appointments are usually unsalaried, they do permit the carrying of concealed firearms and may therefore facilitate private employment. Prior to the establishment and use of contract security personnel, many businesses sought out the services of such private police. Thus, during the early 1890s, for example, the sheriff of Arapahoe County, Colorado, appointed special deputies for such enterprises as the Tramway Company, the Union Brewery, the Electric Light Company, the Windsor Hotel, Elitche's Garden, the Arcade, and so on (Prassel 1972, 133).

Service on a sheriff's posse in the old western tradition was obligatory. Individuals could be jailed or fined for failing the call to duty. As a system of policing, then, the posse depended on community members' ability to drop whatever they were doing (Klockars 1985). Farm and ranch work, significantly, more easily permits such disruptions than does factory or office work, and there was a great deal more of the former type of activity than the latter in the West. It was also no doubt a happy coincidence that westerners were more likely to be equipped with horses and firearms.

The modern version of the posse, in contrast, is an entirely voluntary undertaking, and posse duties now involve a much wider range of assignments. The modern "posse" is no longer a temporary summoning of "the power of the county," but a specialized branch of a larger volunteer reserve police force.[3] Today, although the use of the old-style posse is a rare event, it is still authorized in many jurisdictions.

Another facet of the evolving roles of volunteer and regular police during the antebellum period can be ascertained from studying the ordinances of one particular community, Milledgeville, Georgia, from 1823 to 1831. At the time that these local laws were being adopted, Milledgeville was the seat of state government in Georgia. At first, patrols were to be selected from the general white male population, with exemptions granted for those who could pay various fines for nonservice. After a time, this compulsory system was augmented by allowing some individuals to volunteer for a fixed payment. Finally, in 1831, this system was replaced with one that included a full-time marshal and three sergeants with salaries of one hundred dollars a year. The newly hired full-time police also commanded five private citizens, required to perform nightly patrols (between nine p.m. and three a.m.) on a rotating schedule (Yanochik 1997, 222, 226). In this way, the need for the supervision of slaves led to a combination of paid specialists and unpaid conscripts. Today, such a combination of specialists and volunteers is the norm in those jurisdictions maintaining volunteer police units. Slave patrols and later nineteenth-century northern police also possessed other features similar to those of modern volunteer police organizations, including "specific beats of responsibility, a standardized form of operation, a centralized command, special legal privileges, and preventive policing measures by monitoring trouble spots" (Green 1997, 120).

In the South as a whole, certain features of antebellum policing caused the system to become increasingly obsolete. For one thing, slave-patrol "duty was widely despised," and in time, "the burden of patrol duty fell largely on the poorer, non-slaveholding members of society" (Yanochik 1997, 198, 199). Persons with means could readily afford to pay any required fines for failing to appear for duty, but members of the lower classes could not. Wealthier citizens could also hire substitutes or simply purchase an exemption: "The middle and upper classes just looked at fines paid for refusal to do patrol duty as an additional, but necessary tax" (Yanochik 1997, 202–3). Such evasions led to bitterness among the remaining patrollers and probably contributed to the abuse of slaves (i.e., the inflicting of punishment beyond the usual limits).

One of the most undemocratic features of slave patrol work was that patrollers were (with rare exceptions) draftees. Such military conscription has
been classified into three categories: democratic or universal (no exemptions); autocratic, whereby conscripts are authorized to plunder their victims; and despotic (with exemptions provided for the upper classes)
(Beukema 1982). During the Civil War, riots broke out in many northern
cities because of the "despotic" approach used in the recruitment of Union
troops, adopted by the administration of Abraham Lincoln. Indeed, one of
the worst riots in American history occurred in New York City in July 1863,
fueled by discontent among members of the working classes who felt that
they were being conscripted for the benefit of blacks, while affluent whites
were able to pay for substitutes. Of the more than one hundred persons
killed, at least eleven were blacks murdered by white mobs (Carnes, Garraty,
and Williams 1996, 117). Conscription also led to resistance and sometimes
violence in the Confederacy (see, e.g., Paludan 1981).

Southern slave patrols included both autocratic and despotic features.
Patrols were autocratic because slave patrollers had authority to summarily
punish slaves; they were despotic because of the availability of exemptions
(Yanochik 1997, 219–20).

Thus, the slave control laws of the South had significant nondemocratic
features that affected not only the morale of patrollers (since wealthier
whites could easily escape patrol service) but also the health, safety, and
welfare of both free blacks and slaves: "complaints about patrols abusing
their powers were as common as complaints about their failing to function"
(Stampp 1972, 215). Slaves were abused, beaten, and killed by patrollers;
such "often harsh and arbitrary treatment" probably contributed to patrols'
effectiveness (Yanochik 1997, 206, 237, 242). Indeed, many slaves were de-
terred from escaping because of the threat of punishment from slave patrollers. On the other hand, despite their use of terror tactics, slaveholders
were not able to completely dominate the lives of slaves, hindered by "their
dependence on the labor of slaves, their faulty comprehension of the interior lives of these laborers, and the limited time, effort and will that slave
owners were able to expend" (Kay and Cary 1995, 220).

While former slaves in the South had an opportunity to participate in
public affairs as a unique consequence of Reconstruction, that opportunity
was short-lived. Former slave owners "quickly moved to lay down a color

line that would maintain the old racial distinctions and impress upon the newly freed slaves their place as a separate and inferior people" (Litwack 1979, 262). This separateness, with time, became ingrained in southern statutes. When legal challenges reached the U.S. Supreme Court in the *Civil Rights Cases* (109 U.S. 3; 1883), Associate Justice Joseph Philo Bradley declared that such laws were not indicative of slavery as outlawed by the Thirteenth Amendment, but simply private wrongs. The litigants were then referred to the state courts for any available relief. It would be a long time— until the civil rights movement of the 1960s—before the situation changed.

The activities of the anti-horse-thief detective societies, in contrast, were far removed from the repressive and discriminatory practices of the slave-patrol system. In fact, many democratic features were involved in the formation of the legally sanctioned anti-horse-thief societies. Most had specific constitutions with the usual parliamentary officers (e.g., president, vice president, treasurer, secretary). Annual meetings were held. Individuals were elected or appointed to the position of "rider" or "pursuer." Initiation and annual membership fees were small (e.g., one dollar). Most societies also offered some type of insurance protection against possible loss or damage of property. If a society's treasury needed additional funds, all members were equally assessed. While the rosters of most societies appear to have been composed of males, reflecting the gender restrictions of the nineteenth century, "at least one society employed a woman rider" (Nicolosi 1968, 36–37).

The establishment and methods adopted by Minnesota's Waseca County Horse Thief Detective Society "may be considered typical of the American protective association" (Nolan 1987, 100–101). Its membership list "reads like a 'who's who' of the social and economic elite of the young county" (Nolan 1987, 87). Even the county sheriff was a charter member and was also elected as the first captain of the riders. The person chosen to be the second secretary of the organization also served at various times as county attorney, justice of the peace, state senator, superintendent of schools, and in other public affairs positions. Indeed, throughout the society's history, the pattern of membership "always represented the solid, substantial portion of the county's population, with most of the county officials as conspicuous members" (Nolan 1987, 88, 99).

On the other hand, while most eastern vigilant societies appear to have adhered to their stated policies of assisting sheriffs and constables by refer-ring individuals for prosecution, this practice seems not to have been as rigidly followed in all the midwestern and western states. In the remote frontier regions of the country, summary proceedings were not uncom-mon. Even the administration of "frontier justice," however, was supposed to be accomplished in accordance with an organization's charter. The Waseca County Horse Thief Detectives took the following approach: "If the riders were successful in capturing a thief or thieves, a committee of five members and the president of the society, who acted as chairman, dis-cussed the case and decided upon the course of action to pursue. The con-stitution provided that they were either to 'commence legal proceedings before a civil magistrate, at the expense of the society,' or to 'take the of-fender into their own custody, and when said committee are fully satisfied that the ends of justice may be attained, with less expense and trouble to the society, than by legal process, may satisfy the same as in their judgment may seem just to all parties'" (Du Priest 1932, 155). Only on one occasion, apparently, did the "ends of justice" approach mob violence. Moreover, "any fears by non-members that the indefinite powers of the society might be used unwisely would presumably be laid to rest by consideration of the character of the members" (Nolan 1987, 89).

Although Minnesota never authorized the formation of protective as-sociations and detective societies within its borders, in 1893 it adopted a law that provided that members of legally recognized detective societies in other states could function in Minnesota as livestock law enforcement agents. Such outsiders were required to file a copy of their law enforcement commission and to post an indemnification bond of two thousand dollars. Earlier, in 1873, Minnesota had passed a law providing for a bounty to be paid for the capture and delivery of horse thieves (Nolan 1987, 71–72).

In the West, extralegal vigilante activity took place as a consequence of an absence of laws sanctioning vigilant societies or other adequate means to establish law and order. By the mid–nineteenth century, however, a fairly cohesive body of thought "recognized the legitimacy of self-appointed law enforcement . . . throughout the nation" (Nolan 1987, 226). Eventually, many of the detective and anti-horse-thief associations and protective soci-eties were authorized by statute. These "anti-horse thief societies were much like vigilante movements in respect to organization, objectives, and types of members. However, there was one crucial difference: they did not take the law into their own hands. Instead they restricted themselves to the detection and pursuit of culprits whom, after capture, they dutifully turned over to the local law enforcement officers" (R. M. Brown 1969, 190–91). Many of these organizations were ultimately granted police powers in various states (see table 2 above).

After the Civil War, the proliferation of private charitable enforcement societies in urban areas extended the opportunity to participate in civic affairs to many individuals, including women, as we have seen. By the end of the nineteenth century, for example, more than three fourths of the cases presented to the courts annually by the Medical Society of the County of New York were based on the testimony of women undercover agents (Andrews 1904, 286). The WCTU, although it "appealed most powerfully to the millions of women who defined their roles as wives and mothers," eventually endorsed women's suffrage (Foner 1998, 110). On the other hand, some societies may have abused their special legislative mandates by manifesting a dictatorial and vindictive attitude that invaded the privacy of their clients. At the beginning of the twentieth century, for example, public discussions regarding projects advanced by the American Society for the Prevention of Cruelty to Animals (SPCA) prompted one editorial writer to state, "For our own part, we should have been better content if at least a few of the society's critics had raised the question whether there is a real need for private corporations to execute this or that law, or even to see that this or that is executed" (qtd. in Andrews 1904, 280). Comstock's reckless efforts to suppress vice in America were also widely commented on during his lifetime. One contemporary, for example, noted that "the London Society for the Suppression of Vice was founded three-fourths of a century earlier than its namesake of New York, and was conducted by the same system of espionage, decoying, and informing that has characterized its more modern version" (D. R. Bennett 1971, 1013). One remedial measure for redress of any grievance against a private society agent would be to seek that agent's dismissal: "the contract of employment between the agent and the society does not require charges and a tedious trial before dismissal, as is the case in the police department" (Andrews 1904, 287).

In spite of their occasional shortcomings, however, at least one vital democratic feature was commonly shared by the various public aid societies: they represented an additional check on the traditional branches of government (executive, legislative, and judicial). Their watchfulness may have prompted errant officials to engage in a more responsible mode of activity, to more likely be "alert and anxious and willing to render assistance in fear that their inertness may be commented on to their disadvantage" (Andrews 1904, 286). Thus, the widespread use and presence of volunteers may have provided some oversight of bureaucratic behavior.

Of course, there was little likelihood that slave patrol members would be checking on anyone but slaves, who were routinely surveilled and intimidated. Patrollers could be brutal, "particularly when they encountered groups of slaves at secret religious or other meetings" (W. L. Katz 1990, 47). Patrol duty was undesirable, and patrols were difficult to recruit and deploy. Such difficulty has been documented in South Carolina, Georgia, Mississippi, and North Carolina (see Yanochik 1997; M. A. Henry 1968; Mohr 1989; Flanders 1933; Sydnor 1965; G. G. Johnson 1937). Indeed, from an administrative point of view, "there can scarcely be found any document from the ante-bellum period that praises their conduct or outward competence," although "they were still effective (from the perspective of slave holders) in controlling the movement of slaves and their ability to escape" (Yanochik 1997, 231–32, 233).

The organization of slave patrols in the South may be compared to the use of regular police patrols in the North. Slave patrollers, for example, held special legal privileges that entitled them to enter the homes of slaves, and patrols routinely operated at night in order to detect runaways. Northern police, in comparison, were assigned to regular beats and working-class neighborhoods to deter crime. Both types of police groups were arguably assembled to protect the interests of the wealthier classes (Green 1997).

Overall, by the end of the nineteenth century, a variety of new forms of volunteer police organizations had arisen in response to specific needs. Some, like the western posse and the vigilant and detective societies, engaged in primarily reactive roles, while others undertook decidedly more active roles in their ongoing investigations of welfare applicants and their efforts to prevent delinquency.

After the Civil War, units of the militia were still being drilled for local emergencies, but they were less frequently called upon (Curriden and Phillips 1999). In New York City, two notable instances of the use of militia forces to quell riots took place at Astor Place in 1849 and during the draft in 1863. The establishment of New York City's police department was, in part, due to a desire to limit the need for reliance on the militia (Burrows and Wallace 1999). The regular police in big cities were, for the most part, a reactive institution, although they did serve the public in unique ways. For example, "the police cleaned streets and inspected boilers in New York, distributed supplies to the poor in Baltimore, accommodated the homeless in Philadelphia, investigated vegetable markets in St. Louis, operated emergency ambulances in Boston" (Fogelson 1977, 16). Moreover, by the end of the nineteenth century, police departments, along with other governmental departments, served as places of employment for thousands of recent immigrants and second-generation Americans who "counted on these municipal agencies for their livelihood" (Fogelson 1977, 18).

Classifying the groups discussed here according to the traits laid out earlier in table 1, some general conclusions may be drawn. Slave patrollers may be classified as Type IV volunteers (special purpose/proactive). They did not hesitate to use punitive means to carry out their specific duties and were aggressive in their role as guardians of the southern slaves. In some ways, posse members were similar to slave patrollers because of their special purpose and their combative style. Posse members acted under the color of legal authority. They were, in fact, sworn in for a limited purpose (i.e., pursuing criminals). Furthermore, they sometimes resorted to their own forms of justice, as they were only temporary peace officers and were often assembled with little preparation. On the other hand, their role was a rather limited one in that they only acted when called upon. Thus, they fit more into the Type III category of volunteer police (special purpose/reactive).

The activities of anti-horse-thief and detective societies were authorized in most states (through the recognition of their corporate charters and/or by specific statutes), and they were deployed for the special purpose of pursuing horse thieves. Ultimately, their continued existence was dependent on their adherence to the rule of law and their keeping of adequate records for reimbursement of expenses. Moreover, the mere existence of such societies was often sufficient to deter crime. Therefore, they can also be characterized as Type III organizations (special purpose/reactive).

While the work of the WCTU does not fit the definition of volunteer police, since it was mainly of an educational and advocacy nature, the WCTU played an important role in helping to pay for and recruit women to work in the justice system. On the other hand, such groups as the New York Charity Organization Society, the New York County Medical Society, the SPCA, and the New York Society for the Suppression of Vice had significant law enforcement roles. Since Anthony Comstock, of the lattermost organization, undertook his work with excessive zeal that sometimes had calamitous consequences for the persons he arrested, his work and that of John Saxton Sumner (his successor) can be readily classified as Type IV (special purpose/proactive).

Toward the end of the nineteenth century, the role of volunteer police in American society was seriously waning, ill defined, and narrowly focused. It was nevertheless certainly not invisible to the participants in its various organizational manifestations. Slavery's Jim Crow legacy was also having an impact, a negative one, on the lives of most Americans. Jim Crow remained very much a part of American culture until a turning point was reached near the end of the1960s, at the explosive height of the civil rights movement. Even by the end of the twentieth century, the wretched conditions of various hidden forms of involuntary servitude or forced labor were still prevalent in the United States and other nations.[4]

Several months after the events of September 11, 2001, President George W. Bush proposed that all Americans should become more vigilant. A special "TIPS" (Terrorism Information and Prevention) program was devised that neighbors could use to report suspicious activities. Broadcasters and interest groups ranging from liberal to conservative condemned the idea, and in a few months, the program disappeared from the president's official list of citizen-involvement initiatives for homeland security. Clearly, many commentators and average American citizens had instinctively recoiled from the suggestion of having neighbors reporting on neighbors. However, in the nineteenth century and the early part of the twentieth, such an instinct had not yet been ingrained in the American psyche.

4

The Spy Era From the 1880s to 1920

Life has risks. No one has absolute security. In their quest for it, Americans should not be too eager to sacrifice essential freedoms.
Editorial, *Winston-Salem Journal,* August 15, 2002

After September 11, 2001, the Bush administration tried hard to develop programs to involve the American public in homeland security efforts. One program that was thought to be on solid ground was "Operation TIPS." The TIPS program was envisioned as a national system for reporting suspicious and potentially terrorist-related activity to a government telephone hotline. The U.S. Department of Justice advertised the program on its Web site, indicating that it would involve "millions of American workers who, in the daily course of their work, are in a unique position to see potentially unusual or suspicious activity in public places" (Eggen 2002). The program, however, was opposed by many key lawmakers from across the political spectrum. In due course, even the U.S. Postal Service declined to participate. News columnists, think-tank experts, and editorial writers also helped defeat the idea, some even comparing the TIPS program to the network of thousands of "citizen spies" who were recruited during World War I—the volunteer operatives of the American Protective League. Gene Healy, for example, at the Cato Institute, in Washington, D.C., made a point of noting the earlier organization's abuses of civil liberties: "the APL was a volunteer organization," he wrote, "250,000 strong, which worked closely with the Justice Department identifying potential 'subversives.' When the APL couldn't find enough German spies to keep busy, its members quickly turned to harassing labor organizers and turning in draft dodgers" (2002). John Whitehead, president of the Rutherford Institute, characterized the proposed program as "essentially turning the average citizen into an extension of thought police" (qtd. in Hentoff 2002). Columnist Debra Pickett of the *Chicago Sun-Times* wrote, "It's also easy to see the potential for racial profiling and even vigilantism, as a million citizens bring their own agendas to bear on their newly empowered roles" (2002). And Utah's well-known Republican senator Orrin Hatch bluntly stated to Attorney General John Ashcroft, "We don't want to see a 1984 Orwellian-type situation here, where neighbors are reporting on neighbors" (qtd. in Bunker 2002). The failure of the TIPS program, then, was due in large part to recollected events of the past.

In the 1870s and again in the 1890s, America experienced severe economic depressions. Unprecedented episodes of labor violence also took place in the late nineteenth century, as well as in the early part of the twentieth (Carnes, Garraty, and Williams 1996). In addition, in 1877, when the federal government agreed to end Reconstruction and withdraw its military forces from the South, "the dike that had laboriously been constructed against racist retaliation was suddenly broken" (H. Williams and Murphy 1990, 9). Adding to the turmoil, the U.S. Supreme Court, in 1883, declared that the Civil Rights Act of 1875 was unconstitutional; by the mid-1890s, in *Plessy v. Ferguson,* it had affirmed the principle of "separate but equal." The late nineteenth century, in other words, was a time of tremendous upheaval in the United States, the nation striving to adjust to a changing world and a restless populace.

The violent strikes of 1877, which involved the railroad and coal industries, led politicians and industrialists to utilize federal troops to restore order. Militia units—some of which had been revitalized after the Civil War—had been unable to handle the strikers. Toward the end of the nineteenth century, however, the militia began to gain in strength as it became clear that the Volunteer companies raised for the Civil War may have suffered high rates of loss because of their inexperience: "the resurgent organized militia—or as it was increasingly called, the National Guard—began to wrest from the Volunteers the official role as the nation's second line of defense. Unlike Volunteers, National Guard units trained during peacetime" (Stentiford 2002, 11). Still, a debate raged among military and civilian leaders regarding whether it was best to support the emerging National Guard or create a new federal military reserve as the chief secondary force of the nation. The debate seemed to be heading in favor of the National Guard with the passage of the Militia Act of 1903. The new law gave official recognition to the use of the name "National Guard" and established minimum guidelines for drills and other training. However, it also left important operational and constitutional issues unresolved. For example, the Guard was still legally the organized militia and as such could not be used outside U.S. borders. In addition, no federal agency could remove militia officers, nor could National Guard personnel be required to participate as a federal military force. Amendments were made to the 1903 law in 1908 and 1914 to rectify such limitations, but no legal authority was provided for using the National Guard beyond the borders of the United States. The eventual adoption of the National Defense Act of 1916 finally corrected many of the earlier bills' shortcomings: "The new law defined the Army of the United States as consisting of the Regular Army, the Volunteer Army, the Officers' Reserve Corps, the Enlisted Reserve Corps, and the National Guard when in federal service. . . . When the National Guard was brought into the Army of the United States for war, all National Guardsmen were discharged from the National Guard and became soldiers in the federal army, although they would keep their same unit designations" (Stentiford 2002, 17). In the summer of 1917, President Woodrow Wilson drafted the National Guard for service in World War I. Subsequently, many states found themselves "without their principal means for responding to natural disasters, suppressing riots, and assisting local lawmen when mobs threatened to lynch suspects in custody. Only Pennsylvania had a state police force, and most states depended on their National Guard for police functions. To replace the National Guard in its state militia role, many states permitted the creation of loosely supervised units of home guards, while other states created more centralized military forces" (Stentiford 2002, 22). The 1916 law served as the basis for the organization of the armed forces of the United States throughout World War II.

Changes were also taking place in the nonmilitary sphere. Near the end of this transitional era, two remarkable constitutional amendments were adopted. The Nineteenth Amendment granted women the right to vote in every state, while the Eighteenth Amendment (also known as the Prohibition Amendment) prohibited the distribution, sale, and manufacture of alcoholic beverages. The Women's Christian Temperance Union, under the leadership of Frances Willard, played a secondary role in the establishment of Prohibition. Although Willard attempted to have her organization directly aligned with the Prohibition Party, the WCTU's main accomplishment came through the work of its Department of Scientific Temperance Instruction, as laws were established "in every state compelling some form of Temperance Instruction in the public schools" (Gusfield 1963, 86).

Along with the WCTU, members and leaders of many Protestant churches helped ratify the Prohibition Amendment. It has been estimated that as many as fifteen thousand churches were involved in ratification, especially Methodist, Baptist, Presbyterian, and Congregational groups (Odegard 1966). It has also been argued that the most important backers and supporters of the movement for Prohibition were eastern capitalists. Usually, however, the final success of the movement is attributed to the pressure politics of the Anti-Saloon League (ASL) (see, e.g., Blocker 1976; Sinclair 1964; Timberlake 1963; Gusfield 1963; Odegard 1966). ASL operatives and attorneys combined to form a very distinctive type of "volunteer police," especially active prior to the adoption of national Prohibition, when only local prohibition laws were in existence.

Overshadowing these domestic events, however, was the fact that during this period the United States became recognized for the first time as a world power. At the start of America's twentieth century, the nation expanded through the seizure of the Philippine Islands and the annexation of Hawaii and Guam. The Philippines were seized following a declaration of war against Spain in 1898 and the destruction of the Spanish fleet in Manila Bay. Not a single American was killed in the Manila action. The United States also obtained an overwhelming victory in Cuba, where its military forces greatly outnumbered the Spanish troops. The Spanish-American War changed congressional opinion on the issue of Hawaii's annexation. The South voted solidly against it, its opposition fueled by racial prejudice against the inhabitants of Hawaii (its dark-complexioned natives, its Chinese and Japanese residents). Southerners also feared the economic competition of the large Hawaiian sugar-cane industry (Carnes, Garraty, and Williams 1996, 156). Nevertheless, the annexation of Hawaii, spurred by nationalism aroused by the Spanish-American War and America's rise as a Pacific power, and backed both by members of the merchant and professional classes and by President William McKinley, came about in July 1898 and was "the fruit of approximately seventy-five years of expanding American influence in Hawaii" (Fuchs 1983, 36). Later, America's participation in World War I further enhanced its position as a world power.

One factor that contributed to U.S. expansionist activities at the end of the nineteenth century was the proliferation of American Protestant missionary work throughout the world, beginning in the 1870s. Between 1870 and 1900, the number of Protestant missions increased fivefold (Carnes, Garraty, and Williams 1996). Missionary work was especially prevalent in the Far East, including China, Japan, and the Philippines. In addition, although American exports to the Far East in 1900 were not numerous, the market for American goods within this region, then as now, appeared attractive to U.S. business interests. President William McKinley, perhaps motivated by these different concerns, seems to have concluded that the United States needed to control the Philippines in order to "educate the Filipinos, and uplift and Christianize them" (Carnes, Garraty, and Williams 1996, 152).

At home, however, the federal government did not always seem so concerned with the "uplift" of its own citizens. As the federal government backed away from concern about civil rights, abandoning the projects of Reconstruction, the turn of century also witnessed a distinctive type of racism in the United States against blacks, most of whom became progressively disenfranchised (Hastie 1973, 18). "Jim Crow" laws, named after an antebellum minstrel-show character, institutionalized segregation through legal means and were systematically enforced throughout the South. These laws disenfranchised blacks through the adoption of the "grandfather clause," the literacy test, and the poll tax. The "grandfather clause" typically served to allow whites who would have been disenfranchised by poll taxes, literacy tests, or very short registration deadlines to vote. The 1898 Louisiana constitution, for example, granted suffrage to the sons and grandsons of anyone who had voted prior to January 1, 1867, even if they did not meet other requirements (see Hall 1989, 265; Beth 1971, 111). Throughout the South, black children were forced to attend separate schools. Intermarriage of whites and blacks was prohibited, and a broad range of public accommodations (e.g., trains, buses, hotels, parks, theaters, restaurants) were segregated. In 1926, the U.S. Supreme Court, in *Coorigan v. Buckley* (271 U.S. 323) ruled in favor of the existence of racially restrictive covenants in property deeds (Hastie 1973).

America's racial restrictions were rooted not only in the history of slavery but also in the eugenics movement. This movement, which had its formal beginnings in England, exerted a major influence on educated Americans during the first three decades of the twentieth century. Sir Francis Galton (1822–1911) is considered the founder of eugenics, and he gave the movement its name. His first studies examined the backgrounds of famous men to show that mental abilities are inherited. Galton believed that the inherent abilities of humankind could be raised if the inferior races were replaced by superior ones. Galton, however, underestimated the influence environmental factors have on the development of individual personality and the impact of cultural differences among races (Haller 1963, 11–12). Nevertheless, the notions of eugenics held tremendous sway over intellectuals in the earlier twentieth century, and several important developments in the field took place in the United States. Many leading professionals in the areas of crime, insanity, mental retardation (then called "feeblemindedness"), and poverty embraced the precepts of the movement.[1]

After 1930, the worldwide popularity and prestige of eugenics experienced a rapid decline. Nevertheless, Germany's Nazi Party, which espoused a creed of Aryan purity and superiority, showed graphically what use could be made of an emphasis on biological theories of heredity. In 1935 alone, the Nazis sanctioned seventy-two thousand sterilizations, and in the fall of 1939 about fifty thousand insane, "feebleminded," and deformed individuals were put to death in gas chambers (Haller 1963, 180). The same fate was decreed for millions of Jews and other minority-group members beginning in 1941.

Before its American decline, however, the eugenics movement in the United States coincided with a period of history commonly known as the Progressive Era. Significantly, both of these movements also coincided with the "spy era" of volunteer policing. The central theme of the Progressive movement, which lasted from about 1900 to 1914 and reached its zenith just before World War I, was a belief in the possibility of improving public welfare. The Progressives, who believed that unfavorable environmental conditions were the leading cause of social disorder, thought that remedies to public problems could be fashioned through a proper blend of governmental and private interventions. They thus supported a wide variety of legislative initiatives that were designed to improve the urban environment. Progressive programs were "the invention of benevolent and philan-thropic-minded men and women" who came "from the world of the college, the settlement house, and the medical school" (Rothman 1980, 5). The movement's general goals were to restore "a type of economic individualism and political democracy that was widely believed to have existed earlier in America and to . . . bring back a kind of morality and civic purity that was also believed to have been lost" (Hofstadter 1955, 5–6).

The mission of the settlement house was to gather and analyze the social science data derived from the "natural laboratory" of the slum. Progressives, who possessed an abiding belief in the benefits of achieving middle-class status, sought to use the case method to study and resolve social problems. Their key tenets included individualization of treatment, trust in the power of the state to do good, and the need for the state to act for the common good (e.g., by promoting equal opportunity) (Rothman 1980).

The two-decade period just prior to the full-fledged eruption of the work of the Progressives had seen several dramatic and violent encounters between labor activists and police. On the evening of May 4, 1886, in Chicago's Haymarket Square, an unknown person threw a bomb at the police, who had been assigned to break up a strikers' rally. Before the night was over, five persons were dead and scores were wounded. In 1892, violence erupted when the members of a Pinkerton security force clashed with strikers at Andrew Carnegie's Homestead steelworks, near Pittsburgh. In 1894, a strike by the American Railway Union in support of striking Pullman railroad-car workers led to "violent confrontations in Chicago, Los Angeles, Hammond, Indiana, and other rail centers. In Chicago, where more than 14,000 federal troops, deputies, and police patrolled the troubled areas, at least thirteen persons were killed and substantial amounts of railway property destroyed" (P. Boyer 1978, 126). Undoubtedly, such alarming incidents of labor unrest, along with depression-era anxieties between 1893 and 1897 and popular-media depictions of degrading conditions among the urban poor, contributed to the unease of the middle and wealthier classes, eventually helping to stimulate the progressive impulses of some of the more secure members of American society (Rothman 1980).

The Progressives had knowledge of correctional practices. They knew that prisons (an invention of Jacksonian reformers) had degenerated "into more or less lax, corrupt, and brutal places" (Rothman 1980, 18) where staff survival, rather than inmate treatment, was the main concern. They also knew that asylums and prisons had inept board members who consistently deferred to the will of institutional superintendents. Most prisons sold inmate labor to the highest bidder, so that state legislators and taxpayers had little cause to worry about the costs of incarceration.

Subsequently, at the beginning of the twentieth century, the Progressives adopted the concept of the indeterminate sentence (marked by the philosophy that prisoners carry the key to their prison cells in their own pockets) and advocated such well-known practices as probation (with its comprehensive presentence report), parole, juvenile courts, and outpatient clinics for the mentally ill. They also actively lobbied for better housing conditions, organized playgrounds, safer workplaces, and improved health policies (Rothman 1980).

The Progressive movement had mixed success. In the United States, probation became common between 1900 and 1920. The first probation law in New York State, which provided for the appointment of probation officers by justices of various courts, was passed in 1901. Before the New York State Probation Commission was established to supervise the work of probation officers, in 1907, the "visiting agents" of the New York House of Refuge, a juvenile reformatory, served as parole agents. Founded in 1825, and one of the earliest institutions of its kind in the United States, the New York House of Refuge did not appoint its first visiting agent until 1894. These early parole agents helped ease the replacement of the indenturing system of discharging inmates, visiting the homes of new inmates, and the homes and prospective employers of inmates to be paroled, to ensure appropriate placement. They made similar visits to paroled inmates to check on their progress.

Some of the most important reforms achieved by the Progressives were in the areas of probation and parole. Generally, probation involves release to the community under supervision and the suspension of any applicable jail or prison time by order of the sentencing court. Parole involves early release from prison under supervision based on the decision of parole-board members. Each parolee and probationer must adhere to a tailor-made list of conditions in order to satisfy his or her personalized rehabilitation plan.

While such practices have become common nationwide, fulfillment of the promises of individualized treatment, as contained in the conditions set forth for the probationer and the parolee, remains highly problematic. While parole has survived, it is "undoubtedly the most unpopular of all re- form measures" (Rothman 1980, 159). Parole boards have been found to spend little time on their cases, often making decisions in an arbitrary and capricious manner. Moreover, the supervision of parolees is frequently lax or nonexistent. The parole system persists because it has the support of prison wardens, who fear that its removal could lead to inmate unrest. Pa- role also serves as a safety valve for prison overcrowding. In spite of these factors, there is evidence to indicate that parole actually increases the state's period of control, adding to the period of incarceration a further pe- riod of supervision. Some evidence even indicates that in certain jurisdic- tions parole boards have exacted more time from inmates—especially recidivists—than courts have (Rothman 1980, 196). "Parole," according to a 1925 Pennsylvania report, "is not leniency. On the contrary, parole really in- creases the state's period of control" (qtd. in L. M. Friedman 1993, 305).

Nevertheless, Progressives saw such measures as parole as integral to an individualized approach to rehabilitation. While they may have disagreed about the causes of an individual's problem (environmental, psychological, etc.), they agreed that treatment had to be based on a case-by-case analysis. In other words, different persons had to be treated differently. Such individ- ualized treatment was thus a major goal of Progressives, who decried the uniformity and rigidity of institutions that denied a discretionary response to the needs of particular clients. Progressives, however, were eventually proven mistaken in their belief that institutions (e.g., prisons, mental hospi- tals) could work closely with community alternatives and that the creation of such alternatives (e.g., probation, outpatient clinics) could eliminate the need for institutionalization in many cases. The Progressives "were con- vinced that their innovations could satisfy *all* goals, that the same person and the same institution could at once guard and help, protect and rehabil- itate, maintain custody and deliver treatment" (Rothman 1980, 10). Such misguided convictions, and the well-intentioned errors in judgment that resulted, caused the Progressive movement to eventually run out of steam.

During the 1920s, following the decline of the Progressive Era, the na- tional prohibition of liquor gave rise to new vices (e.g., gambling) as saloon owners and workers sought to maintain their livelihoods. Prohibition insti- tutionalized corruption in American political life on a previously unseen scale (Coffey 1975). The liquor business, as one contemporary observed, operated "with a knowing wink in the most smug communities, as well as in the more free and easy cities of the eastern seaboard. No person . . . believes that these organizations . . . could continue to do business year in and year out without active cooperation of duly constituted police authority" (Driscoll 1925, 170).

Before its decline, the Progressive movement had a hand in fashioning certain reforms involving the nation's police and the administration of justice—reforms that were greatly undermined with the spread of Prohibition. After 1915, Progressives helped set the stage for new types of volunteer police—for example, through the creation of junior police programs. On the national level, Progressives also contributed to the 1908 creation of the Bureau of Investigation, the forerunner of the modern Federal Bureau of Investigation. The Bureau of Investigation's appearance "marked the intervention of the federal government into the law enforcement picture in a manner that was without precedent" (S. S. Walker 1977, 77). J. Edgar Hoover was appointed to head the Bureau of Investigation in 1924. Interestingly, most supporters of Progressive causes were male college graduates from urban and middle-class backgrounds with professional careers. Most were native-born Protestants, and most held membership in the Masons (Hofstadter 1968). Historian Richard Powers notes that "J. Edgar Hoover's resemblance to Hofstadter's ideal progressive type is uncanny, even to the detail of Masonic membership" (1987, 519). Hoover's appointment drew little press attention, except in the *Daily Worker*, the chief publication of the Communist Party in the United States. Its front-page report on December 22, 1924, declared: "After public excitement over the Teapot Dome graft scandal and the corruption exposed in the department of justice died down, the promises made by the government prior to the election were conveniently forgotten. Now that the excitement is over, we find J. Edgar Hoover slipping his feet in Burns' shoes" (qtd. in Theoharis and Cox 1988, 100).

In 1919, prior to his appointment, J. Edgar Hoover had played an instrumental role in the deportation of hundreds of aliens, including the best-known radical of her day, Emma Goldman. In 1892, Goldman had conspired with her boyfriend, Alexander Berkman, to assassinate Henry Clay Frick. Goldman and Berkman despised Frick for his treatment of industrial workers and for his role in the battle between labor and management at the Homestead Steel Plant, in which three Pinkerton security guards and ten workers were killed (see M. Walker 2000, 17–32). Frick survived the attempt on his life, and Hoover was eventually promoted, remaining in charge of the FBI for fifty years. While Hoover set high standards for special agents, and his other managerial innovations were recognized as important milestones in the history of police reform, more recent revelations about his use of secret files and his style of leadership have provoked considerable criticism.

Nevertheless, the organization that Hoover headed for so many years had its roots in the reforms of the early twentieth century. In 1905, the U.S. Department of Justice created its first Bureau of Criminal Identification to provide a centralized reference collection of fingerprint cards. In 1907, the fingerprint collection, as a money-saving measure, was moved to Leavenworth Federal Penitentiary, where prisoners were assigned to handle it. Suspicious of this arrangement, police departments formed their own centralized identification bureau maintained by the International Association of Chiefs of Police (IACP). The IACP refused to share its collection of records with the Bureau of Investigation until Congress intervened in 1924; eventually, the federal government's collection of fingerprints and the IACP's were merged (FBI 2005).

Such instances of inefficiency made the need for centralization increasingly clear. Prior to the 1908 creation of the Bureau of Investigation, attorneys in the Department of Justice had to rely on the investigative services of the agents in the Secret Service Division of the Treasury Department or hire the temporary services of the Pinkerton Detective Agency. Frustrated by this arrangement, President Theodore Roosevelt's attorney general, Charles Bonaparte, a grandnephew of Napoleon, obtained congressional support for the new Bureau of Investigation by promising that "particular care would be taken to recruit high-quality professional investigators. Second, the attorney general would personally assume supervisory responsibility over the initiation and operations of investigations. And, third, the newly created investigative division would not investigate political beliefs and affiliations or strictly personal matters; its investigations would be confined to violations of antitrust and interstate commerce laws" (Theoharis and Cox 1988, 43). Both Attorney General Bonaparte and President Theodore

Roosevelt left office in March 1909. According to the FBI (2005), it was actually Bonaparte's successor, Attorney General George Wickersham, who first officially used the designation "Bureau of Investigation" on March 16, 1909.

New federal legislation followed swiftly. In 1910, Congress passed the Mann Act, which made it a federal crime to transport women across state lines for "immoral purposes." In 1912, Congress outlawed the interstate transportation of prizefight films. In 1919, the Dyer Act made the movement of stolen vehicles across state lines a federal crime. These laws and many more that followed added to the responsibilities of the new Bureau of Investigation and created specific mandates for federal crime investigators. Significantly, the opportunity for any future attorney general to "personally assume supervisory responsibility" over particular cases became more and more remote.

Around the same time as this rapid growth of the Bureau of Investigation, many innovative activities were taking place in some police circles. For example, the Los Angeles Police Department set up an antismoking clinic that targeted community members, especially youth. New York City police raised money for homeless men and gave them meal tickets redeemable at local restaurants. Washington, D.C., had two officers investigating child labor, while New York City police had thirteen boiler inspectors. The Seattle police had three truant officers, and Rochester, New York, had six. Finally, Council Bluffs, Iowa; Cincinnati; and New York City had "junior" or "boy police" programs (S. S. Walker 1977, 83–84).

The same time period also ushered in the spy era of volunteer policing, during which many groups became increasingly active: various home and state guard units of militia; the "friendly visitors" of the Charity Organization Society in New York and other cities; the Anti-Saloon League, which undertook specialized law enforcement activities; and the American Protective League, whose undercover agents engaged in relatively short-lived, controversial work.

In the absence of the National Guard, which had been called to active duty, most states established various types of home and/or state guard units during World War I.[2] While specific federal authorization for such organizations was sometimes tenuous, thousands of men served in such units, subject to being called for regular military service. These new types of militia generally had no direct role in federal overseas war planning and consequently received little or no federal support (Stentiford 2002, 23).

In some jurisdictions, home guards were organized at the county and municipal levels. Florida, for example, established a procedure by which county guard units could be organized by local sheriffs and judges for peacekeeping roles. Such work was authorized only for white males between eighteen and sixty-five years of age, who were most commonly assigned to participate in parades and local ceremonies. Alabama initiated a similarly decentralized approach. Most of the units established by sheriffs, however, only existed on paper, and the governor of Alabama received several offers from local citizens to establish more committed and armed organizations. On one occasion, the governor received a letter from a businessman who wanted to form a home guard unit to arrest German spies and disloyal Americans. Alabama's governor consistently denied such requests. Mississippi recruited for companies of the home guard, but for the duration of the war, the troops were unarmed and lacked uniforms and equipment (see Stentiford 2002, 24–32).

In Missouri, a state-directed home guard was established: "At its peak, the Missouri Home Guard consisted of five regiments, six separate battalions, and sixteen separate companies. . . . The Home Guard contained six thousand men, mostly in the infantry" (Stentiford 2002, 37). The recruitment of such a force was facilitated by the existence of the Missouri Militia Act of 1908. This foresighted state law specifically authorized the governor to create a replacement militia for the National Guard when it left the state. One regiment of the Missouri Guard based in Kansas City was successful in controlling labor unrest during a general strike of workers that lasted six days. Most of the time, however, the Missouri units of the home guard merely engaged in training exercises. These activities "may have been enough to keep local opponents of national policy quiet" (Stentiford 2002, 38). Nevertheless, the Missouri Guard did serve one additional function: it provided preinduction training for young men subject to the draft. Nearly "90 percent of the drafted men who had received such training became noncommissioned officers upon reaching federal training camps. For those who took advantage of state military training, the benefits were substantial" (Stentiford 2002, 38–39). More prosperous northern and midwestern states usually opted for the creation of state guard units to replace the federalized National Guard. Other than in Missouri, state-directed guard units were established in Massachusetts, Connecticut, New York, New Jersey, Pennsylvania, Ohio, Illinois, and Wisconsin (Stentiford 2002, 35).

In the northwestern United States, concern over radical factions of the Industrial Workers of the World (IWW) and the protection of industrial and natural resources spurred the formation of new militia units. In Washington, a state guard composed of sixteen companies was formed. At one point in time, a small fifteen-member unit of the guard was assigned to protect the state against forest fires. In Oregon, members of various county defense organizations were deputized by local sheriffs. Some of these units were eventually incorporated into a new statewide force known as the Oregon Guard when the governor of Oregon became concerned about the activities of possible enemy aliens and the radicalism of the IWW. This fear grew to such an extent that a full-time force of 235 men was recruited to relieve the Oregon Guard members who had been posted at the shipyards in Portland. The new force was called the Oregon Military Police (see Stentiford 2002, 57–60). The state guard also maintained a group of officers who formed "an intelligence department" for the express purpose of finding spies, as well as deserters and draft dodgers. As was the case with most of the home and state guard forces formed during World War I, the Oregon Guard and the Oregon Military Police were disbanded by the summer of 1919 (Stentiford 2002, 60).

Some state guard organizations, however, were not disbanded until 1920. In Maryland, many members of the state guard drilled in Baltimore, where they operated a program providing free lodging and breakfast to federal troops. The Maryland State Guard's only other significant undertakings came after the end of the war, when it maintained order in Annapolis during and after the execution of a black man convicted of murdering a white woman and when it protected a black man in Easton, accused of raping a thirteen-year-old white girl, from being lynched (Stentiford 2002, 68–69).

The New York Charity Organization Society

Throughout most of the twentieth century, environmental factors were consistently cited as contributing to the roots of criminality. Progressives made great strides in the field of preventive medicine in order to reduce the ill effects of such environmental conditions. For example, they helped establish city and state diagnostic laboratories for the identification of infectious diseases, made public the bacteriological origins of many diseases, and promoted the basics of modern hygiene in order to prevent disease transmission. As part of the latter effort, nurses, medical inspectors, and physicians visited schools, tenements, and other places of public accommodation in order to reach the most at-risk children and their parents. By 1915, the infant death rate in New York City had dropped from its 1885 total of 273 per thousand live births to 94. The work of local and state departments of health in the dissemination of educational services, initiated during the Progressive Era, continues today (Lubove 1962, 84–88).

Direct charitable aid or relief, however, was organized under a different banner beginning in the 1880s. In 1882, Josephine Shaw Lowell, a commissioner of the New York State Board of Charities, established the New York Charity Organization Society to consolidate New York City's charitable resources under a single umbrella organization. Lowell was concerned that no matter how carefully an agency sought to deliver its aid, "it was impossible to know each applicant or to ferret out imposters who went from charity to charity collecting help" (M. B. Katz 1996, 75). One of the COS's first achievements was the creation of a file system that kept persons in need of financial assistance from receiving duplicate aid: "By the mid-1890s, when COS had files on 170,000 families or individuals, it was making the information freely available, by return mail, not only to agencies considering giving relief but to prospective employers, landlords, banks, and even the police" (Burrows and Wallace 1999, 1159). Requests for aid were also often turned down because applicants did not fit strict selection criteria.

Instead of hiring professional caseworkers to perform the investigations necessary to achieve its ends, the COS recruited "society women" who could serve as role models for the poorer classes. These workers were urged to be friendly but firm. Charity-minded citizens were encouraged not to give needy persons cash donations but to use coupons, each worth fifty cents. The possession of one coupon entitled a homeless person to two meals and a place to rest for one night, but there was one prerequisite: the coupon's recipient would first have to chop wood for a day (Burrows and Wallace 1999, 1160).

Lowell's COS greatly benefited from the advice contained in the Rev-

erend S. Humphreys Gurteen's *Handbook of Charity Organization,* published in 1882. Gurteen had worked for the Charity Organization Society in
London and had helped establish the Buffalo COS, the first in America. The
core tenet of Gurteen's ideal charity organization society was that, instead
of giving direct aid, it would coordinate, investigate, and counsel. As was
the case in New York City, after relief benefits had been approved, regular
visits to recipients' homes were to be made: "In truth, the visitor was to be at
once a sympathetic friend, an official, a teacher, and a spy" (M. B. Katz 1996,
79). In Buffalo, the initial screening of home-relief candidates was conducted by regular police officers, assigned to the task by district police captains. By utilizing the police, "the COS . . . highlighted its own quasi-public
status" (M. B. Katz 1996, 80).

Gurteen's model of charitable relief was adopted first in larger cities and
eventually in smaller ones. After a time, however, the New York COS found
itself unable to recruit all the volunteers it needed for its special type of
charitable work. Initially, it created a Committee on Mendicancy, "which
hired 'Special Agents' who were empowered by the city to arrest beggars"
(Burrows and Wallace 1999, 1160). Eventually, additional agents were hired
to fill the everyday role of "friendly visitors." The New York COS also published a list of persons known to be public beggars and tried to discourage
the use of police station basements as emergency housing for the needy
(Burrows and Wallace 1999, 1160–61). General housing conditions within
the slums of the city, however, were wretched. The slums consisted mainly
of tenements, often poorly ventilated wooden buildings of five or six floors
with communal sinks located in the hallways (Nevins and Commager 1976,
388).

In addition to miserable conditions, Gurteen's model faced other factors
that led to its eventual failure to reduce dependency in America: "the realities of local urban politics defeated even the most zealous reformers" (M. B.
Katz 1996, 83). In particular, charity organization societies were unable to
overcome "the suspicion, hostility, and rivalry of churches and local relief
organizations" (M. B. Katz 1996, 83). In New York City, the organization was
simply overwhelmed. The work of the nation's largest COS had expanded to
include research, public health, and other activities until "the different departments of the New York COS virtually became different organizations"
(M. B. Katz 1996, 86). The short supply of volunteers required the use of

paid agents both to conduct initial welfare investigations and to engage in home visitations. Training for this dual role was implemented by the New York COS in 1898 and expanded in 1903. The roles of the first social workers directly sprang from the duties of the fieldworkers of charity organization societies. Indeed, by the second decade of the twentieth century, the case-worker was, in essence, "a trained, professional friendly visitor" (M. B. Katz 1996, 171).

The eugenics movement also played a role in the welfare work of this pe-riod. Concern about the inheritance of crime and other undesirable cir-cumstances, for example, fostered the movement of over ninety thousand children from urban areas to new homes in the Midwest. This initiative was the undertaking of the Children's Aid Society, under the leadership of Charles Loring Brace. Other work on behalf of children was conducted by the Society for the Prevention of Cruelty to Children, whose agents after 1881 held peace officer status. This "all-male, all elite, and overwhelmingly Protestant organization" (Burrows and Wallace 1999, 1161) concerned itself with finding abused and neglected children and obtaining court orders to remove them from their families.

The Anti-Saloon League

The members of the Anti-Saloon League, only indirectly concerned with children, sought to police the drinking habits of their parents and other adults. Beginning in the 1890s, the main agenda of the Anti-Saloon League "was not to advocate prohibition in the broad sense, but . . . to rally the di-vided temperance forces for the more modest task of saloon suppression" (Timberlake 1963, 127). The ASL concentrated its early efforts on the dan-gers of the saloon, rather than on all liquor traffic, initially seeking to achieve Prohibition through "local option." Through this method, separate political entities (e.g., an election district such as a city, a town, or an entire county) could pass laws to limit the sale of alcohol. The ASL's field tactics in-cluded efforts to educate the public and discredit the saloon (Cashman 1981, 246–67), its overall strategies focusing on political agitation, legisla-tion, and law enforcement. The organization, headquartered in Westerville, a small town near Columbus, Ohio, was run like a business, with salaried leaders, its operations conducted through various departments. It was tightly organized, administered by "a small permanent, self-appointed committee" that "elected its own officers, who ran the League, hiring and directing superintendents, speakers, and other workers. Local Leagues duplicated this form" (Hamm 1994, 382).

The ASL filled an important gap in the movement seeking Prohibition. The Prohibition Party, begun several decades earlier, had been unsuccessful in having its Prohibition candidates elected to high office, and the Women's Christian Temperance Union was becoming involved in wider social interests. In this void, a wide variety of local, citizen-based "law-and-order" groups had sprung up to raise money for the private prosecution of local prohibition laws, using their funds to hire attorneys and pay informers and detectives. In this way, zealous temperance workers hoped to embarrass and coax reluctant public officials into a more serious effort to contend with liquor sellers. At first, ASL officials disapproved of such law enforcement methods, but such activities proved to be popular and were eventually incorporated into manuals of instruction used by local ASL units. Specifically, securing detectives and furnishing attorneys for liquor law violation prosecutions were among the major law enforcement tactics of state chapters of the ASL (Hamm 1994, 390).

Prior to national Prohibition, the ASL fostered the adoption of local prohibition laws within various states and their subdivisions. By 1908, it was operating in forty-three states and territories, as well as the District of Columbia. The central officials of the ASL placed great emphasis on the services of legal experts and encouraged their recruitment (Hamm 1994, 389), and volunteer and paid ASL attorneys worked in each state. Their functions included preparing annotated lists of state liquor laws, drafting laws, assisting local prosecutors by helping to present cases, public speaking, and helping to raise funds (Timberlake 1963, 132, 144).

The ASL was an unaffiliated volunteer police organization by virtue of its direct actions in undertaking extensive private investigations and prosecutions of suspected local-option law violators. The ASL also contributed to the goals of law enforcement through its efforts to encourage citizens to demand better policing by public officials. In 1916, for example, "five hundred League and WCTU volunteers worked as formal informers to the State Commissioner of Prohibition" (Hamm 1994, 393). Although local units of the ASL routinely hired private detectives to gather evidence regarding liquor law violations, ASL officials consistently proclaimed that paid detectives should be used only as a last resort (Hamm 1994, 393–94). Nevertheless, by 1908, the ASL had participated in over thirty-one thousand cases of liquor law enforcement; its ability to mobilize lawyers, government officials, private detectives, and antiliquor volunteers made its system a cohesive and effective one (Hamm 1995, 141). Indeed, ASL detectives "were indispensable to the enforcement program": "They could enter lower-class saloons, black bars, and other places where the average temperance worker stood out like a sore thumb" (Hamm 1995, 148).

ASL-sponsored prosecutions and the use of private detectives were often necessary because public officials were lax or disinterested in the pursuit of local violators of temperance legislation. A storm of controversy arose regarding this privately based approach, however, after several violent episodes. In 1910, for example, ASL detectives operating in Newark, Ohio, raided a number of locations, at one place encountering a hostile crowd. In the course of the ensuing struggle, one of the ASL detectives, Carl Etherington, aged seventeen, shot and killed one of his assailants while acting in self-defense. Although he was placed in the local jail, he was seized by a mob and lynched in the public square (Timberlake 1963, 144, 218).

This episode no doubt added to the costs of securing private detectives, but it did not appear to diminish the significance of the ASL's accomplishments. By 1913, the ASL was specifically advocating on behalf of national Prohibition, claiming that it represented the nation's churches and the majority of Americans. It had already successfully championed the Webb-Kenyon Act—outlawing the shipment of liquor into dry states—through Congress, as well as the vote that overrode its veto by President William Howard Taft. During the next three years, the ASL also continued to lead efforts for the adoption of state prohibition laws, relying on statistics to make as strong a case as possible for its cause. League publications "fairly bristled with charts, tables, and graphs purporting to establish positive or negative correlations between the saloon and death rates, arrest rates, tax rates, divorce rates, wages, insanity, pauperism, bank deposits, industrial efficiency, housing investment, and public-school enrollment" (P. Boyer 1978, 199).

By 1917, twenty-three states had passed antiliquor laws (Engelmann 1979, 66). The Prohibition movement was further aided in 1917 by the American Medical Association, whose members voted to state their opposi-

tion to the use of alcohol (Sinclair 1964). In the same year, at the ASL's annual convention, the Reverend A. C. Baine announced the organization's intention to bring about international prohibition (Timberlake 1963, 180–81).
Prohibition, the Anti-Saloon League declared, "would remove at a single
stroke most of the political, social, and moral problems associated with the
city" (P. Boyer 1978, 208).

America's entry into World War I greatly accelerated the momentum that
had been generated earlier on behalf of national Prohibition. A period of
wartime prohibition was initiated with the passage of the Lever Food and
Fuel Control Act in August 1917 and the War Prohibition Act in November
1918. The former measure banned the production of distilled spirits for the
duration of the war, while the latter outlawed the manufacture and sale of
all intoxicating beverages (including wine and beer) containing more than
2.75 percent alcohol until the end of wartime mobilization (Kyvig 1979,
10–11).

Meanwhile, the Anti-Saloon League successfully lobbied Congress for a
resolution submitting the Eighteenth Amendment to the states. The Senate
adopted the resolution on August 1, 1917, and the House approved it on
December 18, 1917. The necessary number of states had ratified the Eighteenth Amendment by 1919, with only two states failing to ratify: Rhode
Island and Connecticut (Asbury 1968, 132–33). This rather quick ratification
was perhaps due to the fact that the Anti-Saloon League had been manipu-
lating "state legislatures for some ten years, and . . . the drys had brought
most of them into the fold before they went after Congress" (Asbury 1968,
131).

After the Eighteenth Amendment was ratified, the ASL took on the task
of preparing an appropriate set of guidelines for enforcing it. This initiative
was called the National Prohibition Act, or more commonly the Volstead
Act, named for the man who introduced it, Congressman Andrew J. Volstead. Approved by Congress in October 1919, the act was vetoed by President Woodrow Wilson. Congress, however, easily produced the votes necessary to override the veto, and the Volstead Act took effect on January 16,
1920.

Congressman Volstead was apparently "hardly the fanatic that the
statute named after him implies" and in fact had nearly been defeated in
1916 when challenged by a member of the Prohibition Party (Perrett 1982,

169). Through the seniority system, Volstead had attained the chair of the House Judiciary Committee. In that capacity, he had the obligation to report out of committee both the Eighteenth Amendment and its supplemental enforcement statute. In 1922, he lost his congressional seat to an opponent who had accused him of being an atheist.

The Volstead Act prohibited all drinks containing 0.5 percent alcohol or more. This particular stricture came unexpectedly: "The .5 percent provision—advocated by the Anti-Saloon League and other militant drys—surprised considerable numbers of persons who assumed that, as had been the case with many state laws, only distilled spirits would be banned" (Kyvig 1979, 13). While the law did permit home brews of cider and fruit juices, so long as they were nonintoxicating, as well as liquor that had been stored in homes prior to July 1, 1919 (the date when the last special wartime prohibition law came into effect), most common brands of beer and wine were prohibited (Timberlake 1963, 181–83). Liquor could be used as a prescription medication and for religious purposes, and denatured industrial-quality alcohol was also permitted. Passage of the Volstead Act on October 28, 1919, provoked a nationwide drinking spree over Christmas and New Year's that led to some awful consequences as individuals experimented with homemade recipes: "More than a hundred people in New York drank whiskey distilled from wood alcohol and died" (Cashman 1981, 28).

The problem of enforcing Prohibition fell largely on federal officials (S. S. Walker 1977; Nelli 1976). In New York City, for example, police rarely conducted raids on their own initiative. When raids were conducted, any seized liquor was commonly turned over to federal agents, the raided establishments typically reopening for business as soon as the police left (S. Walker 1933, 74, 165): "For the municipal police, national prohibition represented a strong continuity with earlier traditions of non-enforcement and corruption. . . . Prohibition came and went leaving little effect on the urban police" (S. S. Walker 1977, 109).

Prohibition coincided with a time of relative economic prosperity in the United States. When the prosperous 1920s bubble collapsed, however, the nation's worst period of depression was ushered in. Will Rogers, the most famous American humorist of the time, revealed the mood of many when he declared: "What does prohibition amount to, if your neighbors' children are not eating? It's food, not drink, is our problem now. We were so afraid the poor people might drink—now we fixed it so they can't eat" (qtd. in Severn 1969, 167).

The Anti-Saloon League, which had played a very large role in the enactment of Prohibition in 1919, found itself incapable of sustaining the necessary momentum for its continuation. The ASL had adapted business managerial techniques to accomplish its primary objective, but it was not able to reconcile competing views and enunciate a clear strategy for a dry America.

These events and other factors—such as the change in public opinion expressed in the 1932 general elections—marked the end of America's "Noble Experiment." The Twenty-first Amendment, repealing the Eighteenth, was officially ratified on December 5, 1933, President Franklin Roosevelt expressing the hope that "this return of individual freedom shall not be accompanied by the repugnant conditions that obtained prior to adoption of the 18th Amendment and those that have existed since its adoption" (E. Allen 1979, 279). It seemed at the time that the only lasting result of all this effort was that the word *saloon* had become taboo. Such institutions themselves, of course, have flourished ever since, whether known as the corner bar and grill, a cocktail lounge, a tavern, or by the name of the once-popular television show *Cheers*.

Today, scholars remember the ASL for its pioneering role in running an effective single-issue campaign. Indeed, "by the late twentieth century countless observers of American politics were wondering how the nation could survive the single-issue, interest group political structure the league had promoted" (Kerr 1985, 282). In some ways, the ASL's early efforts, which combined volunteers with attorneys, detectives, and public officials, bear some resemblance to current programs in "community policing." One hallmark of community policing, for example, is building community partnerships. A key difference, however, is that the earlier partnership often met with the indifference of the police. Nonetheless, the ASL, at least in its early years, persisted in its enforcement efforts.

One lasting effect of the Anti-Saloon League is related to its widespread use of private detectives. The ASL, along with various industrial giants like Frick and Carnegie, helped popularize the work of private detectives for future generations. In 1948, there were about six hundred independent detective agencies (Kakalik and Wildhorn 1977, 57–58), and in the decade following World War II, the number of detective agencies doubled. By the latter half of the 1990s, it was estimated that there were five thousand investigative agencies in the United States, with approximately two hundred thousand employees. Many of these workers today assist law firms in the preparation of civil and criminal cases, especially with respect to insurance fraud. Investigators are also employed in the detection of pilferage and shoplifting, as well as in the "high-tech" fields of white-collar crime and computer fraud (Hess and Wrobleski 1996, 33–34).

The American Protective League

While the activities of early temperance groups eventually contributed to the formation of the Anti-Saloon League, the events surrounding World War I were most responsible for the rise of the American Protective League. On April 4, 1917, the Senate voted for war against Germany, and in the ensuing months, thousands upon thousands of American troops were sent to the battlefields of Europe.

Also at this time, in 1917, J. Edgar Hoover obtained his first job with the Justice Department, as a clerk. In a short time, he was promoted to the position of Justice Department attorney because of his wartime expertise in deportation matters. In the coming months, his zeal in enforcing the Sedition Act of 1918 would result in massive dragnet raids and the arrest and detention of thousands of suspected alien radicals. Under the Sedition Act, any alien belonging to an organization determined to be anarchistic or revolutionary could be deported at the sole discretion of the secretary of labor (Theoharis and Cox 1988, 46–50). While 1917's Espionage Act made the utterance of false statements for the purpose of interfering with the war effort a federal crime, the Sedition Act went even further, making the utterance of "disloyal" statements a federal crime.

On June 2, 1919, a bomb exploded on the front porch of Attorney General A. Mitchell Palmer; at least a dozen more bombs simultaneously exploded in other parts of the country. In September 1920, the public fear generated by the 1919 bombings reached even greater proportions when a bomb exploded in front of J. P. Morgan's Wall Street offices, killing thirty-eight and wounding several hundred (Horan 1967, 496). Hoover, whom the attorney general had appointed as his special assistant for investigating radicals of any kind, was now empowered to establish his own General Intelligence Division within the Bureau of Investigation, and he thus began his lifelong career of compiling reports on individuals and organizations. During a period that has come to be known as the "Red Scare," he began to target various Communist sympathizers and arrange for their arrest and possible deportation. Hoover became the assistant director of the Bureau of Investigation on August 22, 1921, and its acting director in May 1924 (Theoharis and Cox 1988).

However, it was during America's involvement in World War I, just prior to the Red Scare, that the first unit of what was to become the largest body of secret agents ever assembled in the United States—and perhaps in any nation—was formed: the American Protective League. This group was the inspiration of Albert M. Briggs, an outdoor advertising executive. Briggs was able to convince the head of the U.S. Department of Justice's Chicago office of the APL's value. He offered a volunteer solution to the problem of how to investigate suspected German agents at a time when funds and departmental equipment were in short supply. Briggs promised personnel and automobiles that could be used by the Justice Department at the discretion of the chief of its Bureau of Investigation (J. M. Jensen 1968).

President Wilson had desperately tried to avoid going to war with Germany, but the nation was soon in need of all the help it could attract. The recruitment of volunteers for the APL was fostered by rumors of sabotage and the threat of invasion. Many conservative businessmen also joined the APL because it gave them an opportunity to learn about the activities of labor unions (J. M. Jensen 1968). Many large contributors paid for APL activities; the Chicago office, for example, was funded by a public utility company. In general, contributors included banks, owners of large industrial plants, and prominent corporations. Many wealthy individuals gave additional amounts, a very considerable sum raised from the sale of badges to volunteer operatives "at a profit to the League" (Hough 1919, 32). During U.S. involvement in World War I, the APL was authorized to protect property, investigate violations of the Espionage Act, locate draft evaders, arrest deserters, report all disloyal or suspicious activities, and enforce vice and liquor regulations in areas around army camps and naval bases (J. M. Jensen 1968, 180). Their most notorious activities, however, involved investigating and reporting "disloyal and seditious utterances" (Hough 1919, 120) and participating in raids in which volunteer APL agents joined with police personnel in rounding up suspected draft evaders.

The first letter of recruitment drafted by Briggs as the APL's general superintendent invited certain men to become the leaders (chiefs) of local units:

> I have been authorized by the United States Department of Justice, Bureau of Investigation, to organize confidentially in your town, a division of the American Protective League. . . . The object of the American Protective League, which is entirely a patriotic one . . . is to work under the direction of the United States Department of Justice, Bureau of Investigation . . . in securing information of the activities of agents of foreign governments, or persons unfriendly to this government for the protection of public property, etc., and any other work that may be assigned to us by the Department at any time. . . . As Chief of your local Division you will report daily or as often as necessary, personally or by telephone, telegraph or mail, to your nearest Special Agent of the Department of Justice . . . and you will properly enroll and swear in each member of your organization. . . . It is essential that the greatest possible secrecy be maintained, both in forming the organization and in conducting it. (Hough 1919, 501–2)

APL members were not made peace officers, nor did they have any powers beyond those of a private citizen. Their membership did not confer any special authorization to carry firearms beyond that extended to private citizens by local laws. Moreover, members were not exempted from selective service regulations and were instructed to avoid making any representation that they were government officers. On the other hand, APL members were permitted to state that they were conducting an investigation "for the Department of Justice" (Hough 1919, 499). In addition, they were organized along a military-style chain of command, their hierarchy including a local chief, an assistant chief, inspectors, captains, lieutenants, and general members (Hough 1919, 497–98).

In Chicago, from July 11 to July 15, 1918, the APL conducted a "slacker drive." In order to find draft dodgers or other persons in delinquent status with their draft boards, hundreds of APL members visited hotels, restaurants, saloons, ballparks, motion picture theaters, railroad stations, and other places of public assembly. About two hundred thousand persons were questioned and some forty thousand apprehended and escorted or referred to local draft boards in order to straighten out their records. According to Hinton Clabaugh, superintendent of the Chicago division of the Bureau of Investigation, "not one word of criticism was heard of the Chicago raid." The Chicago division of the APL, Clabaugh stated, "did seventy-five percent of the Government investigating work throughout the war" (qtd. in Hough 1919, 491).

An important World War I–era case involving many members of the APL was the prosecution and conviction of nearly a hundred members of the Industrial Workers of the World for violating the Espionage Act. The IWW began in 1904 with the merger of the Western Federation of Miners and the American Labor Union. By World War I, the IWW had over one hundred thousand members from many trades, mostly in the western part of the nation. The indictments were framed in general terms, the charges including fostering strikes to delay the output in war munitions, spoiling industrial material, committing acts of violence against persons not of their views, violating the postal laws, and conspiracy. The trial, which took place in Chicago, lasted for five months and was judged by Kenesaw Mountain Landis, "famous for running his court with an iron hand and theatrical gestures" (Reppetto 1978, 275).

Preparation for the trial took nearly two years, and APL members were involved from the start of the investigation. For an entire year, fifteen volunteer APL lawyers worked under the supervision of the Bureau of Investigation to prepare the trial evidence. At the time, trial preparation was said to be the most elaborate work ever done in any case at law: "no one knows how many APL operatives . . . worked on this case for months before an arrest was made" (Hough 1919, 133). The tasks of APL members included shadowing suspects, intercepting mail, going undercover within IWW circles, and preparing reports. On August 17, 1918, the jury received its instructions from Judge Landis; in a little less than one hour, it returned with its finding: ninety-seven persons were convicted, most of them receiving prison sentences that ranged from one to twenty years. A few months later, a similar trial with evidence collected by APL members was conducted in Sacramento, California; forty-six IWW defendants were convicted in that trial. Curiously, the APL performed its work on these trials, and many other related activities, without governmental or legal status (Hough 1919, 133, 137–40, 163).

One contemporary history of the APL indicates that most cases investigated by its members took place in the New York division, "some 300,000 in all" (Hough 1919, 201). The New York division, with over forty-five hundred officers and operatives, covered territory that extended from Poughkeepsie (about seventy-five miles north of New York City) to Montauk Point, at the eastern end of Long Island. Many of the cases the New York division investigated concerned selective service matters. APL members also provided assistance in locating deserters from various military camps on Long Island and dealt with vice and liquor cases involving servicemen. Cases were referred to the APL from a variety of military and governmental intelligence agencies, including the Department of Justice, the State Department, the War Department, the Navy Department, the Alien Property Custodian, the Civil Service Commission, the War Trade Board, the U.S. Shipping Board, and the Treasury Department (Hough 1919, 205–9). The "most notorious" slacker raid occurred in New York City in September 1918, with at least ten thousand persons arrested but less than 1 percent found to be draft dodgers (R. J. Goldstein 1978, 112).

The Cleveland division of the APL, which recruited over fifteen hundred volunteer operatives, was most active beginning in May 1917. During the next fifteen months, the Cleveland APL conducted over sixty thousand investigations concerning failure to register; failure to report for training or physical examination; desertion; seditious and treasonable utterances; loyalty matters; suspected enemy agents; the activities of Socialists, the IWW, and Bolsheviks; and industrial sabotage. The Cleveland division also investigated violations of the food, fuel, gas, and electric rationing regulations; handled registration of enemy aliens; conducted background checks of Red Cross overseas workers and applicants for citizenship; and provided volunteers with automobiles to assist the Cleveland Police Department. On occasion, women were deployed as volunteer operatives within the ranks of the APL. In one case, a young woman undercover APL volunteer was placed in a Cleveland factory that was manufacturing wartime aircraft parts. After a period of about three weeks, she discovered that defective parts were being produced (Hough 1919, 256–59).

The Cleveland division of the APL also played a very prominent part in the case of Eugene V. Debs. Debs, a gifted orator and a committed Socialist, began his public career during the economic depression of 1893, when he helped form the American Railway Union. His union's support of strikers at the Pullman car factory plant in 1894 led to a nationwide strike. In Chicago, thousands of special railroad deputies, federal troops, local police, and members of the state militia were used to break the strike. On one terrible day in July 1894, thirteen people were killed, fifty-three seriously wounded, and seven hundred arrested. Debs was arrested for violating a court order that barred him and other union leaders from assisting in the strike and was imprisoned for six months (Zinn 1990, 272–75). During World War I, Debs deliberately sought prosecution by making antiwar speeches. He was arrested for violating the Espionage Act in June 1918, when he talked for two hours, urging listeners at an open-air meeting in Canton, Ohio, to avoid the draft. At Debs's trial, evidence was introduced to indicate that there had been draft-age males in his audience. He refused legal assistance and called no witnesses on his own behalf. His only statements to the jury occurred during his closing argument: "I abhor war. . . . I have sympathy with the suffering, struggling people everywhere" (qtd. in Zinn 1990, 358). Debs was sentenced to federal prison for ten years, and his sentence was upheld by a unanimous Supreme Court, although it was later terminated by a 1921 presidential order (Reppetto 1978, 276–77; Zinn 1990, 358–59).

In late December 1918, after Debs's conviction, the Cleveland APL went public, volunteering its service to the police department during a period of rising crime. Subsequently, on a few weekends, beginning six weeks after the war with Germany had ended, regular police and members of the APL openly patrolled the streets of Cleveland in automobiles (Hough 1919, 265–66). This trend was not isolated to Cleveland. As early as the summer of 1918, for example, the Washington State division of the APL decided to allow its local units to publicize their activities. Posters in Washington and elsewhere were displayed in elevators and streetcars, on factory bulletin boards, and in store windows, requesting citizens to report violations of the war statutes and disloyal activities to the local APL office. In Buffalo, New York, one such poster read: "Report the man or woman who spreads pessimistic stories; divulges or seeks confidential information; cries for peace or belittles our efforts to win the war. . . . Use your eyes and ears and report these people to the American Protective League" (qtd. in J. M. Jensen 1968, 171).

During World War I, the APL had units in six hundred cities and towns and a membership of nearly one hundred thousand. The zeal of these volunteers, and the nearly two thousand prosecutions under the Espionage Act (only about half of which were successful), have been attributed to the fact that many Americans resisted American entry into the war, especially the new mandatory conscription policies (Zinn 1990). For example, sixty-five thousand men sought conscientious objector status, and Jeannette Rankin, the first woman to serve in Congress, voted against American participation in the war (Zinn 1990, 362–63).

The tactics used by the APL to stifle dissent, and its participation in raids to find draft evaders, earned the organization periodic criticism from liberal leaders, but in the main its practices led to little public outcry. The Justice Department decided to disband the APL at the end of the war. Its members received "honorable discharge" papers and gold badges from APL leaders as symbols of their dedicated service. Some subsequent peacetime vigilante groups, however, were composed of former APL members, particularly in Minneapolis, Cincinnati, Seattle, and Chicago. These individuals hoped for the return of the APL and periodically offered their services against Bolsheviks and other radicals who they believed were seeking to destroy American society. During the Red Scare, former APL members and

Membership card, American Protective League, c. 1918, which confers upon the bearer the "rank of Operative"

chiefs were recruited to participate in raids. When APL members again sought to assist the federal government at the start of World War II, however, J. Edgar Hoover rejected their offers. He believed that counterespionage work should be undertaken only by highly trained and carefully selected personnel (J. M. Jensen 1968).

One has to search very hard to find any historical counterpart for the volunteer undercover operatives of the American Protective League. Two aspects of the APL, however, make it similar to an organization known as the Auxiliary Military Police (AMP). The Auxiliary Military Police consisted of industrial plant guards at war-production sites and other facilities considered of strategic importance during World War II. Both the APL and the AMP involved tens of thousands of Americans during a state of national emergency, and there was some confusion over the powers of members of both organizations. The APL and the AMP, however, greatly differed in the nature of their recruitment, visibility, and responsibilities. The service of all APL members was entirely voluntary, while the plant guards were drafted. AMP members wore uniforms, while APL members wore civilian clothes. Fortunately, following World War I, the model for future volunteer police organizations was not the APL but the New York City Reserve Police.

The Spy Era in Retrospect

These organizations all left their mark on American history. The history of the ASL and its volunteer police, for example, was substantially bound up with the phenomenon of saloon life in America: "In the five or six decades before 1920, the saloon was an almost ubiquitous structure on the American landscape" (Engelmann 1979, 3). The saloon, which fostered an array of social benefits, played an important role in the life of working-class Americans. The urban saloon, however, also became a primary target of Progressives, who associated it with the brothel and other aspects of moral decay (P. Boyer 1978). The ASL concentrated its early efforts on the dangers of the saloon rather than on all liquor traffic, initially seeking to achieve prohibition through "local option." The ASL made efforts to educate the public and discredit the saloon (Cashman 1981, 246–47) and also, controversially, tried to directly aid law enforcement by using hired and volunteer lawyers and laypersons to help arrest and prosecute county and state violators of prohibition laws. The activities of these "volunteer police" were proactive or aggressive in nature, and such agents played a major role during the early years of the spy era of volunteer policing in America.

The attorneys and private investigators of the ASL, although privately retained, performed the essential police functions of surveillance, investigation, arrest, and prosecution. They volunteered for their assignments, and after arrests were made, their activities were publicized, both attorneys and private investigators appearing in court. Generally, during the post–Civil War era, the work of private investigators overshadowed that of public detectives, since "municipal governments were prevented from developing effective forces by their low quality of personnel . . . and, most importantly, [by] the political influence present in local police departments (Reppetto 1978, 256).

Unlike many members of the ASL, all APL members involved in law enforcement activities were unpaid volunteers. Both groups, however, were proactive or aggressive in their approach and performed a variety of special-purpose police functions. APL volunteers performed investigations for various federal agencies, especially the U.S. Department of Justice. While their activities were initially of a covert or secret nature, in time the APL went public.

There are various lessons to be learned from the activities of the ASL and the APL about detracting from and adding to the democratic process. The ASL effectively dismantled the saloon business in America. For sixty years prior to the advent of national Prohibition in 1920, saloons in big cities served as the storefront offices of local politicians and as "election-day recruitment centers where drinks bought votes" (Kyvig 1979, 9). On the other hand, the social services provided by saloons were of strategic value to members of the working class and recent immigrants. The saloon's demise no doubt contributed to difficulties confronting new arrivals to the United States. Still, the ASL did try to educate the public about the sordid side of the saloon trade (Cashman 1981, 246–67): its numerous publications, widely distributed, were a remarkable contribution to the free trade in ideas and the ultimate enhancement of the democratic process. On the other hand, the ASL also created a legacy of claims of undue influence by lobbyists. Today, for example, America's number-one gun lobby, the National Rifle Association (NRA), is known for its high-pressure tactics. It is interesting to speculate what would happen if the NRA decided, like the ASL, to directly aid law enforcement, in the NRA's case for the purpose of suppressing illegal gun traffickers.

The short-lived but checkered career of the American Protective League provides another infamous example of how an early twentieth-century volunteer police organization (although perhaps with good intentions) trampled the rights of individuals and inhibited the growth of democratic institutions: "German-Americans became the most numerous victims of the APL . . . [which] claimed to define the meaning of '100 percent Americanism'" (Abrahamson 1983, 122). During America's participation in World War I, many German Americans were tried and convicted for inconsequential statements regarding the war effort. The APL also assisted the federal government in its attempt to repress the activities of the Socialist Party and the International Workers of the World (Abrahamson 1983). On one occasion, a captain in the Chicago branch of the APL boasted that his unit's most valuable work during the war had been not tracking down enemy agents but "breaking up the activities of the labor agitators and anarchists" (J. M. Jensen 1968, 57). Even after the APL was officially terminated, APL veterans were active during the Red Scare, in the summer of 1919. Forty APL veterans, for example, were part of a team that included police officers from New York City and New York State (J. M. Jensen 1968). The group was assembled to gather information about the possible activities of Red radicals in the New York area. On June 21, 1919, this joint squad conducted raids at such locations as the Rand School of Social Science and the New York headquarters of the IWW. One of the regrettable legacies of the APL is that Klansmen adopted some of the APL's surveillance techniques in conducting certain vigilante activities conducted in the South and Southwest during the early 1920s (J. M. Jensen 1968, 289).

One lesson of the spy era of volunteer policing is that while citizen involvement in crime control is an important feature of American democracy, the nature of the supplemental support offered by concerned groups needs to be carefully reviewed before it achieves the endorsement of public officials. The rise of such volunteer police groups is not hard to understand. At the beginning of the twentieth century, most of America's regular policing establishment was still in its infancy and vulnerable to political manipulation. Moreover, the zeal of early saloon reformers was religious in its fervor;

in fact, the movement was led by leading members of the Protestant clergy. The police at the beginning of the twentieth century and during national Prohibition lacked strict discipline, strong leadership, and quality personnel: "most officers followed the paths of least resistance laid out by ward bosses and precinct captains. Now and then, when pressure from reformers built up, they raided a joint or arrested a crook; but most of the time they kept out of sight and away from trouble" (Fogelson 1977, 51). The urban police of the spy era were also preoccupied with performing a variety of non-law-enforcement duties. They supervised elections; censored movies; operated lodging homes; provided emergency ambulances; disposed of confiscated liquor; and inspected boilers, tenements, markets, and factories (Fogelson 1977, 52). Police preoccupation with all these tasks, along with the political nature of their deployment, no doubt contributed to the ability of ASL and APL operatives to undertake specific law enforcement functions.

Furthermore, in times of national emergency, the democratic infrastructure of the United States has sometimes proven to be quite vulnerable. During the Civil War, Lincoln suspended the writ of habeas corpus in areas surrounding the nation's capital. At the beginning of U.S. involvement in World War II, Franklin Roosevelt ordered a massive evacuation of Japanese Americans from the West Coast and had 120,000 men, women, and children placed in concentration camps for the duration of the war. In 1943, by a six to three vote, the U.S. Supreme Court in the *Korematsu* case upheld the constitutionality of the internment policy of President Roosevelt: "In Congress, only Senator Robert Taft spoke out against the greatest violation of civil liberties since the end of slavery" (Foner 1998, 241). After September 11, 2001, the federal government detained hundreds of aliens without revealing their names, providing them with attorneys, or affording them detention hearings.

The rise of Josephine Shaw Lowell's New York–based Charity Organization Society and its volunteer police—known as "friendly visitors"—sprang from a different source than the ASL and the APL. The New York COS arose in the gap between the rich and the poor, its rise encouraged by the fear that current methods of poor relief (i.e., indiscriminate charity) were worsening the division. Leading COS advocates believed that if then-current methods of poor relief were left unchanged, "pauperism would continue to

grow . . . until it became society's master and destroyed the very founda-
tions of civilized life" (M. B. Katz 1996, 76). Their solution was to coordinate
charitable dispensation through cooperating churches and private associations. Middle- and upper-class women with leisure time would visit recipients of aid to help them achieve independence as quickly as possible.

These "friendly visitors" may be considered volunteer police because of
their close operating relationships with police departments. Buffalo's COS,
for example, obtained the cooperation of the police, who served as the organization's first agents, investigating "the homes of everyone on relief and
help[ing] draw up a central register of the poor" (M. B. Katz 1996, 79). In
turn, the volunteer visitors of the COS maintained contacts with the poor to
ensure that they maintained their eligibility. Significantly, by conducting
these visits in an overt manner, the volunteer fieldworkers were performing
a police function: helping to enforce existing welfare-fraud statutes. Moreover, these workers were also in a position to determine whether family
members were obeying all other laws, especially those that required children to attend school or refrain from work (M. B. Katz 1996, 79). Thus, the
COS "friendly visitors" were members of an organization authorized by governmental action (i.e., engaged in a cooperative agreement) to perform one
or more police functions in an overt manner for minimal or no salary.

"Friendly visitors"—agents of charity organization societies—can be
classified as Type III (special purpose/reactive). COSs were not directly affiliated with any law-enforcement agencies, however, although they did form
close working partnerships with police departments. In Buffalo and New
York City, regular police helped screen candidates for relief by distributing
and collecting surveys provided by the local COS organization. In New York
City, the local COS formed a Committee on Mendicancy that hired "special
agents" who were empowered by the government of New York City to arrest
street beggars. Moreover, New York City's police regularly notified COS
workers when such persons were released from the municipal workhouse.
Generally, COSs existed for the special purpose of coordinating charitable
assistance and were reactive in that they responded to calls for relief assistance. On the other hand, their services were often delivered with a strict
accompanying attitude: only those who did as they were told were likely to
receive assistance (Burrows and Wallace 1999, 1160–61).

On the other hand, Anti-Saloon League detectives and attorneys fit the

Type IV classification (special purpose/proactive). The hired detectives of the ASL were often commissioned by local police jurisdictions, and the ASL's volunteer or retained attorneys always had the status of "officers of the court" in carrying out their prosecutor role. This organization may be said to have existed for a special purpose: detectives secured evidence of local prohibition law violations, and attorneys were engaged in the prosecution of suspected violators. This dedicated type of law-enforcement work, which encountered stiff resistance and had many controversial aspects, was carried out in an aggressive or proactive manner.

The volunteer operatives of the American Protective League may also be classified as Type IV. Although the APL's affiliation with the U.S. Department of Justice was short-lived and somewhat vague, a clear linkage was present. On the occasion of the dissolution of the APL on February 1, 1919, the attorney general of the United States, T. W. Gregory, stated: "Your reward can only be the expressed thanks of your Government. As the head of the Department of Justice, under which the American Protective League operated, I render you such thanks with sincere pleasure. . . . I am frank to say that the Department of Justice could not have accomplished its tasks . . . without the assistance of the members of the League" (qtd. in Hough 1919, 9). The APL, although it was never authorized by the U.S. Congress or any state legislative body, obviously operated with the approval and under the direction of the Bureau of Investigation, the forerunner of the FBI. The special purpose of the APL was gathering intelligence about disloyal utterances, draft evaders, and deserters during World War I. It was certainly a proactive entity: in the course of carrying out assignments, some of its members may have "illegally impersonated Federal agents, conducted warrantless searches, intimidated fellow citizens, and even made arrests" (Abrahamson 1983, 121).

Since colonial times, Americans have used the militia to maintain law and order during both war and peacetime. When the National Guard (i.e., the organized militia) was federalized during World War I, its members subsequently called upon for active military service, a need arose to fill the vacuum left behind. State guard units, created to replace federalized National Guard units, are Type III (special purpose/reactive) volunteer police organizations, their members recruited for the specific purpose of engaging in peacekeeping and other internal security roles in the absence of the Na-

tional Guard. The New York Guard, for example, was formed in 1917 to provide a state security force in reaction to a great concern over the threat of
sabotage. The New York Guard ceased to exist after World War I but was re-
activated during World War II. Subsequently, most state guard units have
been most active at those times when National Guard troops have been deployed for overseas duty.

The Progressive Era coincided with the end of the nineteenth century
and the beginning of the twentieth. In the four decades prior to the beginning of national Prohibition in 1920, reformers centered their interests not
only on the evils of the saloon but also on the problems associated with
almsgiving. This era also saw the birth of settlement houses, the indeterminate sentence, probation, and the first juvenile courts (Nevins and Commager 1976, 388–91).

Indeed, the spy era of volunteer policing was not entirely devoid of democratic developments. The political nature of fledgling police establishments created an obvious vacuum that was filled by differing types of volunteer organizations, whose development was also encouraged by the
conditions of World War I. During the early part of the twentieth century,
then, new avenues for volunteer police coincided with the Progressive Era
(1900–1914) and national Prohibition (1920–33). New state and federal police agencies were created, and women began to take their place on the
front lines of America's justice system. Contributions were also made in the
development of penal reforms, the widespread use of probation and parole,
and the creation of such novel youth educational programs as the junior
police. These developments gained in momentum during the next part of
the twentieth century.

5

The Transformation Era   From 1920 to 1941

The relationship of the citizenry to the state, even in a large city, can take different forms.

A. STEINBERG, *The Transformation of Criminal Justice: Philadelphia, 1800–1880*

The transformation era involved a movement away from special-purpose
volunteer policing to a more general role for volunteer police. This era also
marked the beginning of the integration of volunteers into the structure of
city and county police agencies. The most remarkable evidence of these
changes occurred in New York City when the World War I–era Citizens
Home Defense League was renamed the New York Police Reserve and given
full police authority. This organization, however, lasted only for the decade
of national Prohibition. Elsewhere, on the other hand, especially in the
Midwest and South, new reserve police units were established during the
Great Depression. Eventually, the use of volunteer police as a supplemental
force came into vogue throughout the nation.

After World War I, several of the most important figures in police reform
and professionalism began to place greater emphasis on the crime-fighting
aspects of police work, diminishing the social-service aspects significantly
(S. S. Walker 1977, 79–80). J. Edgar Hoover was one of these early advocates
of the role of police in crime fighting. When Hoover was selected to head the
Bureau of Investigation in May 1924, the agency had approximately 650
employees, including 441 special agents (FBI 2005). Hoover, twenty-nine
years old and an honors graduate of George Washington University Law
School's evening division, immediately fired those agents he considered
unqualified and proceeded to professionalize the organization. Regular inspections of field offices were instituted, for example, and the seniority rule
of promotion was eliminated and replaced by a uniform system of evalua-

tion. Subsequently, all new agents had to be between the ages of twenty-five and thirty-five, they were required to attend a formal academy training program, and a preference was stated for persons with backgrounds in law or accounting. By 1926, law enforcement agencies throughout the nation began contributing their fingerprint cards to the bureau's Identification Division (FBI 2005). Hoover also introduced a strict code of personal behavior for special agents, including a ban on the use of liquor during Prohibition, whether off or on duty (Powers 1987, 152).

Two further significant contributions to the field of policing took place just before World War I and involved the initiatives of women. While these women never formally enrolled in a volunteer police organization, their pioneering work should not be overlooked. Their perseverance is illustrative of the type of community spirit that undoubtedly helped motivate many persons to participate in volunteer police units between the two world wars and throughout the twentieth century.

The first of these contributions involved the creation of the New York State Police. According to that agency's official documents, a 1913 crime contributed to its establishment. The crime occurred in Westchester County, New York, near the site of a home under construction for M. Moyca Newell in Bedford Hills. Four men attempted to rob Sam Howell, the foreman of the home-construction project. Although he was shot several times, he managed to deliver the payroll he was carrying to the carpenters at the site. He died three days later but was first able to identify two of his assailants as men he had hired. The prime suspects were still close to the scene of the crime when local police arrived, but even though their general location was known, they were not pursued and were never arrested (New York State Police 1967).

Newell, with her friend Katherine Mayo, a writer, witnessed the ineptitude of the local police officials at the scene of the crime. Justly outraged, the two women initiated an effort to create a state police force that would bring an adequate police response to the state's rural areas. Through their direct efforts, a lobbying committee was established, and Mayo later authored a book about the need for a state police force that included research on the Pennsylvania State Police. At the time, Pennsylvania had the nation's most recognizable state police department: it resembled a military force in every sense, its troops housed in barracks throughout the state, and had extensive authority. However, its early role in policing labor strikes associated with the coal industry, and other disputes involving the average working-man, had made it very unpopular among the working classes.

Consequently, it was not surprising that the initial bill drafted for the creation of the New York State Police was opposed by organized labor, Democrats, and some upstate Republicans. The bill also gave nearly unlimited power to the head of the proposed organization with respect to the selection of personnel, causing some critics to take the position that the bill was not in keeping with civil service reforms and was merely designed to benefit existing economic interests. New York's governor, Charles Whitman, however, strongly favored the bill, and a new clause was inserted stating that the use of state police would be prohibited "within the limits of any city to suppress rioting and disorder except by the direction of the Governor or upon the request of the Mayor of the city with the approval of the Governor." Governor Whitman urged that the shortage of National Guard recruits could be alleviated by the bill's adoption, since National Guard troops would no longer be required to perform domestic police duties. In the past, these duties had taken guardsmen away from their families and regular employment, resulting in substantial personal inconvenience and financial loss. Officials also wanted the new state police force because it could deal with labor unrest: it could engage in surveillance activities, as well as turn out for strikes and remain on duty until they were settled. The National Guard had traditionally been used to control strikers, but its effectiveness was hampered by its members' short terms of duty. When it became clear that labor unrest was not an isolated problem—that it would, indeed, be ongoing—employers had begun docking the pay of guardsmen on active service, and recruitment for the National Guard had subsequently become difficult (Ray 1995b).[1] The state legislature eventually approved the bill by only a small majority, and it became law on April 11, 1917, just five days after Congress had declared war on Germany (New York State Police 1967).

A surgeon from Kingston, New York, as well as a major in the U.S. Army, George F. Chandler became the first superintendent of the New York State Police. He recruited the first troopers, personally conducted all their physical examinations, oversaw their training, arranged for their barracks, ordered their equipment, and wrote their rules. Near the end of 1923, when the time came for Chandler to return to his Kingston medical practice, he even selected his successor with the blessing of New York's new governor, Alfred E. Smith. Chandler's most important contribution to the emergence of police professionalism was perhaps successfully convincing Governor Smith of the value of the new force. In 1919, the prolabor Smith had recommended that the newly created state police should be abolished (New York State Police 1967). In fact, the New York State Police were called upon to deal with strikes on at least eleven occasions between 1919 and 1923 (see Ray 1995b; Ray 1990). Although it was not his intention, Chandler's early successes with the New York State Police may have motivated political figures in New York City to develop their own quasi-military police force: the New York Police Reserve.

The era's second major contribution to the field of policing that was fostered by women led to the acceptance of some women into the uniformed ranks of urban police forces during the Prohibition Era. Although women had been serving as police matrons (supervising women prisoners) for nearly two decades prior to 1900, their attainment of full and complete equality with male police officers would take the greater part of the twentieth century. Hiring policewomen, as had been the case with appointing the first police matrons, required the lobbying efforts of organized women. Even in "reform minded Cleveland," for example, "the struggle for policewomen took eight years" (S. S. Walker 1977, 88). From 1916 to 1923, Cleveland's Women's Protective Association—initiated after a teenage girl was murdered by a men's club employee—actively campaigned for policewomen and even hired its own "special investigator" to counsel and assist young women (S. S. Walker 1977, 87–88).

The reform impulse that pervaded American life around 1900, contributing to women's suffrage, Prohibition, and a variety of criminal justice innovations, also extended to the administration of municipal police services. Progressive developments, however, came sporadically. Most took the form of new training requirements, achievements related to administrative efficiency, the introduction of some women into police service, and the adaptation of laboratory sciences to the field of policing. A more fascinating aspect of police reforms during the Progressive Era and shortly thereafter was based on "the idea that police should play a positive role in the general reform of society" (S. S. Walker 1977, 79). In many respects, the changes taking place in other areas of the criminal justice system were eventually adapted for the police officer, or more accurately, for the average beat patrolman. Significantly, during the early part of the twentieth century, police in many communities were assigned roles more related to rehabilitation and diversion than to punishment and incarceration. Although this trend was short-lived, these early accomplishments may be said to represent a social work orientation for policing. Indeed, several aspects of this work resurfaced under the heading of "community policing" during the last two decades of the twentieth century.

The foremost advocate of a social-service role for police was August Vollmer, who began his career in police service when he was elected the city marshal of Berkeley, California, in 1905. He owed his popularity to an event that had occurred the previous year, when, as a letter carrier, he distinguished himself by leaping aboard a runaway flatcar and braking it just in time to avoid a crowded passenger train (Carte and Carte 1975, 37). He was the first city marshal to seek out college graduates for policing and to facilitate college-level instruction for in-service personnel. He shared his views in speeches and publications, hoping to convince his fellow police chiefs of the merits of his philosophy. Vollmer believed that police should do more than merely identify and arrest criminal suspects; rather, they should take an active role in diverting potential lawbreakers, for whom he coined the term *predelinquents*. He urged that police work closely with schools and other community institutions so that the most appropriate resources could be brokered on behalf of these young people. Vollmer also encouraged police officers to inform the public about the needs of the poor so that they could obtain support for the delivery of needed services (e.g., youth centers) (S. S. Walker 1977).

In 1925, Vollmer organized a Crime Prevention Division, recruiting Elisabeth Lossing to serve as its supervisor. The division employed social workers who assisted young boys under twelve and women under twenty-one. This pioneering achievement—"the first attempt to bring professional social workers into a police department on a full-time basis" (Carte and Carte 1975, 48)—has seldom been duplicated. Unfortunately, while Vollmer introduced many new ideas to the world of policing, he did not see them become widely accepted. This was partly a result of the difficulty of implementing Vollmer's ideas: "Vollmer's passionate belief that each patrolman could become a 'practical criminologist,'" for example, "was advanced with an excess of rhetoric and a shortage of practical suggestions" (S. S. Walker 1977, 82).

Prohibition itself also complicated the task of the average police officer. Throughout the Prohibition period, profits from organized bootlegging did much to create and maintain a criminal underworld. During the 1930s, J. Edgar Hoover capitalized on the public's fear of gangsters, crime, and general disorder, the fear resulting in expanded duties for the FBI. In fact, public confusion between the Bureau of Investigation's special agents and Prohibition agents led to a new name for the former group when the Bureau of Investigation became the Federal Bureau of Investigation in 1935 (FBI 2005).

During the Prohibition Era, however, some reforms—advanced in large part by Vollmer and Raymond Fosdick—did begin to take hold.[2] Vollmer and Fosdick, a well-known civic official and lawyer during the first half of the twentieth century, were of the opinion that most new police officers were unqualified for their positions, pointing out that most officers hadn't finished high school, scored below average on intelligence tests, received little or no training, and earned inadequate salaries. Many police applicants could even slip through the minimum standards established by civil service commissions: "Under pressure from the ward leaders the civil service commissioners sometimes gave out advance copies of the tests and the precinct captains often ran cursory character checks. The civil service commissioners overlooked serious transgressions if they meant disqualifying a candidate with strong endorsements from influential politicians" (S. S. Walker 1977, 103). The views of Vollmer and Fosdick received considerable press support during the 1920s (Fogelson 1977, 51).

The idiosyncrasies of the system, however, were not easily overcome. It is now widely recognized that the police of this period, along with ward leaders and other politicians, wielded significant influence. Even reform-minded police chiefs and commissioners were often powerless to change the system. In New York City, police were able to exert significant influence through their many rank-and-file organizations (e.g., benevolent associations for captains, squad commanders, and patrolmen). Such groups often lobbied against proposals to enhance central authority. When their interests combined with those of the local politicians who dominated city hall, the city council, police boards, local courts, and other agencies, the united groups were capable of forming a solid wall to resist the efforts of even the most reform-minded officials (Fogelson 1977).

Still, some progress was made, thanks in large part to the efforts of determined individuals. At the start of the 1930s, for example, the federal-level effort to prohibit narcotics was led by Harry J. Anslinger, who served as the Treasury Department's commissioner of narcotics for thirty-two years. Anslinger advocated harsh laws against the sale, possession, and use of all habit-forming drugs. Despite his unflagging campaign against illicit drugs, Anslinger is credited with having ensured that an adequate supply of drugs was available for medical use during and after World War II. With the aid of drug manufacturers, he arranged for the stockpiling of drugs in the gold vaults of the Treasury Department (Krebs 1975).

Progress in recruiting women for police work, however, was slow. Throughout most of the twentieth century, the duties of women police officers were limited. Women typically only worked on cases involving juveniles, missing persons, consumer fraud, vice enforcement, and searching and guarding women prisoners. Interrogating women suspects and crime victims also became an essential part of their role. In general, the educational requirements for policewomen tended to be much higher than those for men, especially in the first decades of the twentieth century. Moreover, they had to serve in separate units and were not issued regular police uniforms. Two major reasons for this policy have been suggested: first, that women's roles were limited to reduce the criticism that they were taking on a traditional male occupation; and second, that women operated separately because doing so might give them a practical advantage in performing detective work. By the 1930s, for example, members of the Women's Bureau of the New York City police routinely patrolled in uniform at large public events. By midcentury, however, only a minority of jurisdictions permitted the promotion of women. Indeed, a 1946 survey found that only twenty-one cities with a population over twenty-five thousand permitted women's promotions (Schulz 1995, 108–9).

The New York Police Reserves

The two world wars ushered in changes in the world of policing. In the year and a half before U.S. entry into World War I, various American cities took steps to protect their citizens. By May 1916, New York City had enlisted several thousand volunteers, organized by precinct, to serve as members of a "Citizens Home Defense League." Twice a month, drills and lectures were presented in local armories, public schools, and halls. There were no membership restrictions regarding age, weight, or height, and by July 1916, twenty-one thousand civilians had been enrolled (*New York Times,* July 6, 1916). When American Protective League units began to be organized, members of local New York Home Defense units operating in Syracuse and Utica, along with various other existing volunteer police groups, were directly merged into the APL. Even a small group of African Americans in North Carolina became a part of the APL in order "to check on possible disaffection among members of their . . . race" (J. M. Jensen 1968, 47).

The new U.S. Army was created under the Selective Service Act in May 1917, and the first American troops arrived in France in June 1917. This left the ranks of many police departments drained of men. Indeed, by the war's end, the United States would dispatch more than two million soldiers to the battlefields of Europe. To deal with the shortages at home, the New York State legislature took steps soon after the United States entered World War I, on May 25, 1917, formally authorizing the city's police commissioner to appoint citizens to perform duty in the New York City Police Department "during the continuance of the state of war now existing" (Laws of New York, 1917, chap. 651).

Contemporary newspaper reports suggested that New York City might be bombed because of Germany's desperation at U.S. entry into the war. The public was warned that U-boats could launch an attack against U.S. coastal cities. German submarines at the time were capable of carrying six seaplanes that could drop bombs (Stevenson 1918). Such statements aroused the people to further strengthen their home defenses.

U.S. entry into World War I coincided with the election of a new Tammany Hall mayor in New York City, John F. Hylan, who promptly butted heads with Arthur Woods, the city's reform-minded police commissioner. Woods had established the Citizens Home Defense League and had created an internal affairs unit to assist in weeding out police corruption, trying to limit "strong-arm" measures and the widespread illegal practice of making arrests only on suspicion of evidence. Hyland abolished Woods's internal affairs unit, discharged Woods, and named Richard E. Enright, "a garrulous and extremely ambitious police lieutenant" (S. Walker 1933, 154) and a known antagonist of Woods, to take his place as commissioner (Fogelson 1977, 100–101). In appointing Enright, Mayor Hylan had taken the extraordinary step of bypassing 122 higher-ranking officers (Lardner and Reppetto 2000, 195).

Enright, who would serve as police commissioner from 1918 to 1926 (Fogelson 1977, 101), possessed his own power base as head of the Police Lieutenants' Benevolent Association, and through this post he also had influence over the larger Patrolmen's Benevolent Association (PBA). A leader of the rank-and-file police who had long opposed Woods's use of an internal affairs unit to oversee police misconduct, Enright had gained a reputation "as the department's first outspoken leader of rank-and-file opinion, inaugurating a long intermittent tradition of acrimony between the various benevolent associations, on the one hand, and the various mayors and commissioners, on the other" (Lardner and Reppetto 2000, 195). When Enright had originally qualified for promotion to captain, becoming first on the civil-service list, Woods had refused to appoint him (Richardson 1974, 76). One of Enright's first official acts was to order the renaming of Woods's "Home Defense League": it would now be called the "Police Reserves of the City of New York." This announcement came after six hundred commissioned officers of the league voted for the change (*New York Times,* February 21, 1918), in large part because of the passage of a new state law that conferred peace-officer powers on all persons belonging to the new organization.

A contemporary journalist compared the new police reserves to the old "rattle watch," which existed under the Dutch in the 1650s: "In organizing these police reservists we are reviving the plan of the old 'Rattle Watch,' . . . when the watchmen were admonished to be on duty before bell-ringing under penalty. . . . At this time when the national German bandits and murderers are at large in the world our precautions for guarding the city cannot be too numerous or too painstaking" (Stevenson 1918, 1). During colonial times, the "rattle watch" was followed by various low-paid or unsalaried compulsory forms of citizen patrols. Similarly, no one was paid for police reserve duty in the 1920s: all service was rendered on a strictly voluntary basis.

The leading proponent of the police reserves was Lewis Rodman Wanamaker (1863–1928), merchant, patron of the arts, aviation enthusiast and supporter, and head of the Wanamaker department stores. In February 1918, he was appointed a special deputy police commissioner in charge of the reserves, a nonpaying position. His responsibilities included the task of reshaping the old Home Defense League into a disciplined organization. To accomplish this, Wanamaker instituted a formal interview process for the city's newest auxiliary police force, rather than admitting all comers, as the previous body had. In addition, he oversaw the preparation of a complete set of rules and regulations. Uniforms, badges, service awards, and revolver training had been planned from the beginning; air, harbor, and mounted squads were recruited later. Wanamaker also instituted plans to recruit a unit of one thousand men between the ages of nineteen and twenty-eight who would take all emergency and special patrol-work assignments. After approximately three years of such training, the members of this unit would become eligible for direct entry into the ranks of the regular police service. Formal evening classes for members of the police reserves would cover the same material as did classes for regular police candidates (*New York Times*, February 21, 1918).

The new auxiliary force, forward looking in its approach, also included the first women's division of the police reserves. There were nineteen members in the very first unit formed, all of whom happened to be the wives or sisters of regular policemen (*Brooklyn Daily Eagle*, May 29, 1918). In less than a month, nearly three thousand women had been recruited and were subsequently assigned to police stations throughout the five boroughs. Police inspector John F. Dwyer was given overall authority for the daily conduct and operations of this new reserve force (*Brooklyn Daily Eagle*, June 25, 1918). Skepticism concerning the value of the women's division was voiced in one local newspaper editorial of that pre–women's liberation era: "The natural consequence of giving votes to women is the haste of politicians to confer office upon women and to create positions for them as a lure for women voters. . . . But of all the propositions of this kind so far advanced none seems to us so little justified or to hold so little promise as the Police Reserve of Women to be organized by Commissioner Enright. It is to be a

Lewis Rodman Wanamaker, Special Deputy
New York City Police Commissioner, c. 1920s

volunteer body, organized by inspection districts, and to reach into every block in the city through one resident woman who shall be responsible to the Police Department for the morals of her block. . . . The danger which the plan holds of converting unfounded gossip, or even malice, into official police reports is at least considerable" (*Brooklyn Daily Eagle,* May 10, 1918).

The duties of the women's reserves, however, as outlined in a general order given by special deputy commissioner Wanamaker, appear less suspicious and characteristic of the World War I period:

> The duties of the Women's Police Reserve will be to carry on the Auxiliary Red Cross work now being done by the auxiliaries attached to the different precincts; to be vigilant and alert in their respective localities; to discover irregular and unlawful conditions and to report the same to the department; to teach patriotism and civic duty and aid in the Americanization of the alien elements of the population; to detect and report cases of disloyalty and sedition; relieve cases of distress and destitution; comfort the unfortunate; advise and direct the weak, foolish and idle; and set an example of unselfishness and patriotic devotion. Members of the Women's Reserve

can be very useful also in looking after boys and girls who may be prone to be delinquent, keeping bad company or pursuing such a course that would lead to crime. (*Brooklyn Daily Eagle*, June 23, 1918)

These duties, obviously, were time-consuming enough to prevent women from engaging in the "unfounded gossip" or "malice" that some skeptics had feared.

During the police reserves' first summer, a series of field-day exercises were held to demonstrate the effectiveness of the men's training and to raise money for the purchase of uniforms and equipment. Among the events listed on official programs were air shows featuring planes and crewmen from the First Provisional Wing of the U.S. Army and concerts given by noted artists, sometimes including Enrico Caruso, the famous operatic tenor (*Brooklyn Daily Eagle*, August 20, 1918). In the months to come, Caruso held benefits that led to his appointment as an honorary captain in the reserves (*New York Times*, January 3, 1919). Caruso, however, was not the only celebrity given membership. In 1925, the reserves recruited Babe Ruth (*New York Times*, September 24, 1925). Ruth, assigned to the Aereo Squadron as a police reserves lieutenant, delighted field-day crowds when he attempted to catch baseballs tossed from aircraft circling the field.

Such reserve forces did not operate only in New York City. By the end of the summer of 1918, for example, volunteer police were also serving in the city of Cincinnati. Their services proved key during a brief strike by the regular police force, when approximately six hundred members of the city's home guard were assigned to patrol the city. On the second day of the strike, local Boy Scouts came to their aid when additional personnel were needed to help police a patriotic parade of twenty-five thousand selective service registrants. In spite of concerns regarding the possibility of violence, with anti-German propaganda being spread in a city with a large German American population, the strike ended peacefully on its third day. A few weeks later, police salaries were raised (S. S. Walker 1977, 113). Not all strikes ended so temperately. A major strike by Boston police, which occurred a year later, resulted in injuries and deaths. During the Boston strike, a special volunteer police force of five hundred citizens, including students and faculty from Harvard University, had been recruited. The volunteers, however, were not fully deployed until nearly a day after the strike had begun. It has been argued that "earlier deployment of the volunteers might have preserved order" (S. S. Walker 1977, 117), but units of the state militia were ultimately needed to restore order.

At the height of New York City activities, there were fourteen thousand members in the police reserves. Old photographs show units wearing olive drab uniforms and campaign hats in the style of the era's soldiers. One unit, numbering four hundred men, was equipped with eight Colt automatic machine guns and three hundred rifles. Aptly called the "Machine Gun Battalion," it enjoyed an enviable reputation in police reserve circles for "being the only machine gun unit attached to a regular police department in the world" (*Brooklyn Daily Eagle*, June 1, 1919).

The assistance of police reserves proved necessary on some occasions during the war. On October 4 and 5, 1918, a federal munitions plant located at Camp Morgan, New Jersey, adjacent to the borough of Richmond, exploded. Many persons were killed and injured, and for several hours, officials believed that yet more property would be destroyed and more injuries incurred. When no one knew what might happen next, two members of the women's police reserves helped rescue survivors, while police reserve members attached to the Motor Boat Squadron transported refugees housed in Morgan, New Jersey, to safety (New York City Police Department 1918, 112, 114).

Meanwhile, the fighting in Europe continued to influence the growth of auxiliary units. On November 11, 1918, the struggle on the Western Front ceased when Germany agreed to an armistice, but the war effort was not over until the signing of the Treaty of Versailles, which detailed final peace terms with Germany. Indeed, because some senators objected to a provision of the treaty that called for the establishment of a League of Nations, the war with Germany "did not officially end for the United States until July 2, 1921, when Congress passed a joint resolution declaring that hostilities were over and reserving a victor's rights and privileges" (Hofstadter, Miller, and Aaron 1972, 653). Throughout this extended period, the New York Police Reserve helped keep the nation's largest city safe.

From August 1, 1918, to August 31, 1919, members of the police reserves were assigned to over two hundred city theaters during evening performances. They were to guard against the outbreak of any fires through the enforcement of the regulations of the fire department. This duty had previously been the responsibility of firemen, but the war effort had reduced their numbers (New York City Police Department 1919, 143–44). In addition, beginning in the fall of 1920, at the request of the U.S. commissioner of immigration, a detail of about ninety police reserve members worked at Ellis Island each Sunday afternoon (New York City Police Department 1920, 265). Also during this period, the women's reserve began staffing ambulance units in the city's theater district.

The dawn of the 1920s witnessed a shell-shocked world trying to recover from the wounds of World War I and an American desire to come "back to normalcy." Of all the words uttered by Warren G. Harding during his successful 1920 campaign for the presidency of the United States, that one phrase received the most approval (Sullivan 1939). The decade, however, would prove to be anything but "normal." On August 26, 1920, an estimated 9.5 million additional women became eligible to vote as a result of the passage of the Nineteenth Amendment to the Constitution. The Eighteenth Amendment, putting in place nationwide Prohibition, had been in effect for over six months when women's suffrage became a matter of national policy, rather than local initiative: for the first time in American history, women in every state had the right to vote.

Urbanization had also taken place, more than half the population now living in or near cities. Urban growth was fostered by at least five causes: (1) migration from the farm to the city as a result of better farming techniques;

Members of the Theatrical Ambulance Unit of the New York City Women's Police Reserve, Twenty-sixth Precinct, c. 1919

(2) the development of manufacturing centers and other expansions of industry; (3) improved systems of transportation, including railroads and some new highways, linking the nation's cities with rural areas; (4) the development of elevated and underground urban electric railways with low fares; and (5) successive waves of immigrants, especially from eastern and southern Europe and Asia.

Conditions within the cities, as we have seen, initially gave rise to a new sense of "social consciousness" when Progressives began to introduce their programs. By the 1920s, however, the tide of Progressivism had begun to recede. President Calvin Coolidge, who succeeded Harding after his untimely death in August 1923, is today remembered for having "chloroformed the remnants of the progressive movement" (Parrish 1992, 52). Coolidge believed that the country had too many laws and would be better off without any more: "The greatest duty and opportunity of government," he stated, "is not to embark on any new ventures. . . . It does not at all follow that because abuses exist . . . it is the concern of the federal government to attempt their reform" (qtd. in Parrish 1992, 52).

The 1920s also witnessed the rebirth of the Ku Klux Klan after a fifty-year dormancy. Although the revived Klan had no actual connection with the original Ku Klux Klan of the days of Reconstruction, the new organization adapted its rituals and dress (Slosson 1958, 308). Consequently, white-robed and masked figures began to assemble in both southern and northern states. On June 24, 1922, a mass initiation of Klansmen took place in a pasture near Tulsa, Oklahoma. Over one thousand men were inducted into Tulsa Klan No. 2 in a ceremony witnessed by a huge crowd of thousands who had driven to the site in their automobiles. The ceremony took place after dark and lasted for several hours. It was illuminated by two fiery crosses, the larger measuring seventy by twenty feet. One young boy who witnessed the spectacle said: "It was awful solemn and spooky. White figures were every place" (qtd. in Sullivan 1939, 574). The new Klan viewed Jews, Roman Catholics, and recent immigrants with equal hostility. The Klan's view of blacks was summarized by Hiram Wesley Evans, a Texas dentist, who became the Klan's new imperial wizard in December 1922: "The Negro is not a menace to Americanism in the sense that the Jew or the Roman Catholic is a menace. He is not actually hostile to it. He is simply racially incapable of understanding, sharing in or contributing to Americanism" (qtd. in Slosson 1958, 309). From October 1920 to October 1921, newspaper reports attributed a variety of atrocities to the Klan: four killings, one mutilation, one incident of branding with acid, five kidnappings, and forty-three persons driven from their communities (Slosson 1958, 311). Whether all these and subsequent acts of brutality were committed by Klan members or pretenders has been a subject of dispute; perhaps the truth falls somewhere in between. Nevertheless, the screening of Klan applicants was minimal, and Klan "membership became a convenient refuge for criminals who wanted protection and politicians who wanted a ready-made 'machine'" (Slosson 1958, 312).

It was during this period that Americans restricted immigration; discouraged international organizations; banned the teaching of evolution in some states; limited the possibility of procreation by insane, retarded, and epileptic citizens in many states by authorizing the practice of sterilization; and, in Oregon, briefly banned the attendance of elementary-age schoolchildren at nonpublic schools. The Oregon law, adopted through a ballot initiative at the general election held in 1922, was declared unconstitutional by the U.S. Supreme Court in 1925 (Sullivan 1939, 613).

The nation's tendency toward isolationism and prejudice, even violence, was not limited to the common citizen. In the halls of Congress, southern senators repeatedly used the filibuster, which allows senators to talk indefinitely on any topic, to block a vote on a federal antilynching statute. Even though presidential administrations from the 1920s until World War II requested and supported such a law, the tactics of a few southern senators could not be overcome (Murray 1969, 402).

The turmoil the nation found itself in made the need for additional police forces even more clear. In the spring of 1920, New York governor Alfred E. Smith signed a new state law that provided for a permanent force of police reserves as an adjunct to the regular police in New York City (Laws of New York, 1920, chap. 711). The original bill was introduced in the legislature by state senator Charles C. Lockwood, who foresaw the necessity of maintaining an emergency pool of trained, disciplined, and equipped citizens. The law provided that the new reserve police force could not have more than five thousand members, that members would serve without pay, and that when ordered to active duty they would have all the powers of police officers (*Brooklyn Daily Eagle*, May 16, 1920).

Under the mandate of the Lockwood Bill, Commissioner Richard Enright picked the most active members from the old reserves and recruited others. All were to have the same authority as the regular police when assigned to duty and would be subject to the rules and regulations of the police department. The city would provide a regular police uniform for each member. New orders were also established for the mobilization of reservists for extended periods of service. The immediate impact of this command was to deplete the force of many workingmen, who could not afford to lose their wages under the new requirement that they could be called upon to devote eight straight hours at a time to a volunteer activity (*New York Times*, September 10, 1920).

Nevertheless, this reorganized special branch of the city's police performed increased tours of duty on a number of assignments. They assisted the police in the Brooklyn Rapid Transit strike in 1920 (*New York Times*, September 10, 1920), worked on traffic duty, served during a milk-truck drivers' strike in 1921 (*New York Times*, November 26, 1921), and participated in a massive drive to put an end to a rising crime wave in 1922 (*New York Times*, April 11, 1922).

The police reserves' 1922 mobilization to aid the police in their efforts to cope with violent criminal acts demonstrated the mutual dependence between the city's police force and its unpaid police auxiliary. Reservists who owned fast-running automobiles were asked to devote them to their crime-prevention assignments; a similar request was made to members owning horses. Soon members were working both evening and daytime patrols, some in uniform and others in plainclothes (*Brooklyn Daily Eagle*, April 10, 1922). Every member was urged to carry his revolver at all times, even when out of uniform. The reserves continued to carry firearms in civilian clothes until 1926, when a new order barred this practice (*Brooklyn Daily Eagle*, April 11, 1922; June 27, 1926).

The order that barred the reserves from carrying arms was issued by Richard Enright's successor, George McLaughlin. The new commissioner was probably aware of Enright's recent difficulties over the status of the reserves and the "political football" it had become. After Mayor John Hylan was defeated by James A. Walker in 1926, Enright had retired, having been ridiculed by his political enemies. In a report in the *New York Times* on October 7, 1925, Enright had been severely rebuked by Otto Rosalsky, presiding judge of the Court of General Sessions, for the fact that criminals were "running riotous in New York City." Judge Rosalsky also stated that "Enright has been told repeatedly by Judges to augment his department with a citizen reserve, and it is absolutely essential that he do so." On the same day, a Manhattan alderman, Bruce Falconer, remarked that "the root of the trouble was that Commissioner Enright was nothing more than a petty politician whose handling of the police force was governed by personal favoritism." Enright replied that "a limited reserve, provided by law, already existed, but difficulty had been experienced in recruiting it to full effectiveness" (*New York Times*, October 8, 1925). McLaughlin, chosen to be commissioner because of his background in public administration, had a mandate to do something about organized crime and police corruption. At the time of his appointment, McLaughlin was the superintendent of banking in New York State (Reppetto 1978, 176–79). Perhaps, when he barred the reserve police from being armed, he sincerely believed that New York City would be safer if fewer civilians were carrying weapons. At the time, the War and Navy Departments prohibited all reserve officers of the U.S. Army and Navy from carrying pistols when not on actual military duty (Cuvillier 1926). There was, however, a significant amount of lobbying to override this federal military policy and grant pistol permits to reservists. One editorial stated: "By arming and placing a certain amount of responsibility on the reserve officers—and those of the militia should be added to the army and navy men—the size of the police force, for this particular purpose, would be doubled. . . . They would be 'plain clothes men,' too—a fact that would add to their efficiency as detectives, for the robbers could not identify them in advance" (*New York Times*, August 16, 1926). In any case, McLaughlin's career was brief: he resigned when he fully realized the unseemly nature of Mayor Walker's character and the enormity of the task to which he had been assigned (Reppetto 1978, 179).

As the "Roaring Twenties" unfolded, the police reserves program gradually ebbed. A number of causes contributed to its decline. Although reservists shared all the hazards of police work when called to duty, they received few of the privileges accorded regular officers. For example, reservists had to pay for their own carfare, their own pistol, and all their incidental expenses. Over a period of nine years, more than 10,500 recruits paid for their own instruction and practice in marksmanship at a private training school. It was reported at the time that attempts to qualify for the expert's gold badge, the highest award presented for revolver proficiency, gave rise to the phrase, "Ten dollars for the medal and a thousand dollars worth of ammunition" (*Brooklyn Daily Eagle*, June 20, 1926). Too, many members of the reserves were doubtless disappointed when they were denied the authority to carry firearms when out of uniform. Morris Joseph, a chief of staff of the New York Reserve Police, declared in a letter to the *New York Times*: "These men are proficient in the use of small arms, as they have been instructed by competent teachers in the armories of the National Guard. There were prior to Jan. 1 nearly 2,500 trained men in this organization, and it seems to me that if the Police Commissioner felt the need of civilian assistance he would issue such orders as to make the Police Reserve of real worth at all times" (August 18, 1926).

Reserve activities were also curtailed because of weakness in the administration of city government under Mayor James A. Walker, whose tenure lasted from 1926 until 1932. Beginning in 1926, New York had three successive police commissioners in as many years. While the purposeful utilization of the reserves required attentiveness and resourcefulness, Walker's appointees had other interests and concerns, and the reserves were disregarded. By 1928, many members of the New York Police Reserve had been given discharge notices. Some demanded that a thorough investigation be made into the recent management of the police reserves, but their public appeals failed to prevent their final release (*Brooklyn Daily Eagle*, January 17, 1928).

These events were in stark contrast to the reviews, drills, and thrilling air shows held only a decade before, when such officials as Mayor Hylan were more encouraging:

> In training and being prepared for any emergency the officers and men enrolled in your ranks are a mighty factor in the cause of law and order, which this Administration is confident can be relied on whenever needed. . . . You set a fine example of patriotic and high public spirit. You sacrifice your time, comfort and convenience by drilling and training so that you may fit yourself to be able to efficiently perform police duty in time of need, without compensation of any kind or hope of reward. In doing this you are rendering real service. And, besides training, you have responded promptly

whenever called upon for duty. . . . Your faithful service to the city in the past and your desire for further service are appreciated and will be rewarded as far as is legally possible. Let me assure you I am with you to the end. (*Brooklyn Daily Eagle*, April 13, 1918)

A third factor also influenced the deactivation of the police reserves: in 1928, Lewis Rodman Wanamaker died. While his donations of funds and personal attention to all reserve activities were important, in the long run his preoccupation with the commercial world and aviation interrupted his devotion. Lindbergh's 1927 achievement preceded by only one month the success of Wanamaker's tri-motored airplane in crossing the Atlantic (*Brooklyn Daily Eagle*, March 9, 1928). It is thus probable that the reserves were made to take a backseat while the aviation industry was born.

Police officials probably found it very difficult to justify the existence of a volunteer reserve police force when its regular force was involved in nonenforcement of the federal Prohibition law. In New York City, during the Prohibition era, neither the beat patrolman nor his superiors appeared to favor Prohibition: "the police raided usually only on specific complaints from persons who had been robbed or otherwise mistreated, or from neighbors who objected to noise and other forms of annoyance" (S. Walker 1933, 74). Some people even believed that if the police really wanted to eliminate the speakeasy, they could have done so in about a week (S. Walker 1933, 160–61). By 1930, illegal stills within the United States were the main source of American liquor, although the choicest types were being "smuggled in from Canada and from ships anchored on 'Rum Row' in the Atlantic beyond the twelve-mile limit of United States jurisdiction" (Kyvig 1979, 21). Throughout most of Prohibition , special speedboats were constructed for the specific purpose of unloading liquor from offshore "mother ships." Abner (Longie) Zwallman, one of the leading bootleggers of his day, operated a fleet of speedboats off the coastline of New Jersey. He made millions and at the peak of his illegal enterprise was "importing about 40 per cent of the bootleg liquor flowing across the nation's borders" (Cook 1974, 75). The success of his operation has been attributed to corrupt law enforcement officials.

In addition, throughout the 1920s, New York and other cities had to contend with the lawlessness of not only suppliers and corrupt officials but also consumers of bootlegged liquor. Members of the volunteer police reserve were never matched with these lawbreakers. Even the U.S. Coast Guard, along with an array of other federal and state law enforcement organizations, was unsuccessful in contending with the illicit liquor trade, stymied particularly by the clandestine manufacturing of domestic varieties of liquor, or "bathtub gin." The federal Prohibition enforcement statute—the Volstead Act—contained a variety of loopholes. Doctors could prescribe alcoholic drinks, and druggists were empowered to fill their prescriptions. Millions of gallons of industrial alcohol were being diverted, watered down, flavored, bottled, and sold with bogus whiskey labels and stamps. Federal and state enforcement agencies were underfunded, understaffed, and inexperienced in rendering each other mutual aid. Although the states were encouraged to initiate and lead policing efforts, "by 1927 their financial contribution to the cause was about one-eighth of the sum they spent enforcing their own fish and game laws" (E. Allen 1979, 189). Courts even set aside certain days to receive guilty pleas for Prohibition violations. Often, the small fines paid on these days allowed bootleggers to return to their trade without much interruption in business (Severn 1969, 129). By the 1930s, Prohibition had led to a racketeering problem of significant proportions.

Prohibition, of course, was not alone in complicating the effectiveness of the volunteer reserves. Phenomenal growth in the readership of the urban press and the popularity of press photography may also have led to the reserves' decline. Between 1925 and 1930, rural subscriptions to city newspapers doubled (Sinclair 1964, 312), and throughout the 1920s, the press meticulously covered police activities. It would have been highly embarrassing for the regular forces if reserves had begun upstaging them by making arrests. Certainly, opportunities to make arrests during the lawless years of Prohibition were frequent. The actions of New York City's police commissioner, Richard Enright, support this speculation. On at least one occasion, for example, Commissioner Enright warned his officers about "leaks" to the press, noting that such leaks interfered with the work of the department. He pointed out that revealing information (which he called "inside stuff") can defeat the ends of justice, urging especially that police detectives should not pose for photographers since such pictures would allow criminals to become familiar with their appearance (New York Times, November 18, 1924). Clearly, then, Enright had encountered difficulties in controlling contacts between the police and the press and consequently may not have wanted to face the same problem with the reserves. This worry may have led him to begin to curtail their services.

As the twentieth century moved on, opponents of Prohibition began to speak openly, further complicating the role of regular and volunteer police forces. In the first quarter of the twentieth century, new pressure groups eventually came to prominence. The efforts of the Anti-Saloon League, for example, were soon followed by the establishment of the Association Against the Prohibition Amendment (AAPA), which launched a major media blitz in the late 1920s, issuing a series of pamphlets that were widely circulated throughout the United States. These publications bore such titles as "Scandals of Prohibition Enforcement," "Cost of Prohibition and Your Income Tax," and "Reforming America with a Shotgun: A Study of Prohibition Killings." The pamphlets, in general, were carefully prepared, containing, aside from their titles, only a relatively small amount of editorial or rhetorical comment. As a result, they were cited by newspaper wire services as regular news items, consequently serving as effective tools for anti-Prohibitionists. March 1929, for example, saw the publication of a pamphlet entitled "Scandals of Prohibition Enforcement." It summarized official reports from five major cities—Philadelphia, Chicago, Pittsburgh, Detroit, and Buffalo—involving gross instances of police corruption. Another pamphlet, "Prohibition Enforcement: Its Effect on Courts and Prisons," summarized research conducted by the U.S. Department of Justice, organizing the material to suggest the increased burden that Prohibition had placed on federal courts and prisons and implying that key elements of the nation's criminal-justice system were being prevented from dealing with other forms of crime (Kyvig 1979, 106–8).

Prohibition inarguably caused enforcement problems of massive proportions. In Pittsburgh, for example, immigrant steelworkers frequently gathered at local saloons to unwind from their long days at the mills. A year after the enactment of Prohibition, Pittsburgh had over five hundred speakeasies and cabarets, and by 1926, about ten thousand stills were operating throughout the region. In downtown Pittsburgh, whiskey was sold at $16 a quart, $150 for a case. The city's major bootleggers traveled in fancy new automobiles and were considered celebrities: "Police and racketeers formed a liaison: bootleggers received protection, speakeasies and stills were allowed to function; for their services policemen received fat fees" (Lorant 1975, 335–36).

Thus, it is quite possible that the regular police and their political colleagues did not want volunteers present in the precinct houses of the late 1920s. The active presence of community members, participating in their own policing, would have provided a direct channel for members of local electorates to learn about the functioning of many public agencies, perhaps influencing their votes on election day. In 1929, New York City's police commissioner Grover Whalen stated that the city contained thirty-two thousand speakeasies. The operators and owners of these speakeasies were "dependent on corrupt policemen and agents who drank too much of their liquor and extorted too much of their profit" (Cashman 1981, 44).

The corruption of police and other local officials engendered by Prohibition was widespread. Indeed, it has been argued that the real tragedies of Prohibition took place among the nation's citizens: more than half a million people were convicted of violations of liquor control laws and related crimes, and thousands died in gangland warfare and from poisonous liquor (Cashman 1981). Ironically, the three groups who had been most active in opposing the use of liquor were in fact the only three groups allowed by law to make, prescribe, or sell it after the adoption of the Volstead Act: "the ministers, the farmers, and the doctors and druggists" (Sinclair 1964, 73).

Although those dark days mark the antithesis of the modern-day concept of community policing, the era was not without its positive developments. America's largest city, for example, launched an ambitious innovation. In 1929, New York City's police commissioner Grover Whalen launched the College of the Police Department of the City of New York, faculty members from the College of the City of New York (CCNY), New York University, and Columbia University collaborating in its establishment (Whalen 1930). While the school never awarded college degrees, it did contribute to increasing the effectiveness of the police and standardizing police methods.[3] This "college" opened one year after the New York Police Reserve ceased to function: in 1934, the police reserves had been officially abolished by the current police commissioner, John F. O'Ryan (*Brooklyn Daily Eagle*, March 31, 1934).

In addition to the AAPA, the period spawned other groups concerned about the enforcement of Prohibition. Pauline Sabin, a member of the Republican National Committee and the wife of Charles Sabin, treasurer of the AAPA, founded the Women's Organization for National Prohibition Reform. In time, her organization's membership greatly exceeded that of the AAPA: by 1932, its membership had surpassed one million, adding half a million more supporters by December 1933, making it three times the size of the AAPA (Kyvig 1979, 120–23). Prohibition opponents were often prominent members of society; in Pittsburgh, for example, the anti-Prohibition movement was led by Samuel Harden Church, the president of the Carnegie Institute (Lorant 1975).

By the end of the 1920s, national Prohibition was doomed, in large part because of such new technologies as the automobile, talking movies, and the radio. These new instruments brought the city to the country and helped erode the strength of the drys, which was based in small towns: "For better or for worse, the American films of the twenties had spread everywhere the desire to imitate the life of the rich. . . . And the life of the rich included liquor, its use and abuse. . . . Moreover, the political use of the radio by Franklin D. Roosevelt gave a great popular support to the economic methods which he advocated, such as repeal" (Sinclair 1964, 324).

The police corruption spawned by Prohibition did not go unrecognized. Several years after the New York Police Reserve had ceased operations, in 1931, the National Commission on Law Observance and Enforcement found that obtaining confessions through physical violence was widespread among police (U.S. President's Commission on Law Enforcement and Administration of Justice 1967, 93). The members of the National Commission on Law Observance and Enforcement had been appointed by President Herbert Hoover, but the commission came to be known by the name of its chairman, George Wickersham. Prior to the Wickersham Commission, a plethora of unofficial "commissions" had been created by concerned business leaders—for example, the Chicago Crime Commission, the Los Angeles Crime Commission, and the National Crime Commission. The National Crime Commission, initiated by the head of U.S. Steel in 1925, included such well-known figures as Charles Evans Hughes, former chief justice of the U.S. Supreme Court, and Franklin D. Roosevelt (S. S. Walker 1977).

Junior Police

Another welcome change of the transformation era was the advent of police-sponsored programs for youth. During the first two decades of the twentieth century, various communities began to experiment with a new kind of youth program. Some of the earliest programs, known as either "junior" or "boy police," began in Council Bluffs, Iowa; Cincinnati; and New York City (S. S. Walker 1977). These programs usually included instruction in good citizenship and various recreational opportunities. After 1920, the automobile's popularity created a need for school programs focusing on the safety of school-age pedestrians. In the early 1920s, in recognition of this need, the American Automobile Association and its local club affiliates began their School Safety Patrol programs. Later, in the period just after World War II, the National Sheriffs' Association conceived of a plan for the creation of a Junior Deputy Sheriffs' League. By 1951, the league had a membership of nearly a million boys and some girls. Every state was represented, as were nearly a sixth of the nation's 3,069 counties (Lundy 1952).

Perhaps the largest municipal junior police organization was pioneered by the New York City Police Department. Similar to the Boy Scouts of America, except for its career orientation, the program was created through the efforts of Capt. John Sweeney. The program was thereafter adopted by the current police commissioner, Arthur Woods. Sweeney, concerned about the boys in various districts of his police precinct, and aware of the power of peer pressure to shape human character, designed the junior police to allow boys to channel their energies into something constructive. He met with the youth of his precinct, sharing his vision of turning the "gangs" of boys in each district into more structured groups focusing on police work. His ideas gained acceptance, and the first group included twenty-one boys. Sweeney personally appointed five of the boys to serve as leaders, and they were given the usual military-style ranks (e.g., captain, lieutenant, and sergeant). The group was based at the school its members attended, and Sweeney made a point of carefully defining the geographical boundaries of the territory in which they would be able to carry out their activities, which extended a few blocks from their school. Several residents donated funds for police-style uniforms, and the group's activities received other favorable responses. Inquiries were soon received from other parts of Sweeney's precinct, and eventually units were organized throughout the city. Each held regular meetings, members performing assigned duties, attending drills and first aid training, participating in games such as dodge ball, and receiving identification cards and shields. The metal shields were well designed and served a distinctive purpose: the receipt of the police shield was dependent on a good record of attendance and required a fifteen-cent deposit. Boys were required to study the twelve duties of the junior police force, which focused on health and safety issues such as refraining from smoking, breaking windows, and jaywalking and keeping sidewalks and fire escapes clear of obstructions (Crump 1917, 277–84). A system of merits and demerits was used to help regulate the boys' behavior. At its peak, New York City's junior police program had an enrollment of six thousand boys between the ages of eleven and fifteen (S. S. Walker 1977, 84) who were required to learn a pledge and motto to obtain initial membership. The pledge read as follows: "I promise on my honor to do my duty to God and my country, and to obey the law; to obey the motto and the rules and regulations of the Junior Police Force of the City of New York; to keep and never to abuse my Junior Police badge, and to surrender it upon demand to the chief of the force" ("Boy Police" 1917, 1258–59). The junior police motto promised that boys would be honest, trustworthy, loyal, helpful, polite, obedient, and brave ("Boy Police" 1917, 1258).

Young girls also played a role in the New York City junior police, although their numbers were much smaller. Like many of the boys, they wore uniforms and even carried wooden batons. In 1916, Celia Goldberg was one of fifty girls who had served a probationary term of six months and were chosen on the basis of merit from a group of five hundred. About fourteen years old, and with the rank of captain, she was actually assigned to help patrol one of the most congested sections of the East Side of Manhattan. Her duties included observing pushcart peddlers to ensure that only fresh food was sold, safely escorting younger children across busy city streets, keeping tenement fire escapes clear of debris, and helping to monitor dance halls so that underage girls would not enter them ("Juvenile Coppettes" 1916, 1735–36).

Junior police programs, of course, were not limited to New York City. In California, Berkeley's pioneering police chief August Vollmer also organized a junior police program. In 1915, several hundred boys were involved in the program, participating in military drills and becoming involved in various

Capt. John Sweeney and officers of New York City's junior police, c. 1917

community projects (Carte and Carte 1975, 34). Honolulu sheriff Charles Rose began a Junior Traffic Police Officers program in 1923 with thirty-three members of the Boy Scouts of America. There are now over four thousand junior police helping to safeguard 128 schools in the city and county of Honolulu (Honolulu Police Department 2000b). One of the earliest known school-based pedestrian-safety patrols, initiated in Newark, New Jersey, in 1917, trained both boy and girl patrollers to assist children on their way to and from schools and playgrounds (Rosseland 1926). By 1931, Milwaukee had an organization, coordinated by the Milwaukee Safety Commission, consisting of 2,619 junior safety cadets for all of its public and parochial schools. The commission issued a pocket-sized handbook detailing the qualifications and duties of these student cadets and captains (Corbett 1931). Some schools assigned entire classes of older students to assist in escorting younger students across dangerous street intersections.

In the early 1920s, the superintendent of recreation in York, Pennsylvania, established a junior police organization whose members served as traffic police in the city's parks. Each boy was given a badge with the words "junior police" in its center, surrounded by the name of the playground for which the boy was responsible. Each badge, color coded to coincide with one particular city park, could be worn only by the boy to which it had been assigned. The boys were examined on their duties and given promotions based on their exam results. Boys who passed a "house officer" examination were authorized to go to the homes of children to find out why they had not been coming to the playground ("Junior Police" 1922). In this manner, the city of York created the first (and perhaps the only) junior truant playground officer program in the nation.

The emergence of the automobile also changed the nature of the nation's law enforcement. In 1921, there were nine million autos in the United States; by 1929, there were more than twenty-three million. Cars gave the workingman the means to go where liquor was sold and to bring it back home. They were also used to take liquor to prospective buyers: "Criminals penetrated the trucking companies and the Teamsters' Union, in order to acquire control of fleets of trucks to transport their supplies of bootleg from still to sale" (Sinclair 1964, 318). On the other hand, automobiles were also hailed by some police reformers as a panacea for crime control, since they could help create a more omnipresent police force: "beginning in the 1920s, the police increasingly equated progress and professionalism with the latest in automobile equipment" (S. S. Walker 1977, 136). Ironically, by the second half of the century, this technological improvement would come to be regarded as a cause of citizen insecurity, placing an obstacle between the police and the public. In addition, the automobile certainly contributed to thousands of road accidents and made school safety patrollers necessary.

By the mid-1920s, while some cities—such as Honolulu, Newark, and Milwaukee—had adopted their own independent youth safety patrol systems, the American Automobile Association had begun to sponsor a national program. Over the years, the AAA program has been credited with saving the lives of many schoolchildren. In 1931, for example, forty-two boys received awards for exceptional acts of heroism that resulted in saved lives. In that year, the typical patrol consisted of four to twelve boys, depending on the size of the school and the number of hazardous intersections around it. Selected for service based on their good grades and leadership qualities ("Guarding Five Million Children" 1932), patrol members were commonly seen stopping traffic by raising their hands and then escorting groups of students across city streets. The boys wore white "Sam

Browne belts" with badges attached to denote their rank. Some had bright-colored felt armbands. During inclement weather, poncho-type capes and rain hats were added to the uniform.

Nationwide, about two hundred thousand safety patrollers, serving in over eighteen hundred cities and towns, had been selected by 1933 ("Schoolboy Patrols Approved" 1933). In his book *Why Not the Best,* former president Jimmy Carter refers nostalgically to his AAA school safety patrol participation: "One of the proudest moments of my life came when I was given a white canvas belt and a tin badge and sworn in as a School Boy Patrolman. My job was to enforce all the safety precautions, but also to go to the nearest house for help when our makeshift bus frequently slid into a ditch during rainy weather" (1975, 35).

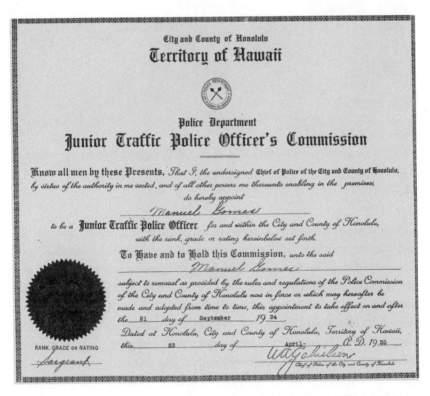

Certificate of appointment, Junior Traffic Police Officer's Commission, Honolulu, Territory of Hawaii, c. 1935

Bobby Senise on safety patrol duty at his school in Blue Island, Illinois, c. 1943 (Library of Congress, Prints and Photographs Division, Farm Security Administration—Office of War Information Photograph Collection, reproduction number LC-USW3-017011-E DLC)

Junior police programs also had more tangible benefits. In Flint, Michigan, the junior safety patrol program, supplemented by required daily traffic-safety instruction for all of Flint's schoolchildren, was organized in 1927. Safety lessons in Flint were enhanced through the use of slogan and poster contests. In 1930, at the start of America's Great Depression, the safety division of the Flint Police Department reported that about eight hundred boys were deployed at some 114 intersections throughout the city, estimating that the use of the school patrols rather than regular police officers was saving local taxpayers $228,000 each year (Demaroff 1930).

In 1938, nearly two decades after the New York City junior police had been disbanded, a similar program was established by the Boston Police

Department through the efforts of Joseph F. Timiltry, the city's police commissioner. Within a year, the Junior Police Corps of Boston included more than five thousand boys from twelve to sixteen years of age. More than ten thousand boys had expressed interest in the program, but with only fifteen police officers assigned to supervise it, the corps' resources were limited. The boys accompanied regular police on their tours of duty and were shown the details of police work. The police department also provided instruction in basic criminal legal procedures, as well as classes in wrestling and boxing. After sufficient training, the junior police were assigned to direct traffic at school crossings and provide supervision at police station Halloween parties and other functions for community youth. Any violation of the rules of the corps, which had its own rank structure, was brought before a trial board consisting of corps members (Timiltry 1939).

In the same year that the Boston organization was initiated, boys ten and older were being recruited in Akron, Ohio. The new Ohio group held its first

"Keeping order in the bus": unidentified teenager in the rear of a school bus in Charlotte County, Virginia, performing his duty as a safety patrol member, c. 1943 (Library of Congress Prints and Photographs Division, Farm Security Administration—Office of War Information Photograph Collection, reproduction number LC-USW3-033458-E DLC)

meeting at the local YMCA, led by Lt. John Struzenski, head of the auto theft unit of the Akron Police Department. In a newspaper interview conducted in 1938, Struzenski commented on why each member would receive a real badge, saying that the badges "signify they are members of our second police force" (Musarra 2000).

In 1946, although the city of Phoenix had only a single traffic police officer assigned to school crossings, it had a record of no traffic accidents involving schoolchildren in the past five years. Instead of traffic cops or other paid workers, the city relied on a corps of junior police. They received their uniforms from local organizations and their authority to perform traffic duty from the Phoenix Police Department. The junior police watched school crossings, directed traffic, handed out tickets, and performed other tasks associated with traffic control ("Stop-and-Go Kids" 1946).

Other kinds of junior volunteer police units were also initiated at the time of World War II. Some were geared to the delinquent or the predelinquent; others simply aimed to promote pride in oneself, one's city, and one's nation. In Providence, Rhode Island, for example, a junior police organization was launched in 1943. Members learned how to march and parade, and basketball and baseball teams were established in each precinct. Some members even participated in a music program, while others were encouraged to audition for appearances on a Saturday-morning junior police radio program. Each half-hour weekly program began with the junior police song, the audience singing along (Deusch 1997).

In 1944, William D. Brogan, an investigator for the San Antonio sheriff's office, was inspired to organize a junior deputies program. Brogan, outraged by a teenage gang fight that led to dozens of injuries, was able to bring together the two rival gang leaders and convince them that their actions were disrupting the U.S. war effort. Many former gang members were among the eight hundred teens, aged fourteen to eighteen, who joined the new organization. Within six months of the establishment of the new "Junior Deputies of America" corps, San Antonio's juvenile crime rate had been lowered by one half, Investigator Brogan crediting his junior deputies with helping to solve various car, bicycle, and horse thefts ("Bill Brogan's Boys" 1945).

The year 1944 also saw the beginning of a rather unique youth program when the state of Mississippi created a junior state guard. This program, designed to provide military training for males under age eighteen, had over

850 boys participating in fourteen different high schools by 1947. Initially, the program encouraged youth to enter the Mississippi State Guard and later the National Guard. Students learned basic military and leadership skills, first aid, and marksmanship and engaged in physical-fitness activities. Credits toward high school graduation could be earned by attending the junior state guard program. In later years, the program was replaced by Junior Reserve Officer Training Corps programs (Stentiford 2002, 182–83).

An important breakthrough in the junior police movement occurred in 1947 when the National Sheriffs' Association (NSA) launched its Junior Deputy Sheriffs' League. In order to spur the growth of the league, the NSA published and distributed a junior-deputy manual. When Grover Combs, sheriff of West Virginia's Logan County, received his copy in 1949, he announced the program, and more than two thousand boys from twelve to seventeen years of age quickly responded. Successful units of the league were established in such diverse communities as Flagstaff, Arizona; East Baton Rouge Parish, Louisiana; and Lafayette County, Arkansas. The existence of league chapters provided juvenile courts with an alternative form of community corrections. In 1952, the NSA reported that more than six thousand juvenile delinquents had been referred to the league. According to Charles Hahn, the executive secretary of the NSA in the early 1950s, the basic reason for the organization's success appeared to be that it "offer[ed] youth in small towns and rural areas a chance at organized sports: hockey, rodeos, boxing, swimming, judo, rifle shooting" (Lundy 1952, 129). The achievements of the league even prompted the Arkansas state legislature to require each county to employ a regular paid deputy to devote full-time attention to the junior-deputy program (Lundy 1952).

Most junior police activities of the nation have now been taken over by the Law Enforcement Explorer division of the Boy Scouts of America and Police Athletic League (PAL) programs. The Explorer programs (which can emphasize any career) started in the mid-1970s, and PAL over fifty years ago. Law Enforcement or Police Explorers are usually between the ages of fourteen and twenty. They may be of either gender and are insured by the Boy Scouts of America. Members of units, which must have local police agency sponsorship and guidance, usually receive extensive training in personal conduct, first aid, police procedures, weapons familiarization, crime-scene investigation, and a wide range of other specialized police duties.

California's Fontana Police Department even uses Explorers to help provide emergency services (Schmidt 1994). In the early 1980s, the Explorer Scouts at a U.S. military base in England produced a variety of training films related to crime prevention for security police (Sellinger 1983). Some police agencies refer to their Explorers as "junior police cadets" or simply as "cadets," and it is common for military ranks to be assigned to members of Police Explorer posts. Explorer and PAL programs continue to grow and find new relevance in today's changing culture. In 1997, there were 250 youths enrolled in the city of Detroit's Law Enforcement Explorers program (Gray 1997). The Portland Police Department initiated its PAL program to deal with increasing gang violence and drug dealing, its members receiving coaching in boxing, wrestling, football, soccer, martial arts, basketball, track and field, and other sports (Austin and Braaten 1991).

No doubt the events of September 11, 2001, and the proliferation of popular television programs dealing with law enforcement have contributed to the phenomenal growth in Explorer programs. Explorer posts have also been established in such related fields as health and hospital careers, medical emergency services, and firefighting. A popular Law Enforcement Explorer activity involves processing mock crime scenes in order to learn about crime-scene investigation. During such exercises, Explorers learn the steps in securing a crime scene, making sure the scene and evidence are safe and secure, marking evidence, and taking measurements and photographs. Explorers also have the opportunity to make field trips. From June 2002 to June 2003, for example, the Schoharie sheriff's Explorer Post 148, in upstate New York, toured the New York State Police Academy and Crime Lab; the 109th Airlift Wing of the Air National Guard in Glenville, New York; and the Schoharie and Schenectady county jails. Reflecting on his department's program, Schoharie County sheriff John S. Bates Jr. indicated that while the program provides hands-on experiences, it also provides "young people a chance with activities that are a positive influence on their lives" (Munger 2003).

Junior police programs provide police an opportunity to foster positive relationships with younger citizens. New York City's junior police evolved into an active PAL program, involving more than sixty thousand youths. The city's PAL program, a nonprofit organization dedicated to the educational, cultural, and recreational enrichment of disadvantaged children, has become well-known for "its programs in athletics, notably boxing, . . . [along with] employment training, courses in remedial reading, drug-abuse counseling, creative writing contests, day-care centers, after-school clubs, and educational summer day camps" (S. Weinstein 1995, 913). By the mid-1970s, nearly thirty thousand teens were enrolled in hundreds of Law Enforcement Explorer posts throughout the nation, their activities ranging from supervised traffic control to various community crime-prevention projects (Renyhart 1975). By 2000, AAA school safety patrols had approximately a half million participants, its roll of former safety patrollers including at least two U.S. presidents (Carter and Bill Clinton); two U.S. Supreme Court justices (Warren Burger and Stephen Breyer); twenty-one astronauts; and an array of other luminaries, including Olympic gold medalists Bruce Jenner, Lynette Woodard, and Edwin Moses (C. King 2000).

Midwestern Reserves

The Progressive, Prohibition, and Great Depression eras witnessed the origins not only of the junior police but also of numerous reserve police units, not just in New York City but especially in the Midwest and the South. During this time, Americans, thanks to expanded use of the automobile, experienced a greater freedom of movement than ever before—a freedom enjoyed by not only the law-observing population but the lawless. This newfound freedom also contributed to the establishment of volunteer police units, which were supported, politically and financially, by the American Bankers Association (ABA). Bankers were troubled by the outbreak of bank robberies in the Midwest that were being committed by notorious criminals such as John Dillinger and "Pretty Boy" Floyd. Many robberies took place in rural areas, where communications could be difficult and regular full-time law-enforcement personnel were scarce. The bankers' group thus urged the formation of volunteer county-wide police units (B. Smith 1960, 94–95).

The ABA supplied members of the new reserve police units with weapons and ammunition and also provided insurance policies for each of the sponsoring county sheriff departments, giving the volunteer police liability coverage. Eventually, there were almost six hundred such units spread across six midwestern states. No doubt, many individuals joined these units because of the opportunity to enforce the law in their own neighborhoods and because of the fringe benefits associated with being a sworn officer. These units were proven reasonably effective: some evidence indicates that their mere existence acted as a deterrent to would-be robbers. On the other hand, problems with volunteers sometimes arose because background checks and training were minimal (B. Smith 1960, 36, 94, 102).

The advent of the reserves, as we have seen, was stimulated by complications arising from Prohibition enforcement and by the need for supplemental police officers, especially in the more rural midwestern and southern states. These new generic volunteer police organizations stood in stark contrast to the volunteer undercover agents of the American Protective League, as well as the hired and volunteer detectives and attorneys of the Anti-Saloon League. Today, the activities of the APL and ASL may provide object lessons about the dangers of overzealous pursuit of law enforcement goals, especially in an age greatly concerned with internal security threats.

The Transformation Era in Retrospect

At the close of the Progressive Era and World War I, New York City established a unique system of volunteer reserve police. Subsequently, many rural jurisdictions implemented similar programs to contend with the lawlessness spawned by the Prohibition period. The use of junior and reserve police—innovations at the time—marked a transformation period in the history of volunteer policing: the reserves took on roles involving general peacekeeping assignments, while junior police units expanded the field by focusing on concern for young people and even the actual performance of police services by youth.

The fact that this transformation involved a shift from reliance on home defense leagues and state guards to a system of reserve police (i.e., from temporary specialists to permanent generalists) is of great significance, given today's domestic battlefront in the war on terror. In various municipalities during World War I (e.g., Chicago and Berkeley), police departments established Citizen Home Defense Leagues. The largest of these, for example, in New York City, was founded chiefly to serve as a source of additional police workers during an emergency. By 1919, New York's league had recruited twenty thousand members; it was transformed into an organized police reserve managed by the New York City Police Department at the war's end. A later law limited its membership to a maximum of five thousand.

According to the classification system detailed in table 1, the police reserves were a Type I organization (general purpose/reactive). They served in a general police capacity, having been initially organized with mounted, motor-vehicle, and motorboat units, with an airplane squadron added later. They were reactive because many of their activities centered on preparedness drills, rather than actual deployment.[4] No member of the New York Police Reserve was compensated.

The junior police and safety patrollers may be classified as Type III organizations (special purpose/reactive). They engaged in a limited number of specific, service-oriented projects (e.g., serving as school crossing guards, providing crowd control at special events, acting as security escorts). They were also primarily reactive organizations: if a crime occurred in their presence, their duty was to call for assistance. Most such groups were authorized to perform their assignments by local police departments that also supervised their activities. Traffic duty was a routine assignment of safety patrollers through at least the 1950s, and recently, older and more qualified Law Enforcement Explorers have been used for limited traffic work alongside regular police in some communities (see, e.g., Munger 2003).

While junior police and safety patrollers generally performed more restricted activities than their volunteer counterparts, on some occasions arrests were made upon the direction and initiative of members of the New York City junior police. In 1914, for example, a thirteen-year-old member of the junior police, Sgt. Louis Goldstein, of the Fifteenth Precinct, caused the arrest of a store owner who was charged with conducting an illegal lottery. Young Goldstein testified about the incident in the Court of Special Sessions of the City of New York. After the defendant realized the strength of the evidence against him, he pleaded guilty. This was not the first arrest in which Goldstein had participated. Previously, he had encountered two men breaking into a display case, each of whom received a six-month jail sentence. This earlier arrest had led to Goldstein's promotion to sergeant ("Boy Police" 1915).

While it is apparent that reserves represent one variety of volunteer police, can junior police, merely school-age children, be considered the same? Clearly, this is the case for the junior police of New York City in the early part of the twentieth century and those in the city of Phoenix in the 1940s. Each group was authorized by a governmental entity (i.e., the police department) to perform one or more police functions in an overt manner without pay. New York City's junior police were specifically charged with such responsibilities as preventing vandalism and bonfires in the streets and ensuring the proper storage of garbage cans. In Phoenix, junior police not only watched school crossings but directed traffic and handed out tickets.

During the first four decades of the twentieth century, new types of volunteer police organizations were established, responding to the exigencies of the times. For example, World War I saw the creation of the ubiquitous American Protective League and various municipal citizen home defense leagues, as well as numerous state guard organizations. During and immediately after Prohibition, there arose new urban and rural reserve police units. These occurrences demonstrate a transformation from special-purpose to general-purpose volunteer policing.

The transformation era of volunteer police played a significant role in fostering democratic institutions in the field of youth development. As we have seen, this era spawned countless varieties of junior police and/or safety patrol organizations. Some evolved into general recreational programs for youth. The opportunities these new organizations afforded for the growth and development of America's youth cannot be overestimated, and the fact that many of these groups were sponsored by police agencies is in keeping with the democratic ideal that government exists to represent and serve its citizens.

On a less positive note, the political manipulations of the 1920s eventually helped unravel the use of the New York Police Reserve. In addition, the strong-arm tactics used by the regular police may have undermined the operations of this urban form of volunteer police force. The 1920s, it has been said, produced some of the toughest police officers in New York City (Reppetto 1978).[5] Administrative efforts to quell the resulting unfavorable publicity for the city's police may have indirectly contributed to the disuse of the reserves, police supervisors concluding that it was safer not to risk such civilians bearing witness to any station-house brutality. When the reserves were withdrawn—when the press's access to the police was curtailed—the democratic ideal of the rule of law in an open government suffered.

Although they often keep a low profile, hundreds of reserve and auxiliary police units currently patrol the nation's rural and urban areas. In 1992, several new graduates of the Los Angeles Police Department Reserve Police Academy said they had volunteered because they wanted to serve the community and help the police keep the streets safe. The academy graduates included a priest, a postal worker, a college student, a purchasing agent, a receptionist, and a deputy district attorney. Los Angeles police chief Willie L. Williams presented the fifty-three new reserve officers with graduation diplomas, stating in his address that "the reserve program is probably the keystone of what community policing is all about" (Hill-Holtzman 1992). About a decade later, Tobias Winright, a professor of religion and ethics and a reserve police officer in Des Moines, Iowa, delivered a graduation talk to twenty-two new police reservists, noting that contrary to dire conclusions about the loss of civic engagement, the class of graduates before him represented at least one countervailing trend (Winright 2001). In the current age of global terrorism, the need for supplemental volunteer police at all levels of government has certainly grown.

6

The Assimilation Era   From 1941 to the Present

During the past several years the concept of an auxiliary or reserve law enforcement unit has become more accepted and is almost a must.

SHERIFF H. P. GLEASON, former president, National Sheriffs' Association

Prior to 1920, a variety of "spy-oriented" volunteer police organizations (e.g., the "friendly visitors" of the charity organization societies, the undercover agents of the American Protective League, and the specialized law enforcement agents of the Anti-Saloon League) dominated the disparate ranks of the volunteer police. In general, the work of these spy-oriented organizations served mainly to diminish the democratic ideal of equality. During the post–World War I era (1920–41), or the "transformation era," volunteer organizations of a more general nature were developed to contend with rising urban and rural lawlessness, as organized crime obtained a firm foothold as a result of Prohibition. In addition, the Great Depression of the 1930s fostered a continuing need for creating junior police and school safety patrols, as well as supplemental reserve units, rather than hiring more professional public-safety workers.

Volunteer police deployment during what may be called the "assimilation era" began in the 1930s but did not reach its full fruition until after both World War II and the Korean War. Today, volunteer police of various types are serving in hundreds of localities throughout the United States. Several states have incorporated volunteer police into their state police organizations (e.g., Arizona, Florida, New Hampshire, New Mexico, Ohio, Vermont). On the national level, the U.S. Coast Guard Auxiliary was founded in 1939 and the Civil Air Patrol in 1941. The U.S. Coast Guard Auxiliary, originally known as the U.S. Coast Guard Reserve, received its official name in 1941, and the Civil Air Patrol became the official auxiliary of the U.S. Air Force in

1948. When Congress passed the Federal Safe Boating Act of 1971, it further expanded the coast guard's role in supervising boating on inland waterways, providing that the coast guard auxiliary would be placed at the service of individual state governments when they asked for its assistance.

While the particular nature and degree of the assimilation of volunteer police have varied over time, random visits to local police department Web sites can quickly reveal the extent of assimilation that has occurred at the town, city, county, and state levels.[1] Overall, the volunteer police organizations of World War II and the Korean War, which focused on civil defense, have continued to develop and are now considered an important part of community policing efforts.

Prior to World War II, at least three major trends in U.S. society were firmly in place: the concentration of the population in big cities, the development of new means of public transportation, and the increasing influence of the media on public affairs. A million black Americans had migrated from the South to the North between 1915 and 1940 in search of a better life. In addition, women's suffrage, the Great Depression, and Jim Crow laws had profoundly impacted the development of American democracy and would all contribute to changes in the institutions and procedures of the justice system.

The severest emergency period of the American twentieth century came during World War II, which began with Germany's invasion of Poland on September 1, 1939. The United States entered the war on December 7, 1941, the day after the naval forces of Japan attacked Pearl Harbor, the base of the U.S. Pacific fleet. Millions of Americans were mobilized for the war effort, including state guard units, which patrolled streets, power stations, and water resources. Many of these homeland security patrollers carried their own weapons, while some carried none at all; some were "clothed in their civilian attire augmented perhaps only by an arm band" (Stentiford 2002, 119).

Women were also affected by the coming of war, their role in the workforce taking a major turnaround. Women, needed to produce war equipment and replace male workers throughout the economy, would serve in countless traditionally male occupations throughout the war. While many women afterward returned to full- or part-time domestic roles, the knowledge that they could fill such workforce roles became a permanent part of the public consciousness. The shortage of men on the home front also depleted the ranks of the regular police. Consequently, many new opportunities opened not only for women but also for youth and draft-exempt men to work in civil defense–related activities.

Although the United States and her allies achieved victory in Europe and in the Pacific by May and August 1945, the risks of espionage remained with the advent of the Cold War and the atomic age.[2] To cope with these new threats to American safety, the Department of War was reshaped into the Department of Defense, and such new entities as the Atomic Energy Commission and the Central Intelligence Agency were created. The new Department of Defense established new security guidelines for private industries seeking government contracts. These security standards mandated that defense-related businesses and organizations "designate a 'security officer' who would be responsible for the program's implementation and maintenance" (Burstein 1994, 4). In this way, a major impetus was given to the field of private security; in the remaining decades of the twentieth century, the growth of private security positions exceeded such growth in the governmental sector. By 1990, the ratio of private to public security personnel was 2.4 to 1 (Ricks, Tillett, and Van Meter 1994, 17).

The events of the turbulent 1960s, particularly after the assassination of President John Kennedy, had a powerful impact on the nation's volunteer policing efforts. During the 1960s, the legacy of America's history of racial intolerance, especially in the South, erupted into a new kind of civil war, pitting local police departments against the efforts of African Americans to end segregation. This titanic struggle would lead to the untimely deaths of young children, college students, and ethnic leaders. Few Americans alive at that time will ever forget the newsreel images of the Birmingham police, ordered by their commissioner, "Bull" Connors, to turn dogs and water hoses on civil rights marchers, or the scene in front of the Lincoln Memorial when the Reverend Martin Luther King Jr. uttered the legendary remarks that began with the words "I have a dream." Nor will anyone familiar with the history of the civil rights movement forget the tragic loss of three civil rights workers in Mississippi during the summer of 1964—workers seeking racial justice who were executed by Klansmen (Bailey and Green 1999). Three years later, some of these Klansmen, including Deputy Sheriff Cecil Price, were convicted of the federal crime of conspiring to violate the freedom workers' civil rights. It took three more years for the defendants' appeals to be exhausted and their imprisonment to begin (Cagin and Dray 1991).

Such racial violence was not confined to the South. During the summer of 1967, just a few months before the verdict in Mississippi, the streets of two northern cities—Detroit and Newark—exploded in turmoil. After the assassination of Dr. King in Memphis, Tennessee, on April 6, 1968, urban violence spread throughout the country. In response, Congress passed the Omnibus Crime Control and Safe Streets Act in June 1968. This law created the Law Enforcement Assistance Administration (LEAA) to fund local efforts to improve the administration of justice, making money available for new equipment, police training, and college tuition assistance for persons planning careers in criminal justice or already employed in peace officer positions. The LEAA also funded the National Advisory Commission on Criminal Justice Standards and Goals, which identified four general priorities: (1) preventing juvenile delinquency, (2) improving the delivery of social services, (3) reducing delays in the criminal justice process, and (4) obtaining greater citizen participation in the criminal justice system (Robin 1984, 55–57). These recommendations for improving the administration of justice augmented those of the 1931 Wickersham Commission, the 1967 White House Conference on Civil Rights, and the 1967 President's Crime Commission.

Traditional gender roles began to unravel in the late 1960s. In the field of policing, the role of women took a dramatic shift in September 1968, when two Indianapolis policewomen, Betty Blankenship and Elizabeth Coffal, were assigned to engage in routine marked patrol car duty. The nation's greatest progress in the hiring of women police, however, came as a result of the 1972 passage of Title VII of the 1964 Civil Rights Act, the 1973 amendments to the Omnibus Crime Control and Safe Streets Act of 1968, and the 1973 Revenue Sharing Act. The provisions of these federal laws meant that local jurisdictions that discriminated against women could be denied substantial federal aid. In spite of such progress in local police departments, the FBI did not hire its first women special agents until after J. Edgar Hoover's death, when two women began FBI special agent training in July 1972 (Schulz 1995, 131–34). At that time, the FBI had only 70 blacks and 69 Hispanics out of a total of 8,659 agents. It was not until William Webster became its director, in 1978, that the FBI began to actively recruit women and minority agents. During Webster's nearly ten years of service as director, the number of minority agents doubled and the number of women agents increased fivefold, from 147 to 787 (Kessler 1993, 398–400).

Funding for citizen patrols and other crime prevention initiatives (e.g., Operation Identification, Whistlestop) followed, as an approach known as "community policing" slowly began to be identified. By 1976, there were about 850 citizen patrol groups active in the United States. Most groups worked closely with local police, patrolling on foot or in private cars to deter crime and report suspicious persons or events. One of the most frequently funded types of patrols involved tenants watching their own buildings. Such tenant patrols were established in public housing developments in both New York City and Detroit (Robin 1984, 120–24). The advent of such programs as crime stoppers (involving safe crime prevention practices for businesses) and neighborhood watches appeared to be ushering in a new era of citizen mobilization. At the same time, many police departments had either already taken steps to revamp their old-style civil defense auxiliaries into better-trained and -qualified volunteer police units or had begun to establish new units. In 1988, Sir Kenneth Newman, commissioner of London's Metropolitan Police from 1982 to 1987, referred to the mobilization of citizens in their own defense as an important evolutionary change in traditional methods of policing (Hartmann 1988, 2).

The new cluster of programs—or community policing—was key to the move to involve community members as active participants in the administration of justice. While the precise contours of community policing tend to vary from jurisdiction to jurisdiction, its basic approach usually focuses on finding ways to make "citizens partners with the police in controlling crime, rather than passive recipients of police services" (Albanese 1999, 179). The importance of this movement was further reinforced in the mid-1990s when Congress agreed to fund the training and partial cost of one hundred thousand new police officers.

New technologies have also dramatically changed traditional enforcement strategies. Improvements such as the 911 emergency phone number have altered U.S. policing in a positive direction. Some of these innovations involve greater levels of governmental intrusion than others. New infrared technology, for example, can now detect the number of people in a building and their locations; ion-scanning equipment can detect cocaine residue on money. In some instances, the U.S. Customs Service has used X-ray and/or magnetic imaging machines as alternatives to strip searches. In cities such as New York, Baltimore, and Los Angeles, the use of computers to analyze crime statistics has greatly increased police performance (De La Cruz 1999). In addition, police now have available computer technology for conducting drug market analysis (DMA). DMA provides location-specific information about where drugs are sold and enables police personnel to access this information quickly, permitting the generation of maps that can be used to prepare probable cause affidavits for obtaining search warrants (Hebert 1993). In addition, the concept of "zero tolerance" has fostered the use of "checkpoints" for the control of drunken drivers, drug users, and illegal gun owners.

Law-enforcement conditions, of course, continue to change constantly in response to a society in transformation. Rising concerns about narcotics trafficking and terrorism during the post–Cold War era have led to stateside military deployments. Various branches of the National Guard have been called upon to engage in counterterrorism and counterdrug operations. In recent years, a special Air National Guard unit, consisting of 140 soldiers and with a budget of six million dollars, has been assigned to counterdrug efforts. This unit, based near Schenectady, New York, uses UH-60 Black-hawk helicopters and fixed-wing aircraft equipped with night-vision and thermal-imaging equipment to find marijuana fields. It also lends its high-tech help to local police agencies to locate people in buildings during drug raids (Gardinier 1998). Additional millions are being spent by local and state governments for their own enforcement initiatives. While the law enforcement apparatus marshaled against drug users and traffickers is greater than ever before, however, it has been estimated that nine out of ten drug shipments on interstate highways manage to get through without detection (Huppke 1999).

In spite of such changes, particularly the upsurge in public fears of terrorism, the use of military forces to police the streets of America and enforce nonmilitary law is limited by the Posse Comitatus Act of 1878. This law, however, has been amended in recent years to permit the type of aid being supplied by the Air National Guard in upstate New York. According to

Congressman Charles Bennett, this law was initially "enacted with strong racial overtones as an outgrowth of Southern anger over the use of troops to enforce the edicts of carpetbagger governments" (C. E. Bennett 1981).

The conditions in place today, including the widespread utilization of volunteer police, were fostered in particular by two national emergencies: World War II and the Korean War. While these catastrophic events led to the recruitment of unprecedented numbers of home front volunteers, high enrollments lasted only while the emergencies did. By the close of the twentieth century, however, and as the events of September 11, 2001, and after unfolded, a new awareness seemed to be developing that public safety and national security may be enhanced through a host of specific roles for the average citizen.

World War II–Era Volunteer Police

During U.S. involvement in World War II (1941–45), millions of Americans were mobilized to aid the war effort, transforming American society during and after the war: "the home front was in reality a battleground of ideas, customs, economic theory, foreign policy, and relationships between the sexes and social classes" (Manchester 1974, 1: 354–55). Many Americans not directly engaged in the war effort (e.g., by working in a strategic industry or serving in the military) nevertheless willingly participated in scrap drives, purchased war bonds, and enrolled in various types of civil defense units (Manchester 1974). Indeed, "in the first six months of 1942 the civilian defense corps expanded from 1.2 million to 7 million, and by mid-1943 more than 12 million Americans were registered" (Putnam 2000, 269). Across America, schoolchildren similarly participated in "the Junior Service Corps, the High School Victory Club, the Scouts, the Junior Red Cross, and, not least, the 4-H, which took a lead in the Victory Garden program" (Putnam 2000, 269).

In America's largest cities, civil defense forces were generally divided among rescue and fire units, air raid wardens, and auxiliary police. Air raid wardens helped enforce blackouts and searched the skies for enemy planes. Auxiliary police, in conjunction with fire and rescue units, engaged in numerous exercises, training, for example, to administer first aid and standing guard duty at strategic locations. Police departments that had previously devoted most of their energies toward furthering their own professionalism turned their efforts to recruiting and training new volunteer police units when they discovered that many regular officers were being called to military duty. Many of these volunteer units were kept in place after World War II, some of them evolving into full-service police organizations. By September 1942, for example, the Wichita Police Department had recruited more than one thousand auxiliary police officers, each taking an oath and receiving an armband. Fifteen years later, the Wichita Civil Defense Auxiliary became the Wichita Police Department Reserve, and in 1958, all of its members received full police powers (Wichita Police Department 2000). In Columbus, Ohio, volunteers were used exclusively as air raid wardens during World War II. After the war, their organization was temporarily abandoned until 1951, when the Korean conflict necessitated its reactivation (Columbus Police Reserve 2000).

Auxiliary police at a weekly meeting, Washington, D.C., c. 1942 (Library of Congress, Prints and Photographs Division, Farm Security Administration—Office of War Information Photograph Collection, reproduction number LC-USF34-013375-C DLC)

The original idea for creating the U.S. Coast Guard Auxiliary came from Malcolm S. Boylan, the newly elected head (or commodore) of the Pacific Writers' Yacht Club, based in Los Angeles (Tilley 2003, 1). Boylan first discussed the idea with a member of the regular coast guard, Lt. F. C. Pollard, sending a letter to Pollard in 1934 outlining the basic concept of a coast guard reserve. A copy of this letter was seen by coast guard commander Russell Waesche, who was very impressed with the idea. In 1939, the efforts of Waesche, who had become a rear admiral and head of the coast guard, led to the passage of the Coast Guard Reserve Act. Unlike the army and navy reserves, the new coast guard reserve was to be a civilian organization: members would not hold military ranks, wear uniforms, or receive military training. Except for gas expenses, it was expected that the reserve would cost the federal government next to nothing. The basic unit of the new organization would be the flotilla, consisting of ten or more boats and presided over by an elected civilian with the title of flotilla commander (Tilley 2003, 1–2).

By June 1940, over two thousand volunteers with small vessels had enrolled in the program. On February 19, 1941, Congress passed a law restructuring the coast guard reserve into two components. One, renamed the U.S. Coast Guard Auxiliary, consisted of the preexisting civilian reserve members. The other, a new U.S. Coast Guard Reserve, "was to function on a military basis as a source of wartime manpower, like the reserves of the other armed services" (Tilley 2003, 3). The members of the new U.S. Coast Guard Reserve would be divided into two categories: "regular reservists" and "temporary members of the reserve" ("coast guard TRs"). A coast guard TR "was a volunteer who served only in some designated geographic area (usually near his home or workplace) and less than full-time. Age limits for TRs were seventeen and sixty-four, and physical requirements were not stringent. Members of the Auxiliary were invited to enroll in the Reserve as TRs and bring their boats with them" (Tilley 2003, 3).

A month before Pearl Harbor, in accordance with existing law, President Franklin Roosevelt signed an order transferring the coast guard from the Treasury Department to the Navy Department, and in May 1942, the secretary of the navy authorized uniforms for the U.S. Coast Guard Auxiliary. Between 1941 and 1945, the auxiliary acted as the coast guard's general-purpose assistant. According to John A. Tilley, a historian of the U.S. Coast

Guard, when German U-boats were sighted off the East Coast of the United States, the Navy Department

> ordered the acquisition of "the maximum practical number of civilian craft in any way capable of going to sea in good weather for a period of at least 48 hours . . . to be manned by the Coast Guard as an expansion of the Coast Guard Reserve . . . and operated along the 50-fathom curve of the Atlantic and Gulf Coasts." Motorboats and sailing yachts, with numbers preceded by "CGR" painted on their bows and depth charges stowed awkwardly on their decks, began appearing on patrol stations all along the coasts. Many were donated by temporary members of the Reserve, or bought outright by the Coast Guard. Others were owned and manned by Auxiliarists. Known variously as "the Putt-Putt Navy," "the Splinter Fleet," and "the Corsair Fleet," they made up much of the American response to the U-boat threat in coastal waters during the early months of the war. As newly-constructed warships took over the load, the Coast Guard abandoned the concept. None of the two thousand CGR craft ever sank a submarine, but they rescued several hundred survivors of torpedoed merchant ships and may have driven some U-boats away from tempting cruising grounds. (2003, 4)

Tilley goes on to discuss the auxiliary's contributions in detail:

> Perhaps the Auxiliary's most important contribution to the war effort came in the form of the Volunteer Port Security Force. . . . The task of protecting the hundreds of warehouses, piers, and other facilities that kept the American shipping industry in business fell to the Coast Guard, which in turn delegated it to the Reserve and the Auxiliary. . . . Eventually some twenty thousand Reservists and Auxiliarists participated in port security patrols. About two thousand women enrolled as "TR SPARs," attending to the mountainous paper work that dispatched ships, cargoes, and troops overseas. . . . As the war went on and the Coast Guard's resources were stretched thinner, Auxiliarists and TRs were called upon to fill gaps wherever active duty Coast Guardsmen left them. . . . Auxiliarists manned lookout and lifesaving stations near their homes, freeing regular Coast Guardsmen for sea duty. When a flood struck St. Louis in the spring of 1943, Coast Guard Auxiliarists and Reservists evacuated seven thousand people and thousands of livestock. . . . The Auxiliary and the Reserve attracted their share of

celebrity members. Actor Humphrey Bogart took his yacht on several patrols out of Los Angeles, and Arthur Fiedler, conductor of the Boston Pops Orchestra, put in his twelve hours per week on patrol duty in Boston Harbor. . . . At the end of the war the Coast Guard TRs were "honorably disenrolled." Many remained Auxiliarists for years afterward. Wartime service had earned them no veterans' benefits and precious little other public recognition. In 1946 the TRs were awarded the Victory Medal. Auxiliarists who had not joined the Reserve had to be satisfied with the thanks of Adm. Waesche: "The Auxiliary during the war years was indispensable. Many thousands of you served faithfully and loyally as Auxiliarists and as temporary members of the CG Reserve, performing hundreds of tasks and relieving thousands of Coast Guardsmen for duty outside the continental limits. The Coast Guard is deeply appreciative of this service." (2003, 4–5)

The U.S. Coast Guard Auxiliary was not the only volunteer civil-defense force in place before American entry into the war. In Hawaii, six months before Pearl Harbor, a foresighted chief of police, together with the Oahu Police Commission, set about the task of recruiting over one hundred business and professional men for volunteer service in an emergency police reserve force. When the Japanese planes attacked, these citizens had already been in training for four months and had been commissioned as Honolulu police reserve officers. This group, whose members included R. Alex Anderson, a noted musician and composer of hapa haole songs, was thus able to render invaluable assistance during the emergency. After the December 7, 1941, attack, the territory of Hawaii was placed under martial law. For the rest of the war, both regular and volunteer police were issued a special seven-point star badge, on which were stamped the words "emergency" and "Honolulu" (Honolulu Police Department 2000b).

In New York City, an emergency auxiliary police force was organized in 1942 and designated the City Patrol Corps. Its mission was to assist the regular police in guarding, protecting, and patrolling areas vital to both the city and the war effort. The corps' divisions, one in each of the five boroughs of the city, were each divided into companies. By 1943, there were thirty-two companies in operation, with a total of nearly 4,500 volunteers, including about 525 women. The men who qualified in marksmanship (nearly three out of every four) were appointed "special patrolmen" and authorized to carry a revolver while on duty. They covered over three hundred posts on a daily basis, many volunteers serving four hours twice a week. Regular duty hours were either from four to eight p.m. or from eight to midnight (New York City Police Department 1943, 21).

Division E of the City Patrol Corps, which served in the borough of Brooklyn, routinely dispatched antisabotage patrols to the shoreline underneath the Williamsburg and Kosciusko Bridges. Soldiers from guard units patrolled the highway and walkway of the Williamsburg Bridge, while members of Division E endured long hours beneath the bridge in all weather conditions. In winter, one patrol member, Sgt. Joseph Berkowitz, resorted to standing inside a large cardboard box to endure his post. In summer, the foul odors emanating from raw sewage flowing into the river near the bridge made matters worse. Beneath the Kosciusko Bridge, weeds grew shoulder high, and mosquitoes were a constant menace (Evans 1998).

A women's division of the City Patrol Corps was also organized, its members assigned to perform clerical work at headquarters and division offices; to drive male volunteers to their guard posts; and to assist regular policewomen at parks, beaches, and canteen facilities. Women who only volunteered for clerical work were not required to participate in drills, appear in uniform, or take a physical examination. The fingerprint requirement, however, was not waived (*New York Times,* March 7, 1942).

In the summer of 1941, the Denver Police Department, which was slowly losing men to the military, also created an auxiliary police force. The department initially recruited a small group of men, but by the following year, the organization had expanded to include 600 members, divided into five companies. They were given training in basic and advanced first aid, bomb recognition and disposal, riot control, and protection from gas attack. The auxiliary policemen, also trained in such police procedures as traffic control, self-defense, and the use of firearms. They were also assigned to ride in patrol cars with regular officers to learn about police problems. By the spring of 1942, Denver had 450 trained auxiliaries, about a quarter of whom were equipped with firearms. All members were issued batons (Humeyumptewa 1994).

One of the first incidents requiring the services of the Denver auxiliaries was the flooding of the Platte River in April 1942. Nearly 150 auxiliary police assisted regular force members, using loudspeakers to tell homeowners to evacuate the area. The volunteer police also patrolled deserted areas to prevent possible looting. Later, when a B-24 army bomber crashed in south Denver in 1943, volunteers controlled traffic and guarded the crash site. Throughout the war years, Denver auxiliaries performed crowd control, assisted other civil defense forces during blackouts, and carried out war-related work. Although some suggested that it should be retained after the war, the organization was discontinued in August 1945 (Humeyumptewa 1994). Similarly, the last patrols of the New York City Patrol Corps took place in late August 1945. An editorial in favor of reinstating the corps appeared in the *Brooklyn Eagle,* proclaiming: "they performed many useful services. . . . Why not remobilize the City Patrol Corps?" ("Call City Patrol" 1945).

The Civil Air Patrol was also organized prior to U.S. entry into World War II, under Fiorello H. La Guardia's Office of Civilian Defense, on December 1, 1941, six days before Pearl Harbor (Swansburg 2002).[3] In early 1942, the U.S. military agreed to permit a ninety-day experiment to see if the private pilots of CAP could use their unarmed aircraft to help defend the East Coast from enemy submarines. At first, patrols were initiated from just three airfields— Atlantic City, New Jersey; Rehoboth Beach, Delaware; and Lantana, Florida. Civilian pilots wore military uniforms with a "U.S." insignia to reduce their risk, if captured, of being shot as spies or guerrilla fighters. Eventually, after a crew watched in vain as a grounded sub off Cape Canaveral, Florida, escaped before armed military aircraft could arrive, CAP planes were equipped with bombs and depth charges. By the end of August 1943, patrols were no longer needed, one German commander later confirming that coastal U-boat operations had been withdrawn "because of those damned little red and yellow airplanes" ("Civil Air Patrol Story" 2003, 2). During the war, members of CAP also had other duties: target towing, courier service for the army, and liaison and cargo flights between defense plants. CAP pilots also patrolled the southern border of the United States to prevent enemy saboteurs from entering the country and engaged in air search-and-rescue operations; nonflying CAP members helped guard airfields and train CAP cadets. A total of sixty-four CAP aviators lost their lives during the war ("Civil Air Patrol Story" 2003, 1–2).

Farther inland, Ohio also organized a group of civil defense volunteers. In 1942, the Ohio State Highway Patrol Auxiliary (OSHPA) was formed when many troopers began entering the armed forces, creating a shortage of personnel who could fill the wartime needs of patrolling highways, airports, bridges, defense plants, and military installations. At the time, membership was limited to members of the Ohio American Legion, mostly war veterans who were unlikely to be drafted into the military. The OSHPA's first official meeting for the purpose of organization and enrollment was held in February 1942. By April 1, 1942, 2,650 American Legion members were attending weekly training classes. Members of the new OSHPA were assigned to assist in emergency calls and traffic control. One of the first disasters requiring their assistance occurred on May 31, 1942, when a huge wave from Lake Erie created a great deal of property damage in North Madison. Within an hour, most members of the Lake County unit of the OSHPA were at the scene to aid in rescue and recovery efforts. By 1945, the OSHPA had reached its peak strength of nearly 5,000 members. After the war, it became a critical component of Ohio's civil defense preparation (OSHP Auxiliary 1992).

Walter Spangenberg, a student at Woodrow Wilson High School in Washington, D.C., during World War II, is shown in his Civil Air Patrol uniform at Stevens Airport in Frederick, Maryland, c. 1943 (Library of Congress, Prints and Photographs Division, reproduction number LC-USW3-039504-E DLC)

Not all World War II–era auxiliaries were made up of unpaid civil defense workers; some jurisdictions, for example, employed full-time patrolmen. Under various state laws, however, their services were considered temporary and were terminated as soon as regular officers returned from the military. In San Francisco, twenty-two women were hired to patrol "the streets and bars as part of the Big Sister program" (Schulz 1995, 99). These women routinely checked bars, nightclubs, and other establishments where liquor was sold to prevent minors from entering. The year 1949 saw the termination of these positions after the new civil service position of "women protection officer" was created (Schulz 1995, 99, 107). In the late 1960s, the role of women expanded further as they emerged from their limited social work roles to undertake regular assignments alongside their male counterparts. Although this stands in stark contrast to Alice Stebbins Wells's 1910 experience, when she approached the Los Angeles Police Department with a petition from leading citizens supporting her appointment to the force (Segrave 1995, 13), the path to full equality has been slow.

Another World War II–era organization came into being on July 2, 1942, when the secretary of war ordered civilian plant guards to be designated as members of the Auxiliary Military Police (AMP). By the summer of 1943, about two hundred thousand individuals were enrolled in this program, the secretary's order concerning employees at civilian, municipal, and War Department plants, posts, camps, and stations that were vital to the success of the war effort. The factories affected included not only those that made arms and equipment but also those civilian and municipal facilities essential for power, communications, and transportation. The order's purpose was to increase the authority, efficiency, and responsibility of guard forces at key industrial facilities. It was thought that these guards, if given military training, could provide help in the event of any unforeseen emergency situation during the war (e.g., sabotage, espionage) (Caudry 1981).

The military organization, training, and command of the AMP were the responsibility of the commanding generals of the Service Commands, under the staff supervision of the provost marshal general. Each plant was assigned a member of the military who would act as a "plant guard officer" in command of its AMP unit. The plant guard officer, however, exercised authority through the chain of command established by the management of each plant or post. Each plant's force became a civilian auxiliary to the mil-

Auxiliary Military Police unit, Western Gear Works, Seattle,
Washington, c. 1943 (National Archives and Records Administration)

itary police when three-fourths of its members signed an agreement with
the United States, pledging to defend the Constitution and to discharge
their assigned duties. The signers acknowledged that they had been read
the Articles of War and were now subject to military law. Those refusing to
sign were terminated from their jobs (Caudry 1981).

Each guard wore a uniform provided by the plant, the plant guard officer
deciding whether members of the unit were in the proper uniform. Members were required by the laws of war to wear distinctive insignia or marks
that could be seen at a distance so that their status could be recognized.
This marking took the form of armbands or patches that said "Auxiliary Military Police." Although no ranks were automatically associated with membership, most guard forces did use a system of ranks. Guards attended
one-hour weekly training sessions on such subjects as the Articles of War,

defense against air and paratroop attack, use of weapons, riot control, and tactical problems. Significantly, their quasi-military status did not interfere with their existing method of employment, benefits, and pay: these matters remained primarily within the province of the guards and plant management (Caudry 1981).

Members of the AMP who completed their service with the approval of the War Department were presented with a "Certificate of Meritorious Conduct." Those who resigned without the approval of the War Department were issued a dishonorable discharge. During the course of their service, members could be recommended for the "Medal of Merit," a civilian decoration authorized by the president for outstanding services (Caudry 1981).

The files concerning the AMP, housed at the National Archives and Records Administration in Washington, D.C., contain several pieces of correspondence from local members who were concerned about the exact nature of their authority. It took a long time for this matter to be resolved: in a

A member of the Auxiliary Military Police waiting for a bus in Chattanooga, Tennessee, c. 1943 (Library of Congress, Prints and Photographs Division, Farm Security Administration—Office of War Information Photograph Collection, reproduction number LC-USW3-038067-E DLC)

1981 decision, the Department of Defense Civilian Military Service Review Board determined that the service of AMP members did not entitle them to veterans' benefits (Caudry 1981; Meis 1981). However, the memorandum upon which this exclusion was determined states that "the existence of the Auxiliary Military Police unquestionably removed the pressure for use of combat troops for internal security duties" (Caudry 1981, 1).

Members of AMP units were not the only civil defense volunteers who ultimately felt somewhat overlooked by their countrymen. Perhaps the least remembered homeland defense forces of World War II were the members of state guard organizations. During World War II, the usual stateside missions of the National Guard were conducted by members of the state guard. State guard forces were responsible for maintaining internal security, responding to natural disasters, training at local armories, and marching on public occasions. One likely reason the state guard has been largely forgotten is that the "State Guard looked so much like the National Guard before it entered federal service that most Americans assumed that they were the same thing" (Stentiford 2002, 168–69). Too, former National Guard members released from active duty, or those too old to be eligible for overseas duty, were encouraged to join local state guard units. The presence of these personnel also contributed to the belief that the National Guard, rather than the state guard, was still functioning on the home front (Stentiford 2002, 169–70).

In spite of their lack of recognition, state guard units were indispensable to the war effort. While their members sometimes trained to contend with the threat of an enemy invasion, their primary mission, according to the War Department, was to deal with civil disturbances (e.g., racial violence) and natural disasters (e.g., floods, fires). The Mississippi State Guard, for example, "spent 520 man-days responding to seven separate call-ups for flood emergency duty from 1944 through 1947" and helped prevent racial violence on a number of occasions by keeping "white mobs from lynching black suspects held in custody" (Stentiford 2002, 171, 181). The Ohio State Guard assisted with the enforcement of blackouts in industrial areas. In June 1943, the Texas State Guard prevented the lynching of black prisoners in Beaumont. In Detroit, in April 1942, "several companies of the Michigan State Troops assisted the city police in protecting twenty African-American families that were moving into the federally funded Sojourner Truth

Homes" (Stentiford 2002, 174–75). The Iowa State Guard was twice dispatched in 1945 to the State Training School for Boys in Eldora in order to quell riots. The Virginia State Guard was deployed in 1946 as a "show of force" to help end a strike by power and electrical workers, state guard members and state police working, in this instance, side by side (Stentiford 2002, 188–89). The individual state guards also provided military training for future conscripts: "many former State Guardsmen became NCOs [noncommissioned officers] immediately upon reaching federal training camps, or even received appointments to officer candidate schools" (Stentiford 2002, 172). Forty-four states had created such militias to replace the National Guard since 1916, but by 1947, most states had disbanded their state guard units. No federal recognition of their service was ever forthcoming, even though most of their members were uncompensated and had to use their own personal ration stamps for gasoline and tires to attend weekly drills and other assignments (Stentiford 2002, 189–90, 216). Later, during the Korean War, about a dozen states initiated plans and/or cadre units for the reactivation of their state guard units, but these units "quickly faded away as federal authorization and local concern ended" (Stentiford 2002, 205). Few units ever performed active duty. One that did was the Mississippi State Guard Reserve, whose members assisted in the enforcement of gambling and liquor laws (Stentiford 2002, 204).

Contemporary Volunteer Police Units

The activities of World War II–era state guard and AMP units are seldom recalled today. Indeed, the entire AMP organization is now considered a relic of the past. In most cases, only scattered records of these organizations have survived, while most of their members have grown old and died. Nonetheless, many other varieties of volunteer policing that emerged around this time are still in existence, and new groups have arisen. For example, after World War II and the Korean War, many jurisdictions—for example, Baltimore County, New York City, Denver, and Ohio—continued to maintain their volunteer police units. In addition, in the mid-1960s, the "Keeper Movement"—an entirely new type of volunteer police organization —was initiated in New York State by a coalition of recreational and commercial fishermen who wanted to reclaim the Hudson River from toxic waste. It has since become the leading citizen-based environmental program for policing the nation's waterways. Many volunteer "fire police" units assigned to municipal fire or police departments have also been started since the 1950s, especially in the eastern United States. The National Park Service volunteer program was also well underway by the 1970s.

The extent to which such organizations have become more or less like their professional counterparts varies. Denver's auxiliary police force, for example, has made tremendous progress in achieving assimilation with its parent agency, while others have made only modest gains. The surviving nineteen or so units of the state guard—which might most logically merge with the state police or the National Guard—have been reorganized "to the point of practical dismemberment" (Stentiford 2002, 238, 241). The National Guard, in fact, has impeded attempts by state guard units to take part in "real-world missions" (Stentiford 2002, 240). In 1982, for example, the National Guard Association took the view that such forces were merely state organizations that "could not be brought as units into 'the military service of the United States,' and would not be subject to 'Federal regulation, control, or supervision'"(Stentiford 2002, 218–19).[4] The National Guard, on the other hand, has become part of the military's "Total Force Policy" since the end of the draft in 1973. Under this policy, in times of emergency, all reserve components, including the National Guard, are expected to be fully absorbed "into the Army and Air Force before any new forces are raised" (Stentiford 2002, 214).

Because of their relative success, it is worth examining certain units of auxiliary police in some detail. In the early 1990s, for example, about fifty police reserves were working on the streets of Denver. In addition to undergoing a background investigation, members were required to be twenty-one years of age and to pass written, oral, physical, psychological, medical, and polygraph examinations. After 480 hours of training, they had to work at least one eight-hour shift a month. Their main duty was to handle extra calls for service and to serve as second officers for regular police patrols. During the summer months, they were assigned to patrol city parks (Weinblatt 1993, 118).

New York City in 1992 had nearly 4,400 auxiliaries. Members had to be at least seventeen years of age and were required to attend a training program of about fifty-four hours of instruction spread over sixteen weeks. Members also needed to be able to read and write English, could have no criminal history, and had to either live or work in the city. New York auxiliaries patrol in specially marked vehicles or on foot. Unlike members of the Denver reserves, who will respond to calls for aid, New York City auxiliaries primarily act as the eyes and ears of the police, summoning help by radio when they detect signs of trouble. They wear uniforms like those of regular members of the New York City Police Department, and their tours of duty consist of at least one four-hour assignment each week (Newman 1992). On various occasions, members of the city's auxiliary police have made arrests, and some have even been killed or injured in the line of duty.[5]

The Ohio State Highway Patrol Auxiliary is another World War II–era volunteer organization that is still active today. While active OSHPA membership declined for a short period following the war, enrollment increased as fears related to the Cold War intensified. During the 1950s, the OSHPA helped conduct nuclear-disaster test alerts and other simulated exercises, such as evacuations. Throughout the 1950s and 1960s, the organization's members also helped at crash scenes and other highway traffic incidents (OSHP Auxiliary 1992). Today, 160 men and women, engaged in a wide range of routine patrol duties, serve in the OSHPA. Their average age is forty-five, with eight years of service. Nearly half have one or more years of college. Over one-third are military veterans, and a dozen have been certified as emergency medical technicians (EMTs). About a dozen have completed the entire basic course of training at the police academy ("Profile of the Auxiliary" 1999). Initial training requirements are eighty-two hours. In 1998, a state law concerning reservists' personal immunity from civil liability for damages and limitation of their powers was adopted: "No member of the auxiliary unit shall have any power to arrest any person or to enforce any law of this state" (Ohio Revised Code, sec. 5503.11[A]).

Ohio's, of course, is not the only state-level auxiliary police force. In 1999, OSHPA officer Edwin L. Hyer, a retired sheet-metal worker and U.S. Navy veteran, completed a brief survey of six state police auxiliaries in the United States, including those in Arizona, Florida, New Hampshire, New Mexico, Ohio, and Vermont. Since this survey was conducted, the state of Oregon has also implemented a state police reserve, consisting primarily of retired state police officers and civilian employees. The Arizona state legislature created the Arizona Highway Patrol Reserves in 1956, and by 1985 it in-

THE ASSIMILATION ERA | 169

cluded one hundred unsalaried, fully certified reserve officers. The volunteers are assigned to each of the highway patrol's thirteen regional districts on the basis of each district's needs and each volunteer's residence. Volunteers are required to serve a minimum of sixteen hours per month and obtain the same recertification needed by regular full-time officers. Basic equipment is provided for them, as well as a prorated monthly uniform allowance. Reserve officers perform all the functions of a regular full-time highway patrol officer, except for investigating fatal accidents, since such cases involve such an extensive time commitment (Deitch and Thompson 1985). A full-time officer provides logistical support in each district.

Effective auxiliary police forces also may be found at the county level. Maryland's Baltimore County auxiliary police force was originally formed in 1942 as an arm of the county's civil defense organization. In 1955, the unit was incorporated into the Baltimore County Police Department, and over the last fifty years, its duties and responsibilities have grown in relation to the needs of county residents and workers. Although members of this contemporary volunteer police organization have authority to make arrests, they receive only a modified version of regular police training, consisting of 136 hours of instruction. Members, required to perform a minimum of 160 hours of duty each year, engage in a wide variety of functions, including traffic control, searches for missing persons, and assisting regular officers in calls for service (Baltimore County Police Auxiliary Unit 2003).

Some volunteer policing organizations are not tied to governmental agencies at all; rather, they are linked to the natural environment. The Keeper Movement, for example, has become the Waterkeeper Alliance, an organization that includes more than one hundred separate groups. In 2003, Robert Kennedy Jr. served as the president of the alliance, as well as the chief prosecuting attorney for the Hudson Riverkeeper group. In New York State, a recent addition to the alliance is the Lake George Riverkeeper, begun when the Lake George village board voted to ban personal watercraft from waters under its jurisdiction starting in 2006. Robert Blais, mayor of Lake George, has stated, "You can never have enough people watching out for this great jewel we have here" ("Lake George Watchdog" 2002). In Jacksonville, Florida, another group in the alliance—the St. Johns Riverkeeper—was formed to protect the river that flows directly through the city. The St. Johns Riverkeeper tests the waters of the river's tributaries in order to alert appropriate agencies to pollution problems (Littlepage 2001). Oregon's Tualatin Riverkeeper has a full-time staff of three and nearly five hundred volunteers who engage in public education about the Tualatin River system through a variety of hands-on activities, including paddle trips and wildlife tours. In 2001, the volunteer president of the Tualatin Riverkeeper board of directors was Ron Garst, an employee of the U.S. Fish and Wildlife Service and an expert on marine science and preservation (S. Allen 2001). In South Carolina, the Catawba Riverkeeper organization has a number of covekeeper volunteers who report to the riverkeeper. They are responsible for patrolling assigned sections of the cove once a month and responding to calls on the riverkeeper hotline (Bigham 2001). In 2002, Georgia had five active riverkeeper groups, each responsible for raising its own funds, chiefly from foundation grants and paid memberships, and handling its own legal affairs. When a successful legal action is completed, the legal fees gained can support another case. The original riverkeeper group, the Hudson Riverkeeper, has filed lawsuits against numerous polluters: "The keeper philosophy is based on the notion that the protection and enjoyment of a community's natural resources require the daily vigilance of nearby residents. . . . One of the requirements of using the copyrighted riverkeeper name is that the organization hire a full-time privately funded nongovernmental ombudsperson whose only job is to be an advocate for the river or other water body" (Krueger 2001).

The services of certain kinds of auxiliary forces are necessary only in certain regions of the country. "Fire police," for example, serve in at least ten states. While the title may be unfamiliar to many persons, fire police are widely used in the northeastern and mid-Atlantic regions of the nation, especially in rural areas. Many fire police are former volunteer firefighters who have transitioned to duties that consist primarily of directing vehicle and pedestrian traffic at emergency scenes, enabling other emergency responders to quickly deploy their equipment. The first fully functioning volunteer fire company was established in 1736 through the efforts of Benjamin Franklin, who based his initiative on his knowledge of the Boston Mutual Fire Societies. Franklin's Union Fire Company, however, differed from Boston's early fire-protection societies in a very significant way. In Boston, volunteers only helped put out fires on properties owned by association members; in Philadelphia, the volunteers in Franklin's company responded to any fire call in their area (D. Smith 1978, 12). Fire police function similarly today. In 1998, the Hagerstown, Maryland, fire police, a special unit of twenty auxiliary officer volunteers, served under the police department. They not only responded to fires within the city limits but also provided traffic control at accident scenes, the police department supplying the unit's members with such necessary equipment as uniforms, radios, flashlights, flares, and so on ("WBFD Fire Police History" 2002). In West Babylon, New York, the fire police unit has members from every company in the fire department. The unit was originally formed in 1949, and their duties have changed little over the years: they assist the police with crowd control and security at the scene of an emergency, fire, or auto accident ("WBFD Fire Police History" 2002). From their inception, fire police appear to have been an integral part of their sponsoring agency. According to the qualities outlined in table 1, fire police may be classified as Type III organizations (special purpose/reactive). They have specific functions at emergency scenes (e.g., traffic and crowd control) and respond along with other emergency first responders.

Members of the National Park Service (NPS) Volunteers-in-Parks program also have a very specific function. The primary purpose of the program, authorized in 1970 by Public Law 91-357, is to provide a means through which the NPS can accept and use voluntary help. Volunteers may be recruited without regard for Office of Personnel Management regulations and are provided coverage for tort liability and, if necessary, work-injury compensation. Some of the volunteers' out-of-pocket expenses may also be reimbursed. Over the years of this program's existence, it has grown significantly; it currently involves approximately 125,000 participants, working throughout the country. In 2002, for example, volunteers at Natural Bridges National Monument, near Blanding, Utah, were assigned to help with undercover law enforcement operations. The same year, search-and-rescue volunteers at Grand Canyon National Park assisted over one hundred inner-canyon hikers (NPS 2002, 5, 9–10).[6]

Many thousands of volunteers, of course, serve today in a more traditional capacity, including reserve deputy sheriffs, reserve posse members, and reserve municipal police officers throughout the western, midwestern, and southern regions of the United States. Ohio has the largest number of volunteer officers, with more than eighteen thousand citizens performing a variety of police services, primarily at the local level. In California, which has more than thirteen thousand reserve police officers, the chances are about even, at certain times of the day, that a reservist will respond to a citizen's call for police service, rather than a full-time paid officer. The training of these volunteers has vastly improved overall, and most undergo full background checks. Volunteer reserve police officers in the city of Dallas, for example, attend a 768-hour academy course before qualifying for assignments (Weinblatt 1993). The growth and development of these contemporary organizations were influenced not only by wartime personnel shortages but also by internal population migrations, by an aging America, and most dramatically by such domestic upheavals as the civil rights movement of the 1950s and 1960s.

Indeed, in the late 1960s and early 1970s, volunteer police units were sometimes called upon to assist with unrest caused by protesters. One 1971 case involving volunteer officers in Columbus, Ohio, may help illustrate their role during this turbulent period. When street unrest over the Vietnam War occurred, motor-patrol auxiliary officers were frequently in the middle of the action. On one particular occasion, auxiliary officer Gary Allen, working with regular officer Kelly Arthur, was dispatched to monitor a large hostile crowd, which, along with heavy traffic, had blocked four cruisers and a wagon at Eighteenth Avenue and High Street. Allen and Kelly stopped northbound traffic so the trapped officers could escape, rioters throwing bricks and stones at the two officers while they attempted to control traffic. Fortunately, Officer Allen had purchased a riot helmet at his own expense. This incident helped convince the Columbus Police Department to equip all its auxiliary officers with riot gear (Columbus Police Reserve 2000).

In 1988, the Columbus Auxiliary Police officially became the "Columbus Police Reserve" after the city council determined that a trend had developed regarding the differences between auxiliaries and reserves: most auxiliary units did not possess peace officer powers, whereas Columbus's volunteer police had always been authorized to make on-duty arrests. Moreover, many other volunteer police had already become known as "reserve officers." Columbus police chief James G. Jackson observed that the city's reserve officers "are a valuable part of the Division's effort to combat crime and to make Columbus a better place to live" (Columbus Police Reserve 2000).

In 1975, Los Angeles had about five hundred reserve officers, required to work a minimum of two patrol tours each month. Their training was spread over a seven-month period, with evening and weekend classes for the convenience of the volunteers. By 1992, volunteer reserve police in the city of Los Angeles numbered nine hundred and were saving the city about $4.2 million every year, a sum representing the cost of their services if provided by full-time officers (Hill-Holtzman 1992).

The Los Angeles County Sheriff's Department (LASD) had nineteen hundred reserves in 1975, all required to undergo training similar to that given volunteer reserve police (Hageman 1985). County reserves were mandated to work a minimum of one eight-hour patrol tour each month and were deployed in all stations to supplement regular patrols throughout the unincorporated areas of Los Angeles and in various contract cities. Most reserves worked as the second officer alongside a regular full-time police officer. In some cases, more experienced volunteers were assigned to work as partners or as a single radio motor-patrol unit. Experienced volunteers were also given motorcycle traffic-enforcement duty and were asked to assist with detective work. They were required to serve in mounted units, to work in communications, to take photographs, to guard jails, and to perform mountain rescues (National Advisory Commission on Criminal Justice Standards and Goals 1973). By 2000, the Los Angeles County Sheriff's Department reserve included 720 reservists (see table 3) and 377 Explorers (Los Angeles County Sheriff's Department 2000). LASD reserves today serve in a variety of stations throughout the county. The unit in Crescenta Valley, for example, includes fifteen armed reserve deputies who patrol in marked vehicles, supplemented by additional unarmed volunteers who do vacation checks of temporarily unoccupied homes, participate in limited traffic control during special events, and help enforce the disabled parking law. Several reserve deputies have also been trained to supervise a mobile practice shooting range so that regular deputies can satisfy their mandatory weapons-training requirements. Other reserve officers assist the county's detective bureau with warrant service (G. Berg 2000).

Administered by the Las Vegas Metropolitan Police Department (LVMPD), the LVMDP Search and Rescue Unit was formed in 1986 to provide a technical rescue service to the community of Las Vegas. The unit is on call twenty-four hours a day and responds to the inhabitants of over eight thousand square miles of mountainous desert terrain in Clark County,

Nevada. All members have completed extensive training in such skills as high-angle rope rescue, helicopter operations, desert survival, tracking, land navigation, and emergency medicine. The unit operates by combining several highly specialized groups to complete its missions. The majority of the LVMPD Search and Rescue Unit is composed of over fifty unpaid volunteers. About thirty volunteers make up the bulk of the mountain-rescue team. Mountain-rescue volunteers hold regular jobs in the community, and most maintain their skills outside of the unit as mountaineers, rock climbers, cavers, scuba divers, firefighters, paramedics, and nurses. Each mountain-rescue volunteer is required to maintain minimum certification as a basic EMT in the state of Nevada, although most are trained to higher levels in emergency medicine (LVMPD 2001–5).

Contemporary reserve volunteer police units may also often be found in rural counties. Carter County, Oklahoma, for example, is situated one hundred miles south of Oklahoma City and one hundred miles north of Dallas. On average, each of the county's seventeen reserve deputy sheriffs, who have the same authority as the regular deputy sheriffs, volunteered a total of one hundred hours during 1999. The Oklahoma Council on Law Enforcement Education and Training requires that all reservists successfully complete 120 hours of basic training, as well as a minimum of sixteen hours of annual advanced training (Weinblatt 2001, 31–32). Reserve officers serve in the patrol, jail, and civil-processing divisions. One member is a pilot and flies his own aircraft, while others have special assignments in such fields as communications and cattle-theft investigations. One is the departmental chaplain.

Table 3 LASD Reserve Strength

Uniformed reserves	570
Posses	56
Search-and-rescue teams	94
Total reserves	720

Los Angeles County Sheriff's Department 2000, 2

The members of various small-town reserve units in Arizona must satisfy the regular police officer training requirements established by the Arizona Law Enforcement Officer Advisory Council. In 1985, each was required to attend a reserve academy, offered at a local community college, their curriculum the same as that for regular officers, but scheduled to accommodate the full-time civilian work activities of the reservists. The volunteers' services varied from department to department, because of local needs and agency policies, but their duties included the following (Lesce 1985, 34):

1. Augmentation of the patrol force, either by manning more beats or by operating as the second officer in cars;
2. Providing coverage of wider areas where regular forces are spread too thinly;
3. Working at special events such as parades, festivals, concerts, rodeos, and other sporting events;
4. Helping in emergencies and natural disasters, and participating in search-and-rescue operations;
5. Delivering special services in criminal investigations, crime prevention, and undercover work;
6. Performing administrative assignments involving communications, and record keeping.

As is obvious by now, volunteer police play a vital role in U.S. law enforcement. In 1986, Lt. Frank Woodward of Alabama's Mobile Police Department recognized the importance of reservists, stating, "The reserve law enforcement officer is to his or her community what the military reservist is to our Nation" (1986, 22). The unit that presumably inspired Woodward's enthusiasm, in Mobile, was first organized in 1962; in 1986, it had ninety members, including ten women. All applicants were required to meet the same qualifications as candidates for regular full-time police officer positions. Upon completion of the required academic and firearms courses, conducted at one of the state's certified training academies, reserve officers were assigned to work as the second officer in patrol cars. In order to remain in good standing, reservists were required to contribute at least twenty-four hours of patrol time during a three-month period and to attend all special functions, unless excused (F. Woodward 1986).

The Florida Department of Law Enforcement estimated in 1986 that about fourteen thousand persons were serving as volunteer police officers in Florida. In Tallahassee, Florida's capital, a reserve unit was established that requires its members to complete the same training as regular officers. Tallahassee's volunteers need to be without a criminal history, to have U.S. citizenship, to pass a satisfactory background investigation, and to have two years of college credit. Prospective reserves must also perform satisfactorily in an oral interview, a polygraph exam, a medical exam, and psychological testing. Upon successful completion of the training requirements (a minimum of 360 hours in 1986), members are provided the same uniform and other equipment issued to regular officers. The volunteers also possess the same police powers as regular officers. Studies have shown that while some volunteer police join for a self-serving interest (e.g., maintaining or obtaining police certification), participants also derive an intrinsic sense of satisfaction through fulfillment of their assignments (B. Berg and Doerner 1988, 82–83).

A reserve unit similar to Tallahassee's could be found in Belding, Michigan, in 1986. All Belding applicants are screened as thoroughly as full-time, regular police officers. An extensive background investigation is conducted for each, and selected candidates typically demonstrate strong community roots. The volunteers are trained in basic law enforcement duties, the use of firearms, and emergency medical techniques. In addition to providing extra help during emergencies and special events, Belding reserve officers ride as observers in patrol units, conduct security checks during foot patrols, give safety talks in schools, and direct the Operation Kid Print and Community Child Watch programs. The reserve officers are supervised by a regular full-time officer (Mason 1988).

It is not unusual for volunteer police officers to aspire to full-time law-enforcement work. In 1994, for example, in Paramus, New Jersey, six active reserve members were selected for various full-time police positions ("Paramus Reserve Loses Six" 1995). In 1991, seventy-four members of New York City's auxiliary police force were selected to fill full-time police officer positions (Newman 1992). The reserves in Arizona routinely serve as a pool for regular police candidates (Lesce 1985). In Mobile, in the mid-1980s, "approximately 18 percent of the department's total officer complement and 27 percent of the female officers entered into the regular ranks after serving in the reserves" (F. Woodward 1986, 20).

Community Policing

Contemporary volunteer auxiliary and reserve police represent the epitome of "community policing" by serving to bridge the gap between local community residents and police agencies. In many ways, community policing represents a new paradigm in policing, its outlook regarding police-citizen relationships profoundly different from that of more traditional methods of policing. In considering the key question of who the police are, for example, the traditional view holds that the police are a government agency responsible for law enforcement services. Under the community policing concept, on the other hand, the police are the public, and the public are the police. Police officers are merely those who are paid to give full-time attention to the duties of every citizen (Sparrow 1988). This precise understanding of the nature of the police was initially proclaimed nearly two hundred years ago by the father of modern policing—Sir Robert Peel.

In the United States, the rebirth of the concept of community policing arose from at least three different landmark reports and from the nation's experiences with domestic violence during the 1960s. The first report, that of the Knapp Commission, addressed police corruption in New York City. The second, which appeared in the early 1970s under the direction of the U.S. Department of Justice, involved a nationwide victimization survey that disclosed the fact that many Americans in large cities had a great reluctance to call the police. The third, by the Kerner Commission (officially the National Advisory Commission on Civil Disorders), reinforced the message sent by the urban rioting of the 1960s, indicating that white racism, as the chief cause of urban disorder, greatly contributed to the need for a new style of policing.

At the same time, the 1960s and early 1970s witnessed the initiation of numerous citizen self-defense groups. In Newark, for example, a North Ward Citizens Committee began private patrols. In the orthodox Jewish communities of Brooklyn, the Maccabees Safety Patrol was established (Fogelson 1977, 276–77). In Los Angeles, the Community Alert Patrol of Watts was established. Unlike the first two groups, however, the Watts organization's sole purpose was to observe and document police conduct. In order to accomplish its objectives, the organization's members used cameras and audiotape recorders (Bennett-Sandler 1979). By 1975, it was estimated that more than eight hundred citizen patrols were involved in various functions related to the deterrence of residential crime (Rosenbaum 1989, 208). This trend was exacerbated when, during the 1970s, crime rates increased. Wealthier neighborhoods and individuals contracted with security-guard companies for extra protection and/or installed elaborate alarm systems in their homes or businesses. In 1972, over 1.1 million crime-related security workers were employed in the United States, 429,000 of them privately (Kakalik and Wildhorn 1977, 5).

The concept of "community policing" has not remained static over the years. For example, "a problem-oriented" or "community-oriented" approach to law enforcement has been developed (H. Goldstein 1990). The basic tenets of problem- or community-oriented policing involve the identification of specific neighborhood problems and the development of a plan to address these problems, as well as the implementation of the plan. Feedback is collected to fine-tune operations, each phase of the process involving appropriate community representatives. The effectiveness of the police role in the process is measured in terms of the degree to which public cooperation and satisfaction are achieved. Since so much of this strategy involves communication with the public, it has come to be known simply as "community policing." Some police scholars refer "to community policing as the philosophy and problem-oriented policing as an analytical tool to deal with the causes of crime" (Thibault, Lynch, and McBride 1998, 211). In 1998, the federal government specifically defined community policing as "an operational philosophy for neighborhood problem-solving in which officers interact with residents on an ongoing basis regarding matters of public concern" (Office of National Drug Control Policy 1998, 35). Since its inception, police officials and policy analysts have varied in their views about whether community policing must involve all members of an agency or merely part of an agency.

In spite of such controversies, however, during the 1990s, many innovations in police work were made under the banner of community policing. For example, neighborhood service teams were established in Garland, Texas, each consisting of personnel from the police and fire departments, the planning department, and housing and neighborhood services. Citizens were then asked to identify problems. The residents of an apartment complex near an elementary school worried about drug activity. In response, the Garland Police Department and other team members achieved a 25 percent reduction in serious crime when they adopted a zero-tolerance enforcement approach, enforced criminal trespass laws, and evicted drug offenders. In addition, code enforcement officials were recruited to assist in making certain that needed housing improvements were made (Thibault, Lynch, and McBride 1998, 207).

Yet another manifestation of the move toward community policing involves the identification of "hot spots": locations that make heavy demands on police due to frequent and repetitious calls for service (Sherman, Gartin, and Buerger 1989). In Jersey City, officials discovered that drug hot spots, which made up just 4.4 percent of the points on the city's map, accounted for 86 percent of the city's drug arrests involving sales. Conditions improved at some of these locations after police met with area residents and instituted close surveillance, foot patrols, and other forms of police presence. The project evaluation concluded that it is best to concentrate attention on a few locations in order to conserve police resources (Thibault, Lynch, and McBride 1998, 209–10).

One of the most well-known illustrations of the community policing initiative for reducing drug-related crime involved the fulfillment of a campaign pledge made by President Bill Clinton. Under his administration, the U.S. Department of Justice created the Community Oriented Policing Services program (COPS). Its dramatic goal was to add one hundred thousand new police officers to the town and city streets of America for the express purpose of reinforcing efforts to reduce drug-related crime and violence. In President Clinton's message accompanying submission of the 1998 National Drug Control Strategy to Congress, he made reference to the COPS program, indicating that such efforts were "making a difference: violent crime in America has dropped dramatically for 5 years in a row" (Office of National Drug Control Policy 1998, iii).

In another manifestation of community policing, Boston began to implement "Operation Ceasefire," designed to deter and control gang-related violence, in 1995. The plan was developed by the Boston Gun Project Working Group in accordance with the principles of problem-solving policing. In 1997, Operation Ceasefire received an award from the John F. Kennedy School of Government at Harvard University. Similar operations have been used in Lowell, Massachusetts, and Minneapolis, Minnesota.

On the whole, such initiatives have been largely successful. An interim report on community policing, for example, concludes that cooperation between the police and citizens creates a feeling of security among neighborhood residents. The police supervisor's role, the report also states, had changed from controlling officers to supporting them (Mastrofski, Parks, and Worden 1998).

Today, in some jurisdictions, further refinement of community policing is occurring as a result of the "Compstat" management process. Many feel that this recent innovation is invaluable: "police problem solving activities," one author concludes, "are certainly nowhere as refined, as focused, or as successful, as in the NYPD under the Compstat model" (V. F. Henry 2002, 109). "Compstat," which stands for "computer comparison statistics," is "a management process through which the NYPD identifies problems and measures the results of its problem-solving activities. Compstat involves [weekly] meetings between executives and managers and . . . uses computer-based technology," along with many other devices and processes, to shape a comprehensive response to crime (V. F. Henry 2002, 5). As this new approach becomes more widely implemented by police agencies, it may usher in an entirely new era of professional police service. While Compstat technology is highly affordable, the potential of its overall implementation as a new management tool has been grasped by only a handful of agencies. In any case, its success is dependent "on the commitment, experience, . . . and integrity of those who put it in to practice" (V. F. Henry 2002, 313).

The Assimilation Era in Retrospect

Innovations such as community policing initiatives and Compstat may seem far removed from the World War II–era deployment of state guards units designed to provide backup when National Guard units were called to active duty. Nonetheless, the remnants of the state guard that remain stand ready for a new homeland-defense role should units of the National Guard become federalized. These units and the National Guard itself are inheritors of America's militia tradition. After September 11, 2001, many National Guard units were activated for stateside sentry duty at strategic locations; others were sent overseas to combat terrorism and to fight in Afghanistan and Iraq. Members of the state guards and/or the National Guard engaged in maintaining local order and relief work may be classified as Type III volunteer police forces (special purpose/reactive).

At the beginning of the twenty-first century, however, most adult volunteer police units are of either the auxiliary or the police reserve variety. Such organizations may be classified as Type I organizations (general purpose/reactive). They are affiliated and supervised by a police agency and perform a variety of police functions. In addition, they are generally nonaggressive in nature, for several reasons: (1) they perform subordinate and supplementary roles in the host agency (e.g., as a second officer in a patrol car); (2) they are more likely to be assigned service-oriented roles (e.g., traffic control, acting as a regular officer's "eyes and ears"); and (3) their limited, once-a-week tours of duty, as well as their full-time jobs, tend to inhibit their participation in such aggressively planned initiatives as sting operations.

Nevertheless, while the majority of volunteer police appear to be merely reactive, performing peacekeeping patrols in urban neighborhoods and/or assisting in traffic control at special events, there are some Type II organizations (general purpose/proactive). In recent years, for example, a special group of experienced volunteer deputies in Houston, Texas, has been active in Precinct 6. Their commitment to law enforcement work has resulted in the arrest of over two thousand parole violators. Other Precinct 6 volunteer deputies help reduce truancy rates by initiating family visits (Claiborne 1994). In Honolulu, reservists may be assigned to plainclothes assignments after five years of service. Moreover, a growing number of reserve units in the West may be classified as Type II organizations because of their full-service police assignments. The trend in these jurisdictions is for selection procedures and training requirements for reserves to be the same as those for regulars (Gill and Mawby 1990, 67, 69).

The activities of members of the Waterkeeper Alliance should be closely observed for future trends. While most organizations in the alliance appear to be Type III organizations (special purpose/reactive), any greater involvement in the prosecution of pollution cases is indicative of a distinctive proactive agenda, or of a Type IV volunteer police group (e.g., the Hudson Riverkeeper). It can certainly be argued that the preservation of America's rivers, lakes, bays, canals, and watersheds is deserving of such nongovernmental initiatives when no other entity is willing to enforce the law. Similar reasoning was used by the Anti-Saloon League over one hundred years ago with respect to the enforcement of local prohibition laws. So long as laws exist in support of the environment, riverkeeper organizations will surely exist. The assimilation of these groups, however, with governmental agencies is not likely to occur in the foreseeable future unless the relevant federal and state environmental departments become much more involved and interested in the services of volunteers.

Participants in the NPS Volunteers-in-Parks program are mostly responsible for non–law enforcement duties. In 2002, however, the National Park Service reported that 6 percent of park volunteers had assignments involving protection (NPS 2002, 40), while at least one national park uses volunteers for undercover law enforcement operations. Thus, a small segment of NPS volunteers could be considered Type III (special purpose/reactive) or Type IV (special purpose/proactive) volunteer police. Numerous states, counties, and cities have volunteer reserve park rangers. The park system in Glendale, California, for example, routinely seeks the services of volunteer reserve park rangers. Their duties are to maintain the peace of the parks and to eject or detain for arrest individuals whose actions are endangering life or property ("Reserve Park Ranger" 2002). Such volunteer ranger programs have specific police functions and thus can be readily considered Type III volunteer police organizations.

Community policing, the mobilization of citizen groups, and the trend for volunteer police to undertake general-purpose policing with either limited (Type I) or full (Type II) police authority characterized the last half of the twentieth century. In more recent years, however, significant riverkeeper, park ranger, and NPS volunteer programs with special-purpose responsibilities (Types III and IV) have emerged. CAP, the U.S. Coast Guard Auxiliary, and other units are also playing revised roles in contending with the needs of homeland security. Thus, while a major characteristic of the last fifty years has been the tendency toward assimilation, more and more local volunteer police units becoming completely absorbed by their hosts, new trends may develop as a result of current events. Nevertheless, at least from 1951 to 2001, assimilation has dominated. In other words, organizations that were once independent (e.g., existing as an arm of civil defense) have merged with regular forces, the major differences between the two groups being salaries, benefits, and duty hours. This was clearly the case in Columbus, Denver, and New York. In many instances, reserve units have even been given full police powers, especially in the western part of the United States.

For its part, the National Guard was completely assimilated into the federal military establishment from 1917 through 1922, and again from late 1940 to 1947. Sizable contingents of National Guard troops also saw action during the Korean War; the Berlin Crisis of 1961; the first war with Iraq (1990–91); and the current global war on terrorism, with American forces occupying both Iraq and Afghanistan. Today, state governors "hold command over their states' National Guard only when the federal government permits it" (Stentiford 2002, 242). On the other hand, since the end of World War II and the Cold War, the role of the state guards has been marginal. Nevertheless, these organizations stand ready to engage in local missions that may be unsuitable for the National Guard (Stentiford 2002, 243).

Viable assignment opportunities for state or local units of volunteer police have always been subject to the more powerful influence of other groups. America's unique political system has certainly played a role in the spread and decline of volunteer police groups. The evolution of the volunteer police has also been affected by the development of powerful police unions. In the eastern United States, during the nineteenth century and for about the first half of the twentieth century, either there were no police unions or they never reached their full potential. Consequently, civil service benefits were minimal. Thus, in many jurisdictions, the regular police had less to lose and more to gain from the activities of volunteer police. For example, if charity workers in New York City had not been authorized to aid homeless families in the city and remove beggars from the streets, the responsibility and burden would have rested entirely on the police. During the post–World War II period, however, the power wielded by police unions began to grow. Throughout the 1950s and the Vietnam era, the opposition of police unions, which pressured elected officials, played a key role in limiting the deployment of volunteer police units in the eastern part of the nation. Union officials are concerned that part-time workers will replace full-time workers. The fact that many of these part-time volunteer workers are willing to perform police functions without being paid is highly suspicious to some regular police officers. Thus, union leadership may be strongly motivated to keep the use of free police workers to a minimum (M. A. Greenberg 1984).

In recent years, concern among regular police agencies regarding professionalism has also affected the evolution of volunteer police groups. August Vollmer, the principal architect of the professional model of policing, proposed a model of police professionalism with at least six key attributes: (1) rigorous training, (2) dedication, (3) use of the latest science and technology, (4) community involvement, (5) high standards of conduct, and (6) separation from politics. To a large extent, volunteer police have benefited from the movement toward police professionalism and the development of new accreditation standards for America's police. According to these professional standards, if police agencies want their volunteers to assume full police duties, they must train them in the same manner as regular police. Currently, this assimilatory trend in training volunteer police is particularly strong in the western United States. On the other hand, in several jurisdictions (e.g., Kansas City and Connecticut), the new training standards have been used as the principal justification for phasing out the use of existing volunteer police units. A few police administrators have stated either that they do not have the financial resources to provide the necessary volunteer training or that they doubt that volunteers will be willing to devote themselves to the longer training requirements. In spite of the fact that the leaders of various volunteer police benevolent associations generally disagree with the latter statement, the new accreditation standards, used as an excuse to justify the discontinuance of volunteer police, have benefited regular police union leaders in some jurisdictions in their quest to limit volunteer services.

During the last decade of the twentieth century, the growth of the Internet not only vastly contributed to the American economy but provided a unique opportunity for hundreds of volunteer police organizations to share information about their activities. No doubt, this new source of information may serve as a catalyst for the creation of new units or the greater assimilation of older ones. At the same time, public awareness of such units should help increase membership. Volunteer police organizations may thus be better able to draw on the vast talents and energies of the American citizenry without regard to the color and gender bars of previous eras. As part of this process, such basic democratic organizational attributes as consensus building, community participation in government, and equality of opportunity should grow.

The existence of community crime-prevention programs, with hundreds of thousands of participants, has provided citizens with new opportunities to participate in their own governance, and participation is the hallmark of the democratic process. While the Internet and cable television (especially C-SPAN) have greatly contributed to the spread of knowledge about governmental institutions and the democratic process, the impetus for the development of many newer citizen anticrime groups was the funding provided by two federal initiatives more than a generation ago: 1977's Community Anti-Crime Program and 1980's Urban Crime Prevention Program. These initiatives "provided funds directly to community organizations (rather than law enforcement) to help mobilize neighborhood residents in the fight against crime" (Rosenbaum 1989, 204). Unfortunately, such direct funding sources are no longer available.

More than two decades ago, researchers from Northwestern University concluded that participation in organized neighborhood anticrime activities is more often motivated by "civic-mindedness" than by fear of crime (Rosenbaum 1989, 208). In the last decade of the 1990s, volunteer service again entered the vocabulary of Americans when Gen. Colin Powell, the former chairman of the Joint Chiefs of Staff, became the chief spokesperson for volunteer service in America. Powell, who later served as President George W. Bush's first secretary of state, helped inspire the creation of a network of volunteer programs to assist at-risk youths with tutoring, mentoring, and other services (Alter 1997, 28–30). Overall civic participation, however, has been declining for thirty years. The "baby boomers," for example, are arguably not nearly as committed to their communities as were the members of the generation of Americans who came of age during and immediately after World War II (Putnam 2000). Nonetheless, the "baby-boomers and their progeny still have many years ahead of them in which to deepen their civic commitments" (Lenkowsky 2000, 57).

7

Potential Roles for Volunteer Police Service

Probably no single step would provide more immediate and more appreciable benefits for improving police effectiveness than the creation of auxiliaries on a neighborhood basis throughout our large cities.

George E. Berkley, *The Democratic Policeman*

The growth and development of the United States during the past two hundred years have been extraordinary. Its metropolitan centers of commerce, industry, and technology have made it the greatest economic and military power on the planet. Expanded cities and commercial opportunities, however, have also reduced interest in performing traditional roles involving communal responsibility for public safety. By the nineteenth century, for example, few bankers and merchants could afford to take the time off to join a posse or engage in the watch and ward (Bard and Shellow 1976, 7). Initially, such persons of means chose to absorb the fines or hire substitutes when called upon to serve as constables, watchmen, or patrollers. Sometimes other arrangements were made, such as providing for reimbursement of the riders of the anti-horse-thief and detective societies through the establishment of a common pool of funds. Today, it is considered sufficient by many persons to pay taxes and leave security matters to civil servants. In addition, many condominium dwellers and persons who live in gated communities pay a surcharge for private security services. Although neighborhood watch groups have become more common in recent years, a 1998 nationwide survey of twelve cities found a greater percentage of neighbors investing in guns, dogs, and locks for protection. The watch groups appear to be short-lived, waning "after an initial burst of enthusiasm, unless rooted in neighborhood associations of a more comprehensive sort" (Putnam 2000, 107).

Volunteer police organizations tend to be of a permanent nature and are most often attached to more comprehensive agencies. Moreover, their assimilation into larger agencies may make possible a variety of new roles for police administrators to consider regarding the recruitment, selection, training, and deployment of volunteer police. The current contributions of volunteer police with respect to community participation in government, consensus building, and equal opportunity represent a few of the basic features of a strong democratic society. Today, minority-group members have an almost limitless opportunity to enroll in various volunteer police programs.

In the past, the recruitment and training of volunteer police were an important aspect of homeland security. This can be true again in the future. Such volunteers may also provide additional resources for assisting troubled youth in urban neighborhoods and addressing a wide variety of other community needs. Time may be running out for this aspect of community participation, however. Today, working more to keep up with the rising cost of living and support their families, people are often too busy to consider volunteer work. Big Brother and Sister programs in most communities, for example, are in desperate need of volunteers, as are many volunteer fire departments (Hipp 2000).

We live in a fast-paced world where many city dwellers lead almost anonymous lives. The urban environment is filled with a constant hum: emergency vehicles blasting their sirens, car alarms incessantly ringing, taxis honking, personal communication devices (beepers, cellular phones, iPods) contributing their tones intermittently. While the urbanite may thus often pay little attention to the presence of responding police cars or other types of emergency vehicles, such devices as cellular phones, video cameras, and satellite positioning systems have made an impact on public safety and police response. For example, an incident of police misconduct on a public street at three p.m. in any large U.S. city raises the possibility that it might be videotaped and viewed by millions of people within a few hours. This knowledge probably acts as a deterrent to such misconduct. However, whereas the recording of events by the public is not easily subject to police scrutiny and control, the enrollment of numerous volunteer police is primarily a matter of police initiative.

Volunteers are needed today to help with the difficult task of working with at-risk youth, as well as the equally perplexing problem of substance abuse. They may also help decrease the occurrence of modern-day forms of slavery.

Role in Delinquency Prevention

The Columbine High School massacre, along with other incidents of school violence at the end of the twentieth century, greatly alarmed the American public. Ideas for addressing the perennial problem of juvenile delinquency and its prevention have ranged from imposing longer sentences on youthful offenders to creating more nurturing home and school environments. Frequently omitted from the lists of such recommendations is the idea of making greater use of new or existing units of volunteer police. In 1969, theorist George Berkley proposed establishing auxiliary police units in the schools, recommending that "schoolboys indicating a flair for leadership" could be used to head up such programs.[1] Berkley further declared that "the police should encourage the ancient democratic idea of every citizen treating infractions of the law and the abuse of others as his own concern" (208).

The use of student hall patrol monitors was quite common from the 1920s through the 1970s. Patrol organizations at the junior- and senior-high levels, once major assets to schools, directed hall traffic, kept order while students were changing classes, and saw that school rules were obeyed. Beginning in 1938 in Stevens Point, Wisconsin, for example, the P. J. Jacobs High School established a police cadet organization, functioning under a detailed constitution that listed the duties and powers of the cadets (Bannach 1941, 353).

By adopting another model of crime prevention (see Brantingham and Faust 1976), adult volunteer police could be used in at least three ways to help with delinquency prevention. Volunteers could reduce the environmental and social conditions that provide opportunities for delinquent acts, could focus on factors and individuals that appear to be most closely linked to delinquency activities, and could confront the issues and problems of known delinquents.

Considering this model, volunteer police could probably make their greatest contributions by augmenting efforts to deal with the environmental and social conditions that foster delinquency. They could be trained to conduct security surveys, checking, for example, for adequate lighting, locks, and appropriate levels of access control. Volunteers could help recruit and train neighborhood watch groups and increase the general level of crime deterrence by their presence on routine patrols. Volunteer police could also be used to deliver presentations to community groups on how citizens can be safe from crime. It has been suggested that "the potential impact of neighborhood watch and community crime prevention is untested in the areas . . . where the greatest margin for change exists. It is in these areas where engendering participation is most challenging" (Lab 2000, 70).

Specialized volunteer police units could also be trained and recruited for staffing a variety of other delinquency control programs. For example, they could help organize and staff after-school recreational centers and youth leagues. Volunteers trained in crowd control techniques could be used as additional security personnel at events or locations that attract large numbers of young people, for example, school functions (e.g., dances, sporting events), parking lots adjacent to convenience stores or shopping malls, parks, and concerts.

Volunteers may also help young people in less direct ways. For example, custodial parents are often unable to collect child support, despite the issuance of court orders and even arrest warrants. Some jurisdictions have not pursued nonpayers vigorously because they lack available enforcement personnel. Volunteer police could be used to assist regular police in tracking down such "deadbeat" parents. In light of increasing school violence, volunteer police could monitor school metal detectors and surveillance cameras. In order to better cope with gun violence, volunteers could help process gun registrations and administer amnesty periods during which weapons could be voluntarily surrendered without penalty.

Volunteer police may also aid in the primary prevention of delinquency by augmenting the human resources available for helping children in foster care. Children's Rights, a national advocacy organization, has won various court-ordered changes in foster-care systems throughout the nation, pointing out the harmful effects of keeping children in emergency shelters over long periods and moving children from one foster home to another (Yellin 2000). Volunteer police could help monitor foster-care placements and assist in the search for adoptive parents. Such innovations would require regular police administrators to meet with their counterparts in family service agencies. If it were determined that additional help was needed, volunteer police could be recruited and trained for the appropriate assignments.

A secondary type of prevention, according to the model discussed earlier, focuses efforts on those persons most likely to engage in acts of delinquency, as well as on those places or situations that tend to create an opportunity for such activities (Brantingham and Faust 1976). Police volunteers could also prove highly useful in this effort. Under the supervision of school social workers, volunteers could be assigned to review attendance records and make constructive contacts with students who have dropped out or are at risk of doing so. They could help in the provision of job-placement services for youth. In neighborhoods known for high rates of delinquency, volunteer police could operate storefront police mini-stations. Volunteers could also be assigned to patrol areas where young people commonly commit quality-of-life offenses (e.g., vandalism, graffiti).

Although many states have adopted gun-free and drug-free school zones, laws forbidding the possession of firearms and controlled substances in or near schools are difficult to enforce. The assignment of volunteer police to these areas could discourage such crimes. Clearly, for example, persons loitering in cars or on foot near schools or playgrounds should be placed under surveillance to help deter any possible exploitation of young persons.

Volunteer police units in jurisdictions with established curfew laws could also help with curfew enforcement. They could help locate runaways and assist social workers and police in ascertaining whether runaway children may be safely returned to their homes or are in need of other types of assistance.

Telephone hotlines and/or Internet chat rooms for aiding runaways, depressed young people, battered persons, or other individuals facing crises could also be staffed by qualified members of a volunteer police unit. An alarm device similar to a telephone pager is now available for use by battered parents and children. It can be easily worn and used to alert authorities of an abuse situation or other emergency. Volunteers could be assigned to explain the purpose of such devices, train persons in their use, monitor them, and arrange for the appropriate response.

Secondary delinquency prevention may also be achieved through programs that offer constructive alternatives for persons who might otherwise be inclined to engage in violence. The School of Public Health at Harvard University is in the forefront of the movement to teach mediation and conflict-resolution techniques to youngsters (Bouza 1993). Volunteer police could play a major role in the expansion of conflict-resolution efforts by helping to train more teachers, parents, and youth in these techniques. Using ordinary citizens and teens to mediate disputes builds community cohesion, and evaluations of dispute-resolution programs have been generally favorable, since they appear to divert a large number of cases from the formal justice system (Lab 1992).

In the model discussed earlier, tertiary prevention efforts are directed toward known offenders in an attempt to ensure that they will not repeat their crimes (Brantingham and Faust 1976). Volunteer police could be of value to many of the understaffed and overworked agencies of the juvenile justice system that deal with offenders (e.g., probation, family courts, community-based treatment or diversion programs). Volunteers could serve as additional court security personnel and help escort crime victims and others to and from court. They could help investigate various family court cases (e.g., delinquency, status offenses, abuse, custody, visitation) and serve in other capacities to assist juvenile probation officers with their caseloads. Volunteer police, for example, could help supervise community-service requirements, such as graffiti removal. They could also help coordinate local prison trips for youth under court supervision.

Volunteer police could also play a role in the Compstat process by helping to compile the program's weekly report—a preliminary count of crimes committed throughout a particular community. The Compstat report "is intended as an early warning system that alerts police managers and executives to rapidly changing conditions and allows them to deploy and reallocate resources in response to those conditions," giving each local commander the ability to know "exactly where his or her command stands in relation to all others" (V. F. Henry 2002, 250, 251). In this way, the Compstat report could augment a community's efforts to control delinquency and other types of crime.

As discussed earlier, the use of volunteers of all kinds received a boost in the 1990s when Colin Powell, the first African American to serve as chair of the Joint Chiefs of Staff, was selected by former president George H. W. Bush to lead a national campaign involving citizen volunteer work: "America's

Promise—the Alliance for Youth." Powell is thought of as a charismatic and inspiring leader who might have been anything he chose, from an enormously rich corporate CEO to president of the United States (Raspberry 2000). Born in the Harlem section of Manhattan to immigrant parents from Jamaica, Powell grew up on the rough streets of the South Bronx, later becoming a military adviser to three presidents. As a national spokesperson for volunteering in the United States, then, Powell was tremendously effective. The cover of a 1997 issue of *Newsweek,* for example, shows a color photograph of Powell, wearing a business suit and posed with his right index finger pointing at the reader. Below his finger is the large caption "I WANT YOU." The issue features a ten-page series of articles about the nature of corporate charitable contributions and Powell's plan to mobilize corporate America, the public, and the nonprofit sector for the sake of the nation's at-risk youth (i.e., children who come from poor and often dysfunctional families) (see Alter 1997, 28–30).

Role in Narcotics Control

There have been numerous other recent innovations aimed toward reducing substance abuse. Street drug-enforcement programs, for example, involve increasing police personnel hours and interagency cooperation for the purpose of narcotics control, placing emphasis on the identification of sellers, users, and crack houses, as well as the development of tactical plans and operations in order to make arrests or obtain court orders for property seizures. Special tactics include saturation patrols; "Trojan Horse" runs (undercover buys made by means of a van or similar conveyance); and "reverse sting" operations, in which undercover officers pose as drug dealers. Law-enforcement agencies may pool their resources and create joint narcotics task forces to generate the necessary intelligence to locate and identify the purchasers and sellers of illegal drugs. Such programs have been carried out in both urban and suburban areas. For example, both Lynn, Massachusetts (population eighty thousand), and New York (population over seven million) have instituted specific street drug-enforcement programs that have resulted in substantial increases in narcotics arrests (Hayeslip 1989).

While this strategy may at first sound punitive in scope, and therefore inconsistent with the role befitting modern volunteer police, it is aimed at providing "the breathing room that might enable a stricken community to re-gain enough sense of security to begin to work effectively on its larger prob-lems" (Currie 1994, 204). Indeed, it has been argued that "what drug ridden communities most need is help in protecting their residents from victimiza-tion by highly visible and volatile drug dealing and by the crime and violence that pervades street drug culture. Making the reduction of violence and open drug dealing our first priority could both save lives and reduce the fear that now paralyzes many poor neighborhoods" (Currie 1994, 204).

Volunteer police personnel recruited from the same communities expe-riencing extensive amounts of drug abuse could effectively assist police departments engaged in drug-enforcement strategies by (1) providing de-tailed information about the location of street sales and the identification of sellers; (2) staffing drug hotlines to obtain additional information about drug sales and providing treatment information to drug users; (3) augment-ing the resources needed to carry out civil procedures for the proper imple-mentation of asset seizures (e.g., crack houses); (4) where laws so provide, conducting field investigations for any applicants seeking gun ownership; (5) assisting in the enforcement of building and fire codes; and (6) main-taining crime-prevention building patrols within every housing project (public or private) where concern exists about drug-related crime.

Police sweeps and other types of street drug-enforcement efforts may be short-lived or otherwise come to lose their deterrence effect over time. Such initiatives, therefore, should be coupled with longer-term strategies, which may be developed through "problem-oriented" policing. Under this approach, police identify problem areas and collect and analyze relevant data as the first step in developing prevention or enforcement strategies. The compilation of local and regional crime statistics and trends is funda-mental to this effort. In addition, police may conduct periodic surveys of residents in order to learn about community problems and the effective-ness of policing strategies. Such studies commonly lead to the determina-tion that a community needs improved educational, medical, daycare, housing, and/ or recreational facilities.

In Houston, Mayor Lee P. Brown broadened this concept when he was the city's police chief, referring to it as "neighborhood-oriented policing." The basis for his approach was the belief that the war against drugs can be successful only through community involvement. Brown listed four distinctive steps necessary to fulfill his strategy: (1) developing a partnership between the people of each neighborhood and the police, (2) identifying local problems, (3) forming joint solutions, and (4) jointly carrying out the activities necessary to resolve the problems (L. P. Brown 1988).

One of the most well-known examples of problem-oriented policing emerged from the Boston Gun Project's planning phase. Key members of the planning team were selected from the Boston Police Department's gang unit, the departments of probation and parole, the U.S. attorney's and county prosecutor's offices, the office of the state attorney general, school police, youth corrections, and social services. Together, they created "Operation Ceasefire," a program that involves two types of enforcement strategies: direct assaults on illicit firearms markets and a "pulling every lever" approach when violence erupts. A central goal of the project is to deter chronic offenders from committing further acts of violence. Thus, the "pulling levers" strategy is designed to send a direct message to gang members that crime is costly. Team members first meet with gangs around the city, visit detention facilities, and speak to school assemblies, informing these groups that the city is not going to put up with violence any longer and that if the warning isn't heeded an overwhelming crackdown will be delivered on gang activities. Consequences (levers pulled) might include strict enforcement of trespassing and public-drinking statutes, serving outstanding warrants, cultivating confidential informants, delivering strict probation and parole supervision, seizing drug proceeds and other assets, seeking higher bail, focusing prosecutorial attention on all gang-related crimes, and even possibly adding sanctions from federal enforcement agencies (e.g., the Bureau of Alcohol, Tobacco, and Firearms; the Drug Enforcement Administration; the Immigration and Naturalization Service). Boston's program was successful because gang members discovered that the team was credible: it was actually able to deliver the promised responses. In addition, communication was maintained with targeted gangs as the strategy unfolded, the members of the program regularly meeting to assess progress and select appropriate responses. Operation Ceasefire could be implemented with respect to other crime problems, such as street drug markets (Braga, Kennedy, Piehl, and Waring 2001).

Volunteer police personnel could play an integral role in a program like Operation Ceasefire, not only carrying out appropriate surveys and other forms of data collection but also staffing local task forces whose object is to obtain any needed resources for the community. Moreover, they could serve as the primary liaison between police and neighborhood residents, especially during the critical partnership-development phase of planning. Volunteer police units composed primarily of local residents would be ideal for this purpose, especially in those communities suffering from a breakdown in police-community relations. In a program like Operation Ceasefire, well-trained volunteers could also protect and assist those gang members seeking to become reintegrated into community life.

Preventing children and adolescents from joining gangs is probably the most cost-effective strategy for drug abatement. In the United States, the number of cities with youth gang problems increased from an estimated 286 cities in 1980, with more than 2,000 gangs and nearly 100,000 gang members, to about 4,800 cities in 1996, with more than 31,000 gangs and approximately 846,000 members (Howell 1998, 1). In response to this astounding growth, the Bureau of Alcohol, Tobacco and Firearms (ATF) implemented a school-based gang-prevention curriculum known as Gang Resistance Education and Training (GREAT). Initial evaluation of GREAT has shown positive results. Students who completed the program, for example, reported lower levels of gang affiliation and delinquency, including drug use, minor offending, property crimes, and crimes against persons (Esbensen and Osgood 1997).

While volunteer police could be used to expand the delivery of GREAT and related youth curriculums, it must be emphasized that the results of evaluations of strictly educational programs often turn out to be less than desirable. In 1994, for example, a review of eight previous studies involving DARE (the well-known educational program) concluded that it was not as effective as had been previously believed. Moreover, the studies questioned the use of law enforcement personnel as program teachers, noting that there had been no studies on whether this is an effective use of police personnel (Abadinsky 1997, 213). In a related example, researchers at the Johns Hopkins School of Public Health reported in 1999 that driver education classes do not appear to produce safer drivers. After a careful examination of several previous studies, they could find no evidence that teenagers who enrolled in the classes had fewer accidents or committed fewer traffic infractions than those who did not attend such classes. Moreover, they indicated that these types of classes might actually be contributing to the nation's accident problem by putting more younger drivers on the road ("Classes Don't Make Drivers Safer" 1999).

A third approach, known as citizen-oriented policing, directly seeks to harness the talents and experiences of local residents in order to decrease crime. The support of community groups is sought for tougher laws, clean-up projects, and more jails. In Seattle, for example, citizens were encouraged to set up their own drug hotline (Hayeslip 1989).

One of the most popular citizen-oriented policing strategies has been the establishment of neighborhood watch programs. One of the earliest of these was the citywide "Home-Alert" organization in Oakland, California. Its objective was to provide protection through participation and cooperation, with each member of the group agreeing to observe and report any suspicious behavior occurring in the neighborhood. Information about the Home-Alert program was spread through mass mailings, newspaper articles, television, and the publication of a monthly newsletter to keep members informed of crime conditions and prevention activities. Within six months, more than one thousand groups were active in Oakland (Whisenand 1977).

Unfortunately, the success of many efforts to harness the latent energies of community members has often been brief. In some instances, block meetings have been held and special street signs erected proclaiming the existence of a neighborhood watch, although in reality the group existed merely in name, rather than fact. In Minneapolis, the police department tried to maintain interest in a watch program by having police go door-to-door to chat with community residents about local crime conditions, but only a few officers actively participated (Sherman n.d.).

Some hotline programs have been unsuccessful because people fear adverse consequences if they report a crime to the police. They fear that they may be arrested (especially if they are undocumented aliens) or victimized through retaliation if they are identified. Nevertheless, most police agencies heavily rely on tips provided by informants to control all forms of vice.

Throughout the 1990s, the Office of Juvenile Justice and Delinquency Prevention (OJJDP), within the U.S. Department of Justice, developed and funded a variety of programs ranging from working with high-risk youth in public housing projects to helping communities fight the growing violence of youth gangs. Many of these programs involve training for law enforcement agents and others concerned with the coordination and daily operation of the various segments of the juvenile justice system. Many also feature elements consistent with the attributes of citizen-oriented policing (Munson 1988).

The use of volunteer police personnel would appear to be a natural component of a citizen-oriented strategy for reducing crime associated with drug abuse. Conceivably, many of the frustrations that police have encountered with regard to community organization might be alleviated by having auxiliaries serve as their bridge to community groups. Yet volunteer police are entirely omitted from a prominent summary of local-level drug enforcement strategies, as well as OJJDP initiatives (Hayeslip 1989). Moreover, there is not a single reference to volunteer police in the ten-year strategy for controlling drugs set forth in *National Drug Control Strategy, 1998,* a guide authored by the Office of National Drug Control Policy (1998). Nevertheless, using units of either reserve or auxiliary police would appear to be an ideal approach to trying to cope with the demand side of the drug crisis. Following are sixteen specific recommendations regarding the use of volunteer police in narcotics control:

1. Making presentations to children and their parents about the nature of drugs;
2. Providing reassurance to potential informants and other tipsters about the confidentiality of their communications to police hotlines;
3. Serving as role models for at-risk youth;
4. Providing crisis intervention in community and recreational programs that seek to divert youth from drug use and sales;
5. Holding forums to give diverse sections of the community the opportunity to share concerns about local drug problems;
6. Providing leadership for participants in neighborhood watch groups by planning and implementing programs to maintain community interest;
7. Organizing and operating boys' and girls' clubs in selected housing projects and other neighborhoods;
8. Promoting user accountability by helping to monitor methadone maintenance programs;

9. Assisting alternative school programs by supervising clubs and other after-school activities;
10. Staffing storefront police stations for the purpose of building community solidarity;
11. Establishing citizen police academies;
12. Serving as departmental liaisons to civilian anticrime patrols and contract security-guard employees and agencies;
13. Educating shop owners and tavern employees about the nature and misuse of false identity cards;
14. Running and staffing a new "designated driver" campaign;
15. Acting as aides to court probation officers to assist in the work of night drug courts;
16. Assisting in the preparation of the weekly Compstat report.

While most of these recommendations are self-explanatory, additional comments may be helpful regarding citizen police academies, storefront police stations, an alternative to the popular but misleading "designated driver" program, and the creation of auxiliary police units to assist in the work of drug night courts.

Citizen police academies (CPAs) offer abbreviated versions of some of the curricula actually presented to new police recruits. Generally, classes are held at least one evening a week for about a ten-week period, different topics presented during each class. In 1993, for example, two sessions of the New York City CPA were devoted to police secrecy and cynicism, as well as quality-of-life issues (e.g., graffiti, open-air drug dealing, panhandlers) (J. R. Clark 1993). Storefront (mini) police stations can actually reduce open-air drug dealing and strengthen ties between residents and the police by providing a highly visible, accessible, and permanent police presence in drug-infested neighborhoods.

The designated driver program, initiated in Scandinavian nations in the mid-1980s, was introduced to the American public by the Alcohol Project at Harvard University's School of Public Medicine. The head of the project was able to convince Hollywood writers to include the concept in their television scripts, and the U.S. Department of Transportation used a public-affairs commercial focused on the theme that "friends don't let friends drive drunk." It urged that one person in every group of drinkers should remain sober and serve as the group's "designated driver." Critics of this approach, however, point out that in reality the "designated driver" will most likely become the person who has had the least number of drinks (rather than none) and that the stories and ads imply that "it's okay to get plastered as long as someone else is driving" (Harris 1994, 165–66). Younger drinkers may thus think that they can drink without regard for possible health consequences. Reserve or auxiliary police officers could help point out these problems at appropriate public meetings and could be on call to serve as drivers upon request.

Drug night courts in Cook County, Illinois, were favorably evaluated by the U.S. Department of Justice in 1994. The favorable report, however, also disclosed a variety of serious flaws in such courts, including the small amount of time spent on each case. Night courts were established to deal with the huge number of cases generated by "zero-tolerance" police work, but the system can lead directly to prison for many low-level minority addict dealers when they are given probation but not treatment for their serious drug problems. According to public defender Tim Lohaff, probation gives "them just enough rope to hang themselves" (qtd. in Gray 1998, 27). Volunteer police officers could be used to deal with inquiries from family and friends about such cases and could play a key role in helping to ensure that probationers receive necessary treatment. Qualified volunteers could help reduce the caseloads of night courts by reaching drug users before they are initially arrested or later returned to court because of probation violations.

The possible functions of volunteer police enumerated here are directly and specifically geared to help communities achieve sufficient cohesiveness so that citizens will be better protected in their environments, less likely to become crime statistics, and more empowered to resist drug dealing. Unlike many regular police, volunteers typically live in the areas they police. Thus, volunteer police are strategically located to promote such democratic ideals as consensus building, neighborhood empowerment, and the rule of law. Their leadership and potential contributions should not be overlooked.

These types of community policing strategies are labor-intensive. Carefully selected and trained volunteers are thus an obvious solution to enforcement problems, in part because they can be recruited without cutbacks to other critical governmental services. It is important to keep in mind that none of the foregoing recommendations for the expansion of the citizen's role in crime prevention and law enforcement infringes on the time-honored duties of regular police. Few if any of these proposals call upon citizen auxiliaries to engage in any type of traditional "crime fighting": police union leaders are unlikely to support any type of drug enforcement strategy that empowers citizens to act in their place. Even "the practice of using retired cops as volunteers may be viewed by the police union as 'scab labor': uncompensated labor that would otherwise be performed by regular hires" (Champion and Rush 1997, 363–64).

In the past, strategies police adopted to reach out to the community were primarily designed to strengthen a limited number of local crime-prevention goals: improved street lighting, property identification, home and business security surveys, special crime or neighborhood watch programs that may or may not have had a citizen-patrol component. When officials and thinkers urge the notion of calling upon the community for assistance, this has often been seen as a last resort, the call typically consisting of asking citizens to respond only to a toll-free hotline or an e-mail address. Not surprisingly, police often receive numerous calls that have little validity or value.

Although reserves and auxiliary units have been recruited by many police agencies, regular patrol officers sometimes viewed them as competitors, feeling that their jobs are threatened by the unpaid volunteers. Perhaps the biggest threat posed to regular police by the use of volunteer police may relate to what has been called the "prime directive of patrolling": the need for police agencies to have officers available for any emergency (Bayley 1994). The emphasis placed on this concept is based on an unspoken fear that there may come a time during the course of a given shift when a big incident might develop that could cause the police to lose control due to a lack of human resources. To avoid this possibility, departments seek to maintain a reserve capacity, typically by seeking to have the maximum number of patrol units in the field.[2] It seems logical that if properly qualified and trained volunteer police were available, this issue would be more or less resolved: they could be summoned to handle routine assignments while regular police were reassigned to the big incident. On the other hand, the presence of reserve auxiliary personnel might be interpreted to imply less need for extra regular patrol units always available and ready for service. Indeed, this issue also causes an unspoken but very real fear in regular police since it might mean that they would then be free to spend more time on their calls. Significantly, most unions (of any type) tend to routinely resist the notion of more work. Moreover, part-time volunteers, no matter how qualified and trustworthy, are viewed as outsiders, and their deployment can upset a very delicate and sensitive arrangement: "The phrase 'out of service' is revealing. The primary purpose of patrolling is not to handle requests from the public adequately, it is to be available. . . . Not being able to regain control is the worst nightmare of a police commander" (Bayley 1994, 45).

In spite of such deep cultural obstacles, many agencies (especially those without unions) appear to favor the use of volunteer police. Such agencies have accepted the idea that the purposeful use of community volunteers should be considered a priority in our democratic system. They recognize that the interaction of community members with their police fosters a greater degree of police accountability: "in the case of police and other officials, democracy amounts to public accountability in the truest sense" (Pepinsky 1989, 467). Indeed, volunteer police who become regular police may play a major role in overcoming their reluctance to accept the value of volunteers. The next logical step should be the creative utilization of auxiliary police or volunteer reserves for the purposes of drug-abuse prevention, delinquency control, the abatement of gun violence, and the elimination of modern-day types of servitude.

Role in Preventing Modern-Day Slavery

As previous history demonstrates, the potential role of volunteer police in maintaining democratic institutions has not always been fulfilled. Nevertheless, especially since World War II, many opportunities have existed to foster this role, and the challenges of the present era present no exception. Volunteer police, in fact, may go beyond the activities described above to contribute powerfully to the realization of an ideal contained in Article I of the Universal Declaration of Human Rights (1948): "All human beings are born free and equal in dignity and rights."

Over 140 years ago, the Thirteenth Amendment to the U.S. Constitution was adopted, banning slavery and involuntary servitude. According to combined figures from the U.S. Justice, Labor, and State Departments, however, more than one hundred thousand people are presently being forced into servitude in the United States. In 1999, for example, a conviction for "conspiring to enslave" fourteen women was obtained by the Justice Department. The women had been forced to work as prostitutes in a network of nine brothels in several southern states. In 1993, a conviction was obtained in a case involving U.S. citizens who were employed as migrant laborers but were forced to sleep in a single room and work in fields patrolled by a machete-armed guard. The Justice, Labor, and State Departments established a National Worker Exploitation Task Force in 1998 to investigate and prosecute such cases of involuntary servitude, and in 2000, the task force set up a hotline to take calls from anyone reporting suspected cases involving forced labor or other forms of worker exploitation. Some members of the task force attributed the rise in the number of such cases to an increase in the smuggling of immigrants. When immigrants enter the United States illegally, they have a greater risk of being exploited by criminals since they may be indebted to them. A Rutgers University study of three hundred smuggled Chinese immigrants, for example, found that many of them had been tortured before paying off their debts (Gordy 2000).

Such servitude, of course, is not limited to the United States; slavery can be found in almost every country. It may be manifested in various forms, including contract slavery (an individual initially agrees to engage in work but discovers on arrival, usually in a foreign land, that they are powerless to leave); debt bondage (an individual ostensibly works to pay off a debt, but in reality the obligation is not permitted to end); and chattel slavery (an individual is kept in permanent servitude as a result of having been captured, born, or sold into it) (Bales 1999, 19–20). Such forms of servitude are not always easy to identify: "much modern slavery is hidden behind a mask of fraudulent labor contracts" (Bales 1999, 26). It has been estimated, for example, that there may be as many as one thousand domestic slaves in London. Significantly, if legal questions are raised regarding these individuals, their "employers" can produce a contract to delay detection of the reality of the situation by honest officials or provide a justification for dishonest ones to simply walk away. Many of these workers are told how and what they must answer if questioned by the officials of the host country (Bales 1999,

26–27). One recent study found many drawbacks in prosecuting involuntary-servitude cases: "The cases are complicated and difficult to put together, they fall into the purview of a number of agencies, and it's not always clear who has responsibility. . . . Victims frequently wind up treated like criminals themselves, detained and deported to the countries from which they were seeking to escape in the first place" ("Fighting the Slave Trade" 2000).

Surely, one area in which volunteer police should be welcome to work without too much fear that they will come into serious conflict with police unions, or will face the claim that they are replacing existing workers, is in the field of human rights. There exists a variety of slaverylike practices involving various forms of child exploitation (labor, prostitution, pornography, etc.). In particular, children of migrant workers, children of refugees or displaced persons, disabled children, and other socially disadvantaged groups may be especially vulnerable to exploitation. In 1988, a symposium sponsored by the International Criminal Police Organization (INTERPOL) urged all law enforcement agencies to give priority to investigations into the international market for pornographic material, with emphasis on the welfare of the child. It recommended that prevention of the sexual abuse of children should be included in the public-awareness campaigns of local police agencies (United Nations High Commissioner for Human Rights 1998). Volunteer police could be assigned to play an active role in making the police and the public aware of the nature of various forms of exploitation. They could prepare presentations, address school groups, and help sponsor art exhibitions and essay competitions to help deliver information about the damaging consequences of slaverylike practices. At least one government-sponsored model for citizen participation in the field of human-rights protection already exists: the Long Term Care Ombudsman program, authorized by the federal Older Americans Act of 1978.

An expanded federal role in volunteer policing could thus build on the experiences of the Long Term Care Ombudsman program, administered by the U.S. government's Administration on Aging. This program was initiated in 1971 as a federal effort to improve the quality of care in local nursing homes, and in 1981, Congress added personal-care homes to the program's mission. The program is administered locally through state or county offices and/or nonprofit agencies (e.g., the American Red Cross). This program's success is contingent on recruiting, training, and retaining volunteers, who are assigned to monitor the health, safety, welfare, and quality of life of residents in long-term care facilities (e.g., nursing homes, assisted living, private homes). Since 1987, volunteers in this program have had access to residents themselves and to their records. Volunteers are "trained to handle complaints[,] [d]ocument them and then bring them to the attention of the facility and to other agencies if needed" (N. Weinstein 2004). In New York State, there are one thousand certified volunteers, authorized to make weekly visits to specific facilities. Each ombudsperson is required to complete a thirty-six-hour hour training program and devote at least three to four hours a week to his or her assignments (N. Weinstein 2004). According to the criteria detailed in table 1, volunteers in this program may be readily classified as members of a Type III volunteer police organization (special purpose/reactive). They have only a handful of specific duties (e.g., advocacy, investigation of complaints) and carry out their responsibilities with a maximum concern for individual rights.

Similar to its inauguration of a program that advocates for the elderly, the federal government should encourage existing volunteer police units to assist with the use of new hotlines, the enforcement of laws designed to protect workers and children from exploitation, and the protection of the homeland. Such encouragement could be provided through the establishment of an auxiliary police training division at one or more of the national or regional law enforcement training centers. The centers could teach leadership development, appropriate reporting techniques, methods of crime prevention, and surveillance skills. In view of the increased demand for improvements in homeland security since September 11, 2001, this course of study could also be made available to the volunteer members of the National Park Service, the Civil Air Patrol, the U.S. Coast Guard Auxiliary, and other groups with more limited policing responsibilities. Volunteers could thus be sent for extra training, like local police receive at the National FBI Academy.

Another model for such a program would be the Defense Department's original "Troops to Teachers" program. During the 1990s, this program helped place at least three thousand veterans from all branches of the armed forces into positions within local school districts. For each veteran who qualified by October 1, 1995, school districts received an incentive grant of up to fifty thousand dollars to help pay their salaries over a five-year period. Over thirty-one thousand persons, many of them relatively young, retire each year from the military (Hewitt and Siew 1998). Just as some of them have become schoolteachers, others could draw on their military training to help train and supervise new volunteer police personnel.

The expansion of a federal role in volunteer policing could also pave the way for various other initiatives. Some programs of this nature have already begun, but they could be enhanced through the selected use of volunteer police personnel. For example, during the last half of the 1990s, the U.S. Department of Justice sponsored "Project Exile" in Richmond, Virginia, as a way of combating gun violence through the use of longer prison sentences. Murder and burglary rates dropped sharply in Richmond, and other cities have since adopted the approach (e.g., Rochester, Philadelphia, Baton Rouge, Oakland). The bulk of the program's funding supports the hiring of additional federal prosecutors and their aides. Local and federal prosecutors work together to determine which cases involving guns should be prosecuted in federal court. Federal gun-possession crimes are generally more inclusive and carry greater penalties than do crimes prosecuted at the state level. In addition, since federal prisons are scattered throughout the country, sentenced offenders can be removed (in effect exiled) from their families and associates. Other aspects of the program include enhanced supervision of parolees, investigation of the sources of illegal weapons, support for juvenile-violence-reduction efforts, and funds to help publicize the existence of the program (Kowalski 2000). Volunteer police personnel could greatly assist local police by manning hotlines to obtain tips about illegal weapons dealers, helping to publicize the nature of the program and thus maximizing its deterrent purposes, and providing additional support for juvenile crime initiatives.

An Opportunity for Civic Engagement

Volunteer police at the federal, state, and local levels have a distinct role to play in controlling juvenile delinquency, drug abuse, worker exploitation, and gun violence. No doubt, across the United States, some volunteer police have already performed several of the functions and tasks recommended here. In 1991, for example, the New York City Police Department began using modified recreational vehicles as police mini-stations near schools to offer a variety of services and help establish drug-free school zones. The vans were staffed by regular police, community volunteers, police cadets, and members of the New York City auxiliary police force. All of the participants in this project were trained in such antidrug strategies as how to evict drug dealers, how to deal with family violence, and how to handle complaints affecting the community's quality of life (Timoney 1993).

The routine use of volunteer police personnel would appear to be a natural form of a community policing–based antidrug and antidelinquency strategy. If governments were to recognize their potential, the forces marshaled against these problems could be doubled or even tripled in a short amount of time.[3] In the United Kingdom, a major study involving special constables (volunteer police) found that nearly 80 percent of the regular police agreed that they were a useful supplement to the force (Leon 1991, 668). Synergism occurs when people and governmental organizations channel their energies toward a common purpose and accomplish what they could not accomplish alone. Citizens who are auxiliary police or who have been trained by them (e.g., through CPAs) may serve as a tremendous resource in the prevention of drug abuse and juvenile delinquency. As a result of the events of September 11, 2001, the spirit of the public has been aroused. This spirit is waiting to be harnessed to the same extent as it was during World War II: hundreds of thousands of potential volunteers are waiting for the call. On January 13, 2002, during a National Public Radio interview, Harvard professor Robert Putnam indicated that after September 11, he conducted a follow-up survey of five hundred people he had interviewed for his original study involving civic engagement (see Putnam 2000), finding them less cynical and more trusting in government and their neighbors. Putnam felt it was important for governmental officials to take advantage of this shift by calling for greater civic participation.

Most Americans today believe illegal drugs are a serious problem in their communities, and most would be willing to contribute time and money to help fight them. In one survey, 60 percent of respondents indicated that they would be willing to volunteer five hours a week in their communities to work against the drug problem and would contribute twenty dollars to a communitywide effort to stop the use of illegal drugs ("Poll" 1990). Geoffrey

Canada, a private citizen active in the field of crime prevention, states: "We have failed our children. They live in a world where danger lurks all around them and their playgrounds are filled with broken glass, crack vials and sudden death. . . . And so we must stand up and be visible heroes, fighting for our children" (1995, 178–79).

The recruitment, training, and deployment of minority-group police officers and volunteers have provided a practical way to promote the rule of law. Conceivably, the very presence of such personnel within station houses has helped deter some forms of police misconduct. Such arrangements may also promote the opportunity for dialogue and understanding of diverse cultures. In turn, minority-group members may inform community members about the harsh realities of police work and the need for community support. While some minority volunteers have already undertaken the full-time responsibilities of police work, minority recruitment is still high on the agenda of most urban police agencies. Former FBI director William Sessions notes: "in the early days of our Nation, private citizens kept the peace in their communities, through respect for the law and through voluntary involvement in peacekeeping. . . . As we confront the challenges of crime . . . into the next century . . . the key to our success will be . . . forming strong partnerships with citizens of the community. . . . Indeed, every time a citizen becomes involved in crime prevention, our neighborhoods, our communities, and our Nation are improved" (1990).

The experiences of thousands of volunteer police can provide important object lessons for future endeavors. It is clear that properly screened and trained volunteer police can serve as an important link between minority groups and police. Over time, such linkages have helped reduce the mutual levels of ill will and distrust. It is important, therefore, to continue this trend, although the practical wisdom of former Los Angeles sheriff Sherman Block should always be kept in mind: "A volunteer is not a replacement for or an alternative to a paid employee. The volunteers' function is to enhance existing resources, not replace them. The success of a volunteer program will depend strongly on the ability of department personnel, civilian and sworn, to foster a harmonious working relationship under all sorts of conditions" (qtd. in M. Jensen 1998, 103).

Explicit in the development of new roles for volunteer police is the understanding that unless democratic ends are being served, the tasks in question should not be undertaken. The events of September 11 demonstrated how quickly epochal turns may come. While the mid-twentieth century's great worldwide calamity spurred a tremendous growth in civic engagement, the age of terrorism has surely ushered in an urgent new need for the mobilization of volunteer democratic police.

The Role of Volunteer Police in Terrorism Prevention

The ordinary, loyal and decent citizens are themselves a priceless asset in combating terrorism if only they can be mobilized to help the government and security forces.

PAUL WILKINSON, professor of international relations, University of Aberdeen

Major Arthur Griffith, a British police officer, commented in 1898 that "murderous organizations have increased in size and scope; they are more daring, they are served by the more terrible weapons offered by modern science, and the world is nowadays threatened by new forces which, if left unchained, may some day wreak universal destruction" (qtd. in Laqueur 1977, 227). At that time, British officials believed that "a few police agents strategically placed were quite sufficient" to combat terrorism (Laqueur 1977, 99). These views were probably shared by U.S. police representatives, especially those familiar with the demise of the Molly Maguires, which has been credited to the undercover work of a lone Pinkerton detective, James McParlan.[1] After the September 11 attacks on the World Trade Center and the Pentagon, many persons blamed their occurrence on a breakdown in American intelligence-gathering operations, as well as lack of aviation security. The prevention of terrorism, however, should not be considered the sole responsibility of any particular set of salaried public servants, corporate executives, or security personnel.

New threats to public safety and new modes of delivery may be just over the horizon. In June 2003, for example, an Ohio truck driver pleaded guilty to conspiring with al-Qaida to derail trains and destroy the Brooklyn Bridge. During the same month, Congressmen Jerrold Nadler of New York and George Miller of California addressed the U.S. House of Representatives about the need for the federal government to establish a reliable system for inspecting the contents of the estimated twenty million cargo containers that arrive yearly in the United States by ship, train, and truck. In addition, U.S. senator Charles Schumer of New York called upon the Transportation Safety Administration to require companies shipping hazardous materials to register their trucking routes with the agency. He also asked that the federal government install global positioning satellite (GPS) systems in all trucks, so that appropriate actions might be taken if they deviate from their routes. Schumer stated that "we need to put the same energy in securing our trucks as we do in securing our airlines" (qtd. in Parsavand 2003). There is also concern about the need to revitalize security arrangements at other sensitive and vulnerable locations. Nationwide, tons of jet fuel, gasoline, liquefied natural gas, and munitions and seaport storage facilities may be inadequately protected. Raymond W. Kelly, a two-term police commissioner of New York City, spent a year studying port security, finding that five of the twelve ports he visited did not have a fully trained and equipped security force and many port employees had never received background checks (Haner 2001).

Threats to air safety are also more varied than previously thought. Shoulder-fired missiles have been used in Iraq and Afghanistan. During the 1980s, dozens of Soviet aircraft were destroyed by such weapons during the Soviet intervention in Afghanistan. Stockpiles of these weapons still exist and could be used against civilian aircraft in the United States by al-Qaida, as they have been elsewhere: "In November 2002, al-Qaida broke the taboo on firing at commercial jets outside war zones when operatives launched two SA-7s at an Israeli jet as it took off from Mombassa, Kenya for Tel Aviv" (Benjamin 2003). The SA-7, produced in the former Soviet Union, is currently stockpiled in some seventy countries; the Nicaraguan military alone has at least twenty-five hundred shoulder-fired missiles (Benjamin 2003). Although al-Qaida's Kenya attack failed, a near miss against civilian aircraft in the United States would likely result in the grounding of all commercial flights. As is obvious, effective perimeter security must be maintained at U.S. airports and other vulnerable locations, and volunteer police resources could be tapped for this type of duty.

Defining Terrorism and America's Response

Terrorism has been called "an offense against humanity. . . . It is akin to piracy, or war crime. And like those crimes, terrorism deserves to be dealt with by responsible authority any where and any time" (Harmon 2000, 234). The terms *terrorism* and *terrorist* date back to the period between March 1793 and July 1794, the time of the French Revolution, commonly known as the "Reign of Terror" (Laqueur 1977). Terrorism itself, however, may be a far older phenomenon. In the first century CE, there existed a well-organized religious sect (the *sicarii*) consisting of men active in the Zealot struggles in Palestine. They attacked their enemies during the daytime, when the largest crowds were most likely to gather in Jerusalem (Laqueur 1977, 7). Terrorism, now as then, can occur anywhere and is one of the most dangerous problems currently facing mankind.

Although there exists considerable disagreement concerning a precise definition of terrorism, "some degree of political and/or religious motivation is an element of the final objective" (Ward 1990, 65). Terrorism has been further defined as involving "the use of force or the fear of force to attain a political aim" (Ward 1990, 65) and "as the deliberate creation and exploitation of fear through violence or the threat of violence in the pursuit of political change" (Hoffman 1998, 43). Further, terrorism is "conducted by an organization with an identifiable chain of command or conspiratorial cell structure (whose members wear no uniform or identifying insignia) and [is] perpetrated by a subnational group or non-state entity" (Hoffman 1998, 43). A useful working definition of terrorism has been proposed by Ted Robert Gurr, who calls it "the use of unexpected violence to intimidate or coerce people in the pursuit of political or social objectives" (1989, 202).

During the nineteenth century and continuing into the twentieth, terrorist weapons included individual assassination and the use of various types of homemade bombs. By the end of the twentieth century, some of these weapons mirrored the available technological improvements in society—for example, plastic explosives, portable rockets, and jet airliners. On the other hand, a major tool in countering the threat of terrorism is the use of electronic screening devices at airports and other ports of entry (Crelinsten, Laberge-Altmejd, and Szabo 1978).

During the 1980s, Americans were targeted by terrorists on several occasions. When a suicide bomber attacked a temporary U.S. Marine barracks in Beirut, 241 soldiers were killed. In 1988, 270 passengers and crew members aboard Pan Am Flight 103 died when a bomb hidden in a piece of luggage exploded as the plane was flying over Lockerbie, Scotland. Nevertheless, it wasn't until a series of three terrorism-related incidents that policy analysts began to notice that terrorism seemed to be escalating to higher levels of violence, death, and destruction. The first occurred on February 26, 1993, with the first bombing of the World Trade Center in New York City. Six persons were killed and hundreds injured. Second, in March 1995, the Japanese Aum Shinrikyo religious sect carried out a nerve-gas attack on Tokyo's transit system. Third, on April 19, 1995, the federal building in Oklahoma City was destroyed by at least two native-born Americans who had attended the meetings of a Michigan private militia group. One report indicates that such private militia groups are located in forty states and that they engage in paramilitary training because their members fear that only a resort to arms can protect Americans from being repressed by the national government (Halpern, Rosenberg, and Sual 1996).

In 1980, it was noted that a major effect of terrorism "has been a diversion of resources to internal security functions . . . where the burden of defense is increasingly placed upon local government, the private sector, and the individual citizen" (Jenkins 1980, 106). In 1986, scholars warned that "international terrorists and their patrons are, in effect, at war with the United States, and it is only a matter of time before they decide to carry the war to U.S. shores . . . and the nation must not be found unprepared" (Livingstone and Arnold 1986, 1, 9–10). In that same year, a historian counseled that terrorists do not recognize any rules or conventions of warfare and often favor methods of attack that may cause maximum suffering among civilian populations (Wilkinson 1986, 4). In 1982, President Ronald Reagan had designated the FBI as the lead agency for countering terrorism in the United States, and in 1996, FBI director Louis Freeh stated that the agency's number-one priority was preventing terrorism by conducting investigations so that "we get there before the bomb goes off, before the plane is hijacked, before innocent Americans lose their lives" (1996). Prior to September 11, the bipartisan Hart-Rudman Commission on National Security in the Twenty-First Century warned that Americans will likely die on American soil within the next quarter century.[2] According to Joseph S. Nye Jr., however, such warnings went unheeded in part because of "widespread national complacency in the 1990s about the rest of the world" (2001, 200). In fact, in the decade prior to the attacks on America on September 11, 2001, major television networks had greatly reduced their coverage of international affairs (Nye 2001).

In recent times, various units of U.S. law enforcement have periodically issued alerts about such potential targets as reservoirs, sewage systems, hydroelectric and nuclear power plants, offshore oil wells, gas and oil pipelines, and underwater cables. Following September 11, the United States was also served a major warning regarding the vulnerability of national landmarks, high-rise office buildings, and governmental installations. Whereas in the past, the skyjacking of commercial jets was widely recognized as a terrorist crime, it is now plainly understood that the jets themselves can be used as weapons of mass destruction. President George W. Bush's characterization of the events of September 11 as acts of war and his mobilization of America's military forces to seek and destroy terrorists and weapons of mass destruction in various parts of the world have added a whole new dimension to countering modern forms of terrorism.

After September 11, the United States began to rebuild its sky marshal organization, update its psychological screening profiles, arm its commercial airline pilots, and modernize and federalize passenger and luggage inspection. Such efforts are based on the "target-hardening" approach to crime prevention. In the 1970s, similar efforts significantly helped reduce skyjacking. A unique twist to more recent efforts, however, was the call for the public at large to assume a greater role in controlling terrorism. All Americans were encouraged to be on high alert for any telltale signs that could imply that preparations for terrorist actions were being made. Suspicious packages or strangers, for example, were to be immediately brought to the attention of authorities. The threat of biological terrorism was also publicized after various letters containing a deadly strain of anthrax were found in the mails, several individuals losing their lives as a result. Congress authorized the deployment of troops first to Afghanistan and then to Iraq to deal with regimes considered hostile to America's security. Rebuilding each country's government and infrastructure was deemed to be of strategic importance in the war on global terrorism.

Eventually, a Department of Homeland Security was created that merged over twenty different federal law enforcement agencies. Moreover, Congress passed a comprehensive aviation security bill that included a provision permitting police officers to travel armed so they could assist sky marshals aboard commercial airliners. While the bill stated that such officers must be on board with regular sky marshals (Schiff 2001a), it was unclear if the authorization extended to armed volunteer police officers. The bill also included sections requiring the federal government to take over all security screening at airports. By 2003, a new Transportation Security Administration had been established within the Department of Homeland Security, and over forty thousand security screeners had been hired.

The U.S. Coast Guard Auxiliary

The U.S. Coast Guard Auxiliary, established in 1939 in response to the increasing number of recreational boating accidents, is currently a division of the new Department of Homeland Security. In recent years, the coast guard's role in the suppression of drug trafficking has been significantly expanded. The coast guard has about thirty-five thousand active-duty members and about eight thousand reservists, more than twenty-seven hundred of whom were called up to assist in antiterror efforts after September 11. In addition, as many as twenty-eight thousand U.S. Coast Guard Auxiliary members may have been available to perform volunteer assignments during the emergency (Gilmore 2001).

Typically, many members of the auxiliary operate their own boats to assist in marine safety programs. When so used, these craft are considered to be U.S. government property. Members of the coast guard auxiliary must be citizens of at least seventeen years of age and are eligible to take advanced training courses in navigation, seamanship, communications, weather, patrols, and search-and-rescue procedures. Prior to September 11, the auxiliary had three major missions: public education, the provision of courtesy marine inspections, and on-water operations (e.g., search and rescue, safety patrols) (Kastberg 1998). September 11, however, added a new type of de facto mission to the duties of the auxiliary: security patrols (Bertelsen 2001).

According to coast guard commander Chris Olin, auxiliary members performed approximately 124,000 hours of volunteer duty between September 11 and December 7, 2001 (2001). By January 4, 2002, that number had reached 152,850 hours, an increase of approximately 45,040 hours over the previous year in similar categories ("Operation Golden Eagle" 2002). Hundreds of multimission water- and shoreside patrols were conducted during this time frame, many involving protection of the nation's 360-plus ports, especially some 90 ports and waterway areas that had been designated "security zones," in which boat and ship traffic was prohibited. New York City alone had eight such zones, including areas near the United Nations and the World Trade Center site. Auxiliary coast guard members augmented the work of active-duty personnel during the largest port-security operation since World War II (Gilmore 2001).

The contributions of the auxiliary did not go unremarked. On October 2, 2001, Viggo C. Bertelsen Jr., the volunteer national commodore of the U.S. Coast Guard Auxiliary, announced that he had received a call from Admiral James M. Loy, the commandant of the coast guard. Loy had expressed his appreciation for the auxiliary's service in providing critical support to the coast guard's missions since September 11: "We couldn't have done it without you," Loy had said (Bertelsen 2001).

The Civil Air Patrol

The services of the Civil Air Patrol were also vital in the days following September 11. CAP provided the first direct aerial photos of the World Trade Center disaster site, and the Civil Air Patrol's Mobile Operations Center provided communications support for rescue workers at the crash site in Somerset, Pennsylvania.[3] At the request of the National Guard Bureau, CAP chaplains were also on standby for any stress-related needs that the rescue workers might have (Crowe 2001).

The Civil Air Patrol, a civilian auxiliary of the U.S. Air Force, is organized along military lines. It is governed by a national board whose members are elected, except for the post of senior air force advisor. This position is held by an active-duty air force colonel who also acts as the CAP–U.S. Air Force commander. CAP is organized into eight geographic regions, with a total of fifty-two wings: one for each state, the District of Columbia, and the Commonwealth of Puerto Rico. Each wing is headed by a CAP commander and includes one or two retired U.S. Air Force members who perform liaison duties. The wings are subdivided into groups, squadrons, and flights depending on their size ("CAP Organization" 2002). In addition, the chief academic officer of the CAP National Staff College (NSC) is a retired air force major general. The NSC offers a one-week executive management course that provides CAP officers with advanced leadership training ("CAP News" 2001).

As discussed earlier, the Civil Air Patrol was officially founded in December 1941, one week before Pearl Harbor, by citizens involved in aviation and concerned about the defense of America's coastline. Initially placed under the control of the Office of Civilian Defense, the organization was under the command of the army air force by April 1943. CAP members became known as the "minutemen" of World War II, performing many missions involving coastal patrol to search for enemy submarines and saving hundreds of crash victims ("CAP History" 2002): "Anti-submarine patrol for the Civil Air Patrol lasted from March 5, 1942 until August 31, 1943. . . . [Twenty-six] CAP pilots and observers lost their lives and seven sustained serious injuries. In all, 90 aircraft were lost during [those] 18 months" (Burnham 1974, 28). CAP aircraft and pilots were also used for patrolling the U.S.-Mexican border to spot any unusual activities by enemy agents. The Civil Air Patrol became an official auxiliary branch of the U.S. Air Force by congressional action in May 1948 (Public Law 557). The relevant act provided that CAP would have three major missions: aerospace education, emergency services, and a cadet corps. The organization, whose national headquarters are located at Maxwell Air Force Base in Montgomery, Alabama, today has nearly fifty-three thousand members in nineteen hundred units, all of whom have been screened by the FBI. Since 1986, CAP has provided communications support to various federal and local law enforcement agencies engaged in counterdrug operations, especially in remote and sparsely populated areas. Members, however, cannot carry firearms or act as law enforcement officers ("CAP Support to LEA" 2002).

The day after the attack on the World Trade Center, CAP planes began to fly over the disaster site at the request of New York's governor to take high-resolution digital photos that would be studied by the Graphic Information Program of the New York State Emergency Management Office. These first flights, and subsequent ones, were authorized by the FEMA Regional Command Center, the Federal Aviation Administration, and the U.S. Air Force. CAP volunteers also transported cases of blood, needed medical supplies, and government officials; monitored airspace at many airports; and provided communications support to state and local agencies ("CAP News" 2001).

Community Emergency Response Teams

Civilians may also assist in public emergencies through gaining expertise in disaster management. Since 1993, the Federal Emergency Management Agency's Emergency Management Institute (EMI) has made available various courses and materials to enable private citizens to obtain the basic skills and knowledge to take care of themselves and others in the aftermath of a disaster. If a community desires to supplement its response capability after a disaster, individuals can be organized into special teams to serve as "auxiliary responders." Any neighborhood group, business, or governmental agency can organize a Community Emergency Response Team (CERT) and arrange training for this purpose. CERTs may provide critical services during the first three days of a major disaster when conditions may prevent access by professional emergency-response personnel. For example, a CERT-trained team or individual may provide immediate assistance to victims in the area, organize spontaneous volunteers who have not had formal training, and collect disaster intelligence that will assist professional responders with prioritization and allocation of resources following a disaster (FEMA/EMI 1997a).

Basic CERT training usually consists of about twenty-one hours of instruction, which can be arranged into various sessions, for example, one evening a week over a seven-week period. Sessions cover such topics as disaster preparedness (e.g., actions to take before, during, and after a disaster); disaster fire suppression; disaster medical treatment; search-and-rescue tactics and rescuer safety; disaster psychology; and CERT organization and management principles. A final session includes a review and a simulation exercise designed to reinforce learned skills (FEMA/EMI 1997a).

The Community Emergency Response Team concept was initially developed and implemented by the Los Angeles City Fire Department in 1985. By 1993, the Disaster Preparedness Division of the fire department had trained more than ten thousand people, and 267 teams had been organized. FEMA adopted and expanded upon the Los Angeles materials, making them available on a national basis. In particular, FEMA supports CERT by conducting and sponsoring Train-the-Trainer (TTT) courses for professional members of fire, medical, and emergency-management agency personnel. In turn, the newly trained CERT instructors are encouraged to offer the basic CERT course to community members and help organize teams (FEMA/EMI 1997a). FEMA is now a part of the U.S. Department of Homeland Security.

Community Emergency Response Teams have proven vital to public security on many occasions. In November 1997, for example, the Mohave Valley Fire District and the Mohave County Emergency Services Department established the first Arizona CERT. In July 1997, CERT volunteers were used to assist local fire agencies in the Mohave Valley during a wilderness fire within the Lake Havasu Wildlife Refuge, loading and unloading supplies for three hundred firefighters (FEMA/EMI 1999). In Ewing Township, New Jersey, planning was underway in 2001 to replace the community's auxiliary police program with a CERT (FEMA/EMI 2001). CERT members in Portland, Oregon, worked with the local fire department to establish perimeter protection around downed power lines following an ice storm, freeing fire department personnel to attend to other imminent hazards requiring their specialized training (FEMA/EMI 1997b). In Whatcom County, Washington, CERT members have assisted in such emergencies as the Whatcom Creek pipeline explosion, the Georgia-Pacific pulp and paper mill explosion, Sandy Point winds and floods, and the Nisqually earthquake. They have aided officials by answering phones, collecting and posting data, and surveying and reporting damage to property. In Tennessee, CERTs assisted senior citizens during a water shortage by helping to transport containers of potable water and providing relocation assistance after a fire (FEMA/CERT 2001).

As of September 2001, twenty-eight of Florida's sixty-seven counties had active CERT programs, sponsored by local fire departments, law enforcement agencies, and county emergency-management offices. Florida's Division of Emergency Management coordinates the CERT TTT course to help local agencies start programs. In one southern Florida community, the local emergency-services director provided CERT leaders in several high-rise retirement condominiums with alphanumeric pagers, giving the director the ability to inform CERT leaders about hurricane conditions and evacuation orders. Once alerted, these CERT leaders may contact residents in their building and keep in touch with the emergency director about the status of the evacuation and any potential problems (FEMA/EMI 1997b). In September 1998, Cape Coral utilized CERT members, supervised by the fire department and a public-education specialist, to answer a citizen information hotline during Hurricane George. During 1999's Hurricane Floyd and 2000's Tropical Storm Gordon, CERT members in Alachua County, Florida, contacted special-needs clients regarding available shelters and helped arrange transport for those persons in need of assistance. During the 1998 wildfires in Deland, CERT members assisted firefighters who were temporarily housed at Stetson University (FEMA/CERT 2001).

Community CERT teams may also be formed as a part of existing neighborhood watches. In 1992, for example, a neighborhood watch patrol program was started in Del City, Oklahoma, which has a population of about twenty-two thousand in an eight-square-mile area. Citizen volunteers patrol in six different neighborhoods using their own cars, which can be identified by portable yellow flashing lights and magnetic signs on their doors. In 1999, the city's fire department encouraged the patrol members to undertake CERT training. Courses in disaster preparedness, fire suppression, light search and rescue, medical operations, and topics related to terrorism alerts were set up using the curricula provided by the FEMA's EMI (Gaseau 2002). Fortunately, a variety of existing volunteer search-and-rescue units are in existence, and their members can be tapped to serve as CERT instructors. For example, in Maricopa County, Arizona, senior citizens are trained for search-and-rescue work. The Las Vegas metropolitan Police Department also has a very well-qualified CERT unit.

Technological Developments

Over three thousand years ago, "the Chinese required servants at the Imperial Palace to wear rings engraved with unique intricate designs identifying palace areas they were permitted to enter" (Sweet 2002, 528). Today, systems of security continue to evolve, the newest featuring computers and other electronic components. In May 2003, for example, the National Amber Alert Law (Public Law 108-21), named in honor of Amber Hagerman, was enacted.[4] At the time of Amber Hagerman's abduction, the citizenry could not be effectively mobilized. To rectify this situation, the Amber Alert

Search-and-rescue training exercise conducted in the desert north of
Sun City, Arizona, c. 1980s

system involves radio, television, and highway messages. The highway messages appear on electronic billboards that transverse roadways. Television
stations run alerts across the bottom of the screen, just like weather warnings. America Online, the nation's largest Internet provider, agreed to also
forward alerts to its customers. The new federal law set up a grant program
that can help fund more electronic bulletin boards, as well as other equipment and training, including computer-based systems that send text and
digital photographs to media and law enforcement (Krainik 2002).

There also exists an independent alert system that was developed by Robert Piccioni, a police captain from Mesquite, Texas. This e-mail system, which permits users to send alerts to any part of the country based on specific ZIP codes, may be used to send four types of alerts to subscribers: missing child, missing adult, homeland and community security, and major crime. According to Piccioni, one of the system's unique features is that it allows a customized two-way link so that users can respond directly to an alert if they have relevant information ("CrimeWeb Alert System" 2003).

Guarding against terrorism can also be aided by the use of a credit card, driver's license, or other identification that contains biometric information about the cardholder. Currently, biometric identity information systems, such as retina and/or fingerprint scans, have been tested, various countries exploring how best to use this new technology. Such identity cards may help reduce identity theft and delays at airports and other checkpoints. Police will be able to scan such cards during a routine traffic stop and learn if an individual is wanted by authorities. Howard Safir, police commissioner of New York City from 1996 to 2000, is an avid supporter of this identity technology (see Safir and Whitman 2003, xi).

A fourth type of technology that can be of significant value in assisting in the prevention of terrorism is a tiny video camera, the width of a pencil. A number of companies now have these available. The JonesCamLX, for example, is a wireless, hands-free device that can be mounted on an officer's head to record exactly what the officer sees during a field contact and transmit the images in real time to a remote location for monitoring. Facial-recognition software, which allows the camera to "recognize" suspects when connected to the appropriate database, is also available (Schwartz 2003).

Clearly, such communication systems could be used by both regular and volunteer police.[5] When necessary, alerts to mobilize other related agencies and such volunteer police units as the U.S. Coast Guard Auxiliary, the Civil Air Patrol, Community Emergency Response Teams, Law Enforcement Explorers, or various state guards could also be made. Of course, before such a universal alert is broadcast, there should be enough descriptive evidence about, for example, the child abduction or terrorist threat to determine that such an alert and mobilization will help. Federal funding is needed to ensure that all volunteer police personnel have received the appropriate training and equipment and can be reached in a crisis. Moreover, general oversight of all federal and local volunteer forces marshaled for terrorism prevention should be the responsibility of the U.S. Department of Homeland Security. It would seem plausible to enlist well-qualified volunteer police in the various branches of the Department of Homeland Security for planning, intelligence gathering, and coordination purposes. Frank Cilluffo, former special assistant to President George W. Bush for homeland security, has indicated that "it is essential that any strategy encompass prevention, preparedness and incident response, vis-à-vis the public and private sectors, as well as the interface between them" (2001).

It might also be possible to demonstrate that the use of new computer technology is more cost-effective and productive in aiding homeland security than the current reliance on color codes. The mayor of Boston, Thomas M. Menino, past president of the U.S. Conference of Mayors, has stated that an orange alert costs the city about one hundred thousand dollars per day. Nationally, the Conference of Mayors estimates that municipalities spend an extra seventy million dollars per week when there is a high-level terrorism alert (Dionne 2003).

A major problem with the use of such new technology, of course, is the need for trained and reliable personnel to study the data being received and enter alerts into the relevant computer systems. Personal privacy interests need to be considered along with the survival of the country. Fortunately, volunteer police can be recruited and trained for these specific needs. The nation's localities could save millions of dollars and be better able to mobilize when necessary by combining the available alert systems, new technological aides (e.g., biometric cards, mini–video cameras), and volunteer police mobilization for the prevention of terrorism.

Mobilizing for Homeland Security

In 1986, Paul Wilkinson, who has been researching terrorism and responses to terrorism by democracies for over thirty years, strongly urged that measures to increase the volunteer police reserve as a supplement to regular police assigned to combating terrorist crime be given urgent consideration. He stated, "there is no reason why police reserves could not adequately perform many of the extra duties of patrols, searches, and vehicle checks that may be necessitated by a terrorist emergency" (25). A similar view was expressed by Robbie Friedman, an Olympic Games security consultant, who stated that "the community should be called on to help law enforcement do their job. . . . It's common sense. There are more of them than security personnel" (qtd. in M. A. Greenberg and Cooper 1996, 12). In fact, reserve deputies attached to Georgia's Fulton County Sheriff's Department made a vital contribution to the security of the 1996 Summer Olympics in Atlanta.

When something goes wrong, and a disaster occurs, police auxiliaries are trained to report to their respective units and fill in for regular officers who are being used at the scene ("Auxiliary Police Union" 2001). In New York City, for example, the coordination of auxiliary police response to the attack on the World Trade Center was the responsibility of the auxiliary forces section of the city's police department. Auxiliaries worked alongside regular members of the uniformed forces at precincts, volunteer centers, and around the Ground Zero perimeter.

Volunteers, clearly, may play an important role in preventing terrorism. Israel, for example, has probably survived repeated suicide-bomb attacks because it has mobilized its citizens into a variety of professional and volunteer protective services. In the United States, President George W. Bush has clearly indicated that America is engaged in a war on terrorism. In order to recruit more volunteers to serve in the prevention effort, President Bush has begun to use conventional media resources (i.e., television, radio, and print) to address the nation. While his initial rhetoric suggested that the public should be constantly vigilant regarding suspicious persons and unattended bags and parcels, he later called for the widest possible participation of all Americans in community-service activities, whether directly or indirectly concerned with the prevention of terrorism. Bush's proposals demonstrate an approach that goes beyond having citizens serving as extra eyes and ears in their everyday pursuits to specifically calling for citizens to join local, regional, and national organizations, for example, local volunteer fire, rescue, and police units, as well as CAP, CERTs, and the U.S. Coast Guard Auxiliary.

After the attack on America on September 11, many people asked, "But what can I do?" During the week of October 18, 2001, the *Ridgewood Times*, a local weekly newspaper in New York City, received a letter to the editor in response to this exact question. Its writer, Audrey Eckhardt, an auxiliary police sergeant in the 102nd Precinct, responded that if people really want to get involved in preserving their communities, they should consider joining a unit of the auxiliary police (2001). President Bush has echoed these remarks, stating on a visit to Florida on January 31, 2002, that "if people in this part of the world want to be a part of the first defense in homeland security—and that is, help patrol neighborhoods or industrial complexes— a great program is Citizens Observers, right here in Volusia County" (qtd. in DeWitt 2002). The neighborhood watch program in Del City, Oklahoma, also illustrates the productive use of citizen volunteers for homeland security. In that community, citizens have discussed what to do in the case of a terrorism incident and have learned how to identify potential terrorism suspects and targets. Del City fire marshal Jim Hock has noted that "community involvement is changing as people take more interest in their communities and come out of their homes. . . . It used to be you were an island on your own. . . . Now you have to know your neighbors" (qtd. in Gaseau 2002).

After the events of September 11, 2001, the American Truckers Association (ATA) began to organize a national highway watch program, funded by the Federal Motor Carrier Safety Administration, a subdivision of the U.S. Department of Transportation, to train and enlist professional truck drivers to recognize and report incidents on the nation's highways. As part of this program, a potential three million qualified truck drivers could serve as the eyes and ears of law enforcement officials across the country. A major goal of the program is to help reduce response times to roadside emergencies since truck drivers typically carry cell phones and know exactly where they are at all times. The program has gotten off to a good start. In Arkansas, for example, the Arkansas Trucking Association, the ATA, and the Arkansas State Police combined their efforts to conduct a two-hour course for twenty-four drivers in April 2002. The drivers who attended the session were officially certified as highway watch members and were assigned a personal identification number. Some of the other states that signed on during the program's first few months of operation are Colorado, Oregon, Florida, Virginia, Kansas, Minnesota, and Vermont.[6] On August 16, 2002, U.S. transportation secretary Norman Y. Mineta issued a press release indicating that the trucking industry had created an antiterrorism action plan involving professional truck drivers who "will become 'America's Trucking

Army,' trained to recognize and report suspicious activity that may adversely affect national security" (Federal Motor Carrier Safety Administration 2002).

A similar program was developed for the field of general aviation (GA) that involves more than 650,000 pilots at small airports throughout the country. This program was put into place by the Aircraft Owners and Pilots Association (AOPA), the trade group that represents private pilots, in partnership with the Transportation Security Administration (TSA). The AOPA airport watch, which features a toll-free hotline that went into operation at the end of 2002, includes warning signs for airports, informational literature, and a training videotape.[7] Such cautionary measures could have a tremendous impact on security. Small airports typically do not provide scheduled passenger service, and most do not have high fences, metal detectors, or baggage screeners. Moreover, most private pilots do not have to file flight plans with the Federal Aviation Administration.

Qualified volunteer police officers could be utilized to help screen and train members of the ATA's highway watch, CERT units, and citizen patrol groups and employees in sabotage-prone industries such as general aviation, public utilities, and businesses in industrial parks. The federal government could officially recognize the potential contributions of volunteer police by establishing training sections at its various federal law enforcement training locations that could teach appropriate internal security methods. Alternatively, the federal and state governments could subsidize the cost of classes in safety and security management for volunteer police members at local community colleges, thereby making it possible for such volunteers to fill personnel voids during critical alert periods.

A wide range of potential governmental and civilian responses to the threat of terrorism and homeland security alerts exists. The future will see new national study committees impaneled and new strategies undertaken. In the meantime, localities will have to cope with the day-to-day reality of a changed state of affairs. After September 11, 2001, New York governor George Pataki responded to the new conditions in which the nation finds itself by issuing an emergency order waiving the mandatory retirement age of fifty-seven for state police officers; by mid-December 2001, he had announced the rehiring of over one hundred previously retired troopers, needed to guard the state capitol and other vulnerable locations. In response, Superintendent James McMahon, head of the New York State Police Division, stated, "It was very creative on the governor's part, because it was the quickest way to supplement the force . . . to meet these unexpected needs" (qtd. in Hammond 2001). While state officials were unable to provide an immediate estimate of the costs involved, the delay in deploying these workers (over ninety days from the attacks) and the associated personnel costs probably could have been avoided had there been in existence an auxiliary trooper program or an adequately trained and equipped state guard. Governor Pataki did make use of the National Guard, but their ranks were thinned due to call-ups for overseas duty.

On the other hand, the lack of a dedicated state volunteer police in New York was alleviated to some extent by the existence of a variety of other types of volunteer police, including the U.S. Coast Guard Auxiliary, the Civil Air Patrol, and some CERT units, all given assignments directly in line with their training and experience. For example, after September 11, coast guard auxiliarists began augmenting and backfilling for active-duty service personnel throughout the United States (Gilmore 2001). There was also a resurgence in enrollment in such organizations as the Civil Air Patrol. According to Lt. Col. Ken Jurek of the 560-member Nebraska wing of CAP, there has been a 12 percent increase in enrollment in the unit since the terrorist attacks (von Kampen 2003). Furthermore, the Westchester Hudson Composite Squadron in New York saw its number of senior members doubled (Swansburg 2002).

The regular use of citizen police would appear to be a valuable resource for maintaining homeland security. According to Charles Jones, professor emeritus at the University of Wisconsin, "There's a kind of predictability to conventional war, but with terrorism there is . . . an uncertainty about what might happen, who is being targeted, which government building might be struck" (qtd. in Solomon 2001). In these difficult times, it is of paramount importance that thousands of additional emergency service personnel and other first responders be recruited. They are needed to fill a variety of homeland security roles during this new age of terrorism. At Disney World, nearly every worker, pool, fountain, and flower garden serves as an important component in the park's overall safety system: "Every Disney Productions employee, while visibly and primarily engaged in other functions, is also engaged in the maintenance of order" (Shearing and Stenning 1987,

319). Similarly, whether individuals are inclined to join a volunteer police organization or not, each person has a role to play in defending our nation against terrorism.

This work is meant to serve as a kind of roadmap for those contemplating a contemporary citizen's role in homeland security and community safety. Thus, scant attention has been paid to the individual stories of volunteer police. At this point, however, it seems appropriate to take a look at the average contemporary volunteer police officer. As we will see, such volunteers come from all walks of life and have chosen to serve their country in a variety of ways.

Anne Auxier, a member of the Portland Deputy Reserve, teaches German at the Sam Barlow High School in Gresham, Oregon. She routinely performs patrol work involving responding to family disputes and traffic accidents, as well as the prevention of gang activities ("Off-Beat Teacher" 1996). Tobias Winright, a professor of religion and ethics at Simpson College in Indianola, Iowa, serves as a reserve police officer, regularly serving at least sixteen hours at the Des Moines Police Department every month. Winright spent nearly five months in training to learn how to protect his community (Winright 2001). Robert Karton, who practices law in Chicago, Illinois, has for many years regularly flown his own aircraft on behalf of search-and-rescue missions for the Civil Air Patrol (Chanen 1994). Tom Shaw and Peter Shaw, a father-and-son team that routinely patrols the waterways around Wilmington, North Carolina, use their own eighteen-foot motorboat to help encourage boating safety and conduct hundreds of safety checks for other boat owners each year. They perform these tasks as volunteer members of the U.S. Coast Guard Auxiliary's Wilmington flotilla (McGrath 2002). Randal Leval, a police lieutenant with the Maui Police Department in Hawaii, is also the volunteer commander of the Maui Composite Squadron, a CAP unit. The unit has a C-182 Cessna aircraft that has been used to fly over rural coastal areas to warn residents of tsunamis, to deliver time-sensitive medical materials, and to participate in search-and-rescue operations. Leval, now a lieutenant colonel, began his career in the CAP program as a cadet (Tanji 2003).

The people of the United States through their numerous volunteer police organizations have created thousands of emergency-response, patrol, and communications networks for homeland security and community safety. It is now critically important for the survival of our democratic system that citizens seek membership in such authorized organizations, which have longstanding records of honorable service in defense of America's freedom. At his nomination hearing to be the first secretary of the Department of Homeland Security, former Pennsylvania governor Tom Ridge stated that "in spite of everything we have done, we are only at the beginning of what will be a long struggle to protect this country from terrorism" (qtd. in Shenon 2003).

In light of this coming struggle, the recently released *9/11 Commission Report* includes over forty recommendations for the protection of America from further terrorist assaults, the most well-known being the establishment of a National Counterterrorism Center and a new National Intelligence Director. The report, however, fails to specify a clear delineation of the average citizen's role in protecting the homeland. It says nothing directly about how civilians can assist in the prevention of future attacks on cities and America's vast infrastructure, even though it notes that al-Qaida "considered the environment in the United States so hospitable that the 9/11 operatives used America as their staging area for further training and exercises—traveling into, out of, and around the country and complacently using their real names with little fear of capture" (366). Clearly, some of America's enemies may still be in this country, merely awaiting a signal from abroad to attack—the same approach that was used to attack America on September 11. Protection against saboteurs thus needs to be a central focus of homeland protection efforts.

At the time of World War II, Americans by the millions were enlisted for wartime civilian defense purposes. About two hundred thousand private war-industry plant guards were mustered into auxiliary military police units. In New York City, Mayor Fiorello LaGuardia (not without controversy) recruited a city patrol corps, which served as an armed auxiliary police force. Other major cities, such as Washington, D.C., also recruited a civilian auxiliary force. Nationally, millions of posters and advertisements were produced to foster homeland security and assist in the recruitment of civilian-defense forces. In particular, a volunteer Civil Air Patrol was developed to guard our coastlines against enemy infiltrators and U-boat attacks. After World War II, the Civil Air Patrol's contributions were recognized when Congress made the organization an official civilian auxiliary of the U.S. Air Force. All members of these civilian forces were trained to keep a close eye out for the saboteur. Indeed, the members of the 9/11 Commission may have had some of these civilian forces in mind when they stated that "the men and women of the World War II generation rose to the challenge of the 1940s and 1950s. They structured the government so that it could protect the country. That is now the job of the generation that experienced 9/11" (9/11 Commission 2004, 399).

Although various CERT units are being trained for the day when they will be needed to respond to a disaster, and there have been some initiatives to recruit more members for CAP and other protective units, a major effort still needs to be undertaken to harness the civilian population for the protection of America's infrastructure. The recent recruitment of privately sponsored and informal "watch groups" is inadequate. The country's infrastructure of communication links, energy grids, tunnels, bridges, highways, railways, pipelines, and ports needs to be protected from sabotage. A new civilian auxiliary to the U.S. Department of Homeland Security can and should be recruited without delay. Moreover, the initiation and funding of this new organization should be a federal responsibility: Article IV, Section 4, of the U.S. Constitution requires the national government to protect each of the states from invasion. Though the 9/11 Commission failed to specify civilian roles in homeland defense, the list below, compiled from the 9/11 Commission's own recommendations, summarizes some of the duties a new federal organization might undertake. Specifically, a civilian auxiliary to the U.S. Department of Homeland Security could assist in the protection of America by helping:

1. to track terrorist financing (382);
2. to constrain terrorist mobility (385);
3. to check identification documents (390);
4. to defend potential terrorist targets (391);
5. to check watchlists at points of entry (393);
6. to monitor checkpoints to detect explosives (393);
7. to maintain the infrastructure for emergency response (396);
8. to implement the Incident Command System (397);

9. to establish and staff signal corps units for communications among civilian authorities, local first responders, and the National Guard (397);
10. to ensure that private-sector preparedness complies with the American National Standards Institute's guidelines (398).[8]

The 1998 film *The Siege* contains scenes in which senators and key players from the FBI, the CIA, the Department of Defense, and the executive branch come together to consider such issues as who is in charge in a time of national emergency and the significance of the Posse Comitatus Act, which places restrictions on the use of military force for domestic security. Today, when the need to decrease America's vulnerability by increasing homeland preparedness is of paramount importance, these same issues are being debated not by screen actors but by actual occupants of seats of power. As both national and local civilian authorities plan for homeland defense, they should not overlook the strategic and historic role that citizens have performed in defending America.

APPENDIX A   Volunteer Police Timeline

The following timeline outlines the approximate dates of either the existence or the initiation of various volunteer police organizations in the United States. For reference purposes, major contemporaneous historical events are also identified. The placement of each volunteer unit within the timeline is generalized and approximated and may or may not have had any direct connection with the listed historical event. The dates provided for the existence of Native American military societies are very approximate. In about 1700, the Sioux moved from the eastern woodlands to Minnesota "and then to the Black Hills—forcing the Crows and Cheyennes on just ahead of them. . . . From approximately 1775 on most shifting ceased, the various Plains domains were set, and because of the spread of the horse, a common, buffalo-and-horse-oriented pattern of life . . . emerged which lasted till about 1875, the end date varying somewhat according to what happened to each tribe in its contact with the Whites" (Mails 1972, 2).

Table 4 Volunteer Police Timeline: The Citizens' Role in Homeland Security

HISTORICAL ERA	TIME PERIOD	CITIZEN VOLUNTEERS
Colonial era	1620–1776	Militia captain Myles Standish Constables/watches Militias/slave patrols Native American military societies
American Revolution	1776–83	Constables/watches Militias/slave patrols
Lewis and Clark Expedition	1804–6	Vigilante societies
Civil War	1861–65	Anti-horse-thief and detective societies

Table 4 (continued)

HISTORICAL ERA	TIME PERIOD	CITIZEN VOLUNTEERS
Reconstruction era	1865–77	Slave patrols end Law-and-order societies/posses Charity society volunteers ("friendly visitors") Vice-suppression agents
Progressive movement	1890–1914	Anti-Saloon League agents
World War I	1914–19	Home defense leagues/junior police
U.S. involvement in World War I	1917–18	New York State Guard American Protective League
Prohibition era	1920–33	New York City Police Reserve School safety patrols Midwestern police reserves
Depression era	1929–40	U.S. Coast Guard Auxiliary (1939) Georgia State Guard (1940–46)
World War II	1938–45	Civil defense units Office of Civil Defense created (1941) Civil Air Patrol (1941) Auxiliary military police Ohio State Highway Patrol Auxiliary (1942) New York City Patrol Corps
Korean War	1951–53	Civil defense auxiliaries
Vietnam War era	1964–75	Reorganized auxiliaries/reserves
Watergate scandal	1972–74	Boy Scouts of America Law Enforcement Explorers
FEMA established	1979	Citizen police academies Long-term care ombudsmen
Gulf War	1990	Citizen observer patrols Teen police academies Los Angeles Unified School District Police Magnet program CERT teams (1993)
September 11, 2001, attacks		
U.S.A. Freedom Corps announced	2001	Citizen Corps initiative
U.S. Department of Homeland Security established	2003	Volunteers in Police Service

Information about slave patrols can be derived from a variety of doctoral dissertations on the subject (Green 1997; Hadden 1993; M. A. Henry 1968; Yanochik 1997). Hadden's dissertation was revised and published by Harvard University Press in 2001. At least one dissertation has been devoted to the anti-horse-thief and detective societies of the nineteenth century (Nolan 1987). In addition, various historical archives throughout the country have files related to similar examples of early volunteer police organizations (e.g., the Minnesota Historical Society).

Useful biographies of Anthony Comstock include the works by Richard C. Johnson (1973) and Heywood Broun and Margaret Leech (1927). The records of the New York Society for the Suppression of Vice are housed in the Library of Congress. The best discussions of the history of censorship in Boston are by Paul S. Boyer (1968) and Ralph E. McCoy (1956). Generally, the single best overview of this era involving censorship and the policing of morals is by Nicola Beisel (1997).

Several U.S. studies present data about auxiliary and reserve police officers. In 1969, Virginia's Arlington County Police Department conducted a survey designed to determine the status of volunteer police, taking into account a wide range of variables. The agency contacted all fifty-seven U.S. cities with a 1960 population of over 250,000 and received forty-eight responses, learning that members of the surveyed units typically received two hundred to four hundred hours of initial training, as well as an FBI security check (Rand Corporation 1972). A section of the volume *Report on Police,* prepared by the National Advisory Commission on Criminal Justice Standards and Goals (1973), deals with the need to establish minimum selection and training standards for reserve police officers. The same study also includes information about the recruitment and training requirements for reserve units in California,

Florida, and Arizona. A more recent California survey found that 89 percent of police departments in the Los Angles area have reserve officers (Sundeen and Siegal 1986). Martin Gill and Rob Mawby (1990) trace the history of the British special constabulary, comparing it with similar entities in other countries. Their work, which includes an assessment of the role of special police in relation to that of regular, finds that special police tend to identify more with the police than with the community in their attitudes and self-conceptions. Significantly, none of these studies attempts to present a comprehensive history of volunteer police in the United States.

At least one book and numerous articles consider the operations of auxiliary and reserve units in particular American cities and counties—for example, Dallas (E. Brown 1976); New York City (M. A. Greenberg 1984); Dade County, Florida (Bohardt 1977); Maricopa County, Arizona (Lesce 1985); Mobile, Alabama (F. Woodward 1986); Columbus, Mississippi (Watkins 1979); Belding, Michigan (Mason 1988); Palo Alto, California (Bocklet 1988); and Tallahassee, Florida (B. Berg and Doerner 1988). The only recently published study providing information on state, county, and city volunteer police units was prepared by Richard Weinblatt (1993). However, this work is limited in that it refers only to comparative training standards and the number of auxiliary or reserve law enforcement personnel in the United States. None of these studies attempts to synthesize volunteer police historical materials from the colonial era to the present.

Annual police reports and other government documents (e.g., commission reports, training manuals, departmental regulations, recruiting pamphlets) from many large U.S. cities and the United Kingdom contain summaries regarding the policies and activities of volunteer police units. While such works reveal divergent evaluations of the units' usefulness, they do not focus on historical analysis.

Reports in the daily press, statutes, and court decisions also provide data concerning the powers and activities of volunteer police. For example, the *New York Times* reported on September 13, 1987, that an auxiliary police unit in Quincy, Massachusetts, had ceased to patrol as a result of pressure exerted by regular police officers who felt that their jobs were in peril. In *Fitzgibbon v. County of Nassau* (1989), New York State's Appellate Division, Second Department, ruled that the creation of auxiliary police units does not confer immunity from civil liability lawsuits to the sponsoring county, the auxiliary police unit, or the individual volunteer police officer (Anderson 1989). These and similar materials can serve as valuable sources for information on volunteer police.

Such information has also begun to appear on the Internet. While no one knows how many computers are connected to the Internet, almost every available Internet resource is available via the World Wide Web, an information retrieval system. Via the Internet, numerous police agency home pages exist. Individuals can search for volunteer police programs by category in their community by visiting the following Web site: http://www.policevolunteers .org/programs/. This site is managed by the International Association of Chiefs of Police, in partnership with and on behalf of the White House Office of the U.S.A. Freedom Corps and the U.S. Department of Justice.

Currently only one other English-language work addresses the topic of volunteer police from a historical perspective: Clare Leon's "Special Constables: An Historical and Contemporary Survey" (1991). Leon's thesis discusses four main issues regarding the volunteer police of the United Kingdom: their identities, their deployment, their effectiveness, and their relationships with other law-enforcement agents and with the wider public. He notes that "despite their ancient pedigrees, special constables are the hidden feature of the British policing landscape" (5).

Bibliographic sources regarding the regular police include works by R. Fogelson (1977), Sidney Harring (1983), David Johnson (1981), Roger Lane (1967), James F. Richardson (1970; 1974; 1979), Thomas Reppetto (1978), and Samuel Walker (1977; 1980). Each of these studies concerns the history of American law enforcement, and all are useful for comparing basic trends and issues regarding regular and volunteer police. Walker's two books provide an excellent introduction to the subject and cover some of the main themes (especially the issue of professionalism). Johnson's book emphasizes the development of police agencies. Fogelson focuses on twentieth-century urban police reforms and discusses the impact of police on various social classes and ethnic groups. Richardson's 1974 work addresses police duties and administrative structure as reflections of increasing urbanization. Lane deals with the specific history of the Boston police during the nineteenth century. Harring is especially useful for his meticulous documentation of how the police have aided management when confronted by strikes. He notes, for example, how in 1896 a Milwaukee streetcar-employee strike was broken when lower-level

236 | APPENDIX B: BIBLIOGRAPHIC SOURCES

streetcar officials were sworn in as deputies and many strikers were arrested (1983, 119–20). Reppetto explains how and why policing developed differently in such cities as Boston, New York, Philadelphia, Chicago, San Francisco, and Los Angeles, holding the particular position that policing has been most influenced by the struggle of competing interest groups.

The only significant book that concentrates on the African American experience in policing appeared in 1996. Dulaney (1996) divides this history into three eras: "Crime Fighters" (nineteenth century to World War II), when black police officers were assigned to fighting crime in black neighborhoods; "Reformers," (1950–1960s), when black officers pushed for professional training and advancement; and "Professionals" (1970s–present), when blacks in law enforcement gained leadership positions within police departments across the nation.

NOTES

Introduction

1. Although Kelling and Moore (1988) contribute useful insights regarding the history of policing, H. Williams and Murphy (1990) point out that the roughly indicated eras apply mainly to white majority communities. Blacks and other minorities did not exert any political influence during the political era, nor did they benefit from the legal reforms of the following era. Furthermore, even though significant progress has been made in recent decades toward the creation of police agencies responsive to minority needs, the community era has not been fully achieved. In particular, H. Williams and Murphy note that the analysis presented by Kelling and Moore fails "to take account of how slavery, segregation, discrimination, and racism have affected the development of American police departments—and how these factors have affected the quality of policing in the Nation's minority community" (1990, 1).

Chapter 1 | Unraveling the Concept of Volunteer Policing

1. In the United Kingdom, special constables have evolved from the performance of limited service on special occasions (especially during national emergencies) to routine neighborhood patrol assignments. In addition, the police forces of the city of London and the Metropolitan Police use specials to conduct neighborhood self-defense classes, and specials coordinate the neighborhood watch program in Wiltshire. In 1986, there were over sixteen thousand special constables in England and Wales, including just under a third who were women (Conference on Special Constables 1987).

2. According to Stentiford (2002), the framers of the Constitution "intended that the militia would be called into federal service when needed," since "Article II, section 3 established the president as the commander-in-chief of the militia when in federal service" (11).

3. This figure, however, does not include the various types of federal volunteers— for example, the more than 77,000 people who volunteer in the National Park System. This number also excludes membership in the state guard or the National Guard. The U.S. Army National Guard, for example, has about 350,000 members, and

the Air National Guard has about 110,000 members (Debnam 2003, 24). These present-day guard units trace their volunteer police origins to the militia tradition, which dates back to colonial times. When not called to full-time active duty, National Guard members usually train at least one weekend a month and two full weeks each year (Debnam 2003).

4. Table 1 presents a typology of volunteer police based on the findings of the present research. It should be noted that such entities as the regulators, the Klan, and other vigilante associations are not considered in the typology. Under the widely accepted standard definition of vigilantism, these are extralegal groups (R. M. Brown 1975, 95–97). The goal of the present work is to deal mainly with the phenomenon of authorized law-and-order groups, rather than unauthorized and/or illegal varieties.

While other typologies concerning citizen involvement in crime control have been proposed (e.g., Percy 1979; Marx and Dane 1976; Grabosky 1992), none of these exclusively involves authorized and overtly functioning volunteer police organizations such as those described in the present study. Percy includes independent citizen groups, Marx and Dane include adversarial citizen activity, and Grabosky incorporates private (commercial) security organizations. None of the existing typologies gives prominence to the basic styles of policing involving reactive and proactive strategies, the latter including techniques that seek to aggressively pursue crime prevention. In recent years, these measures have included community empowerment based on educating members of the public about how to protect themselves and their property and generally encouraging them to assume greater responsibility for assisting in crime control (Peak 1997, 398).

5. In order to narrow the scope of this history, individuals who participate in contemporary neighborhood watch groups and ham-radio operators have been excluded. Generally, the main purpose of such groups is the covert and rather passive behavior of watching and/or serving as a vital conduit for the transmission of critical information during emergencies. Travis (1995) defines *neighborhood watch* as "a term generically applied to citizen crime prevention programs involving the mobilization of residents to serve as the 'eyes and ears' of the police and to watch for and report any crimes or suspicious activities" (443). Interestingly, Rosenbaum (1987) concludes that law enforcement "should not be applauded for starting programs, unless we genuinely believe that posting watch signs on the block is sufficient by itself to deter criminal behavior" (129). Occasionally, however, a particular watch program has expanded its activities. For example, watch groups have undertaken community patrol work, sometimes referred to as "citizen observer patrols." Such initiatives extend beyond simply "watching," and duly authorized and qualified participants are here considered to be "volunteer police": meeting and helping crime victims and crime-prevention patrols are routine, overt police functions.

6. Responding to an emergency has never been easy. Coping with fires, floods, hurricanes, and blizzards has always required a unique set of responses. Today, we

must also be prepared to cope with the threats of radiation, toxic chemicals, and terrorism, and new hazards may be just around the corner. The Federal Emergency Management Agency (FEMA) Web site provides important information about how U.S. citizens can better prepare for emergencies (http://www.fema.gov). Prior to the events of September 11, FEMA's Emergency Management Institute and other organizations had developed courses and materials that were in use in at least forty-seven states. New bachelor's degree programs in the field have also been developed, with the following colleges among the first to recognize its importance: Arkansas Tech University, the University of Richmond, Eastern Michigan University, Arizona State University East, the University of Florida, the University of Akron, the University of North Texas, Western Carolina University, and Empire State College. FEMA also plans to establish emergency management associate degree programs in every state of the nation. Onondaga Community College in Syracuse was the first community college in New York to develop such a program. See the following two government-sponsored Web sites for further information on citizen preparedness: http://www.dhs.gov and http://www.ready.gov. Information is also available at http://www.redcross.org. The Red Cross is always in need of volunteers who can help respond to local disasters, teach lifesaving skills, organize blood drives, or make phone calls when the need arises.

7. Although Putnam (2000) points out that since the mid-1960s the membership rolls of a great variety of civic and fraternal organizations have steadily fallen, there are certain notable exceptions, including evangelical Christian groups and inner-city crime patrols (Lenkowsky 2000). Opportunities for minority participation in inner-city crime patrol organizations are high. As a side note, volunteerism among seniors also doubled over the last quarter of the twentieth century (Putnam 2000, 129).

Chapter 2 | The Lay Justice Era

1. A useful timeline regarding the history of firefighting can be found at http://www.auroraregionalfiremuseum.org/history/timeline.htm.

2. T. Thompson (1986), Chapin (1983), and Semmes (1966) all relied heavily on court records in their studies of colonial Maryland. In studying materials from this period, it is critical to distinguish between "the ideal" (found by historians in sermons and conduct books) and "the real" (found carefully described in court dockets and the depositions in court files). Of course, there are serious difficulties in using court records. A summary of the advantages and disadvantages of using court records to discern social history can be found in T. Thompson 1986 (xviii). Thompson's discussion of prenuptial fornication and various other sexual activities seems at odds with Morgan's (1966) discussion of the strict rules of the Puritan family concerning such issues as sex in marriage, disciplining children, reverence for parents, restrictions on church membership, good habits, and family government. The difference appears to be a result of the nature of the primary research materials used by

each author. While Thompson relies heavily on the descriptions found in court records, Morgan emphasizes such prescriptive sources as sermons, tracts, and commentaries by the writers and leaders of the Puritan period (e.g., Thomas Cobbett, John Cotton, John Davenport, Thomas Hooker, Cotton Mather, Increase Mather, Samuel Sewall, Benjamin Wadsworth, Samuel Willard, and John Winthrop). The danger of relying on such evidence is that it is not uncommon for discrepancies to exist between the preachments and the practices of historical figures (see T. Thompson 1986, xiv).

3. Regulators were self-appointed and were not organized by societal action for the purpose of fulfilling police functions on a permanent basis. Consequently, they are not included in the definition of *volunteer police* used in this study. On the other hand, Native American military societies and southern slave patrols do fall within this definition, since they were organizations authorized by legislative enactment (slave patrols) or societal action (warrior societies) for the permanent performance of one or more police functions.

4. Important discussions of slave patrols may be found in at least four doctoral dissertations. M. A. Henry (1968), whose work was originally presented as a dissertation at Vanderbilt University in 1913, studies patrols in South Carolina from their origins in the late 1600s until 1860. He discusses the legal status and punishment of slaves; the role of the overseer; the patrol system; slave insurrections; and a variety of other aspects related to the lives of slaves, runaway slaves, and freed slaves. Hadden's study (1993) addresses the origins of slave patrols, their organization and administration, their methods of appointment and compensation, their routine functions, their responses in times of crisis, and facts related to patrols during the Civil War and at the war's conclusion. (Hadden's dissertation was subsequently revised and published; see Hadden 2001. Currently, this is the most definitive work on the subject of slave patrols.) Yanochik (1997) presents three essays regarding the economics of slavery. The second essay examines the economic effects of the slave-patrol system. Yanochik considers some of the legal aspects of patrols, as well as the personal characteristics of individuals serving on patrols, concluding that slave patrols acted as a subsidy to slave owners, serving to lower the cost of using slave labor. Green (1997) explores the relationship between slave patrols in South Carolina and police in northern industrial centers, noting the similarities in their features and the reasons for their existence. He finds that "each law enforcement apparatus acted to protect the interests of the dominant economic class" (121).

Chapter 3 | The Vigilant Era

1. The following special procedures existed for the recapture of slaves: (1) only affidavits of slave catchers were needed to identify fugitive slaves; (2) fugitives could neither offer defense nor testify; (3) there was no trial by jury; (4) hearing commissioners were paid ten dollars if they found against a fugitive and only five dollars if

they found in a fugitive's favor; (5) federal officials who hampered in any way the seizure of a fugitive could be fined a thousand dollars, and if a fugitive escaped with or without their help they would be responsible for the entire value of the slave; (6) bystanders were required to assist slave catchers if a fugitive tried to escape; and (7) a fine of a thousand dollars or imprisonment for six months was established as the penalty for assisting a runaway slave (Buckmaster 1941, 176–77). The Fugitive Slave Law of 1850, part of the great compromise made to avoid the breakup of the Union, did not deter the workers of the Underground Railroad, however. The "fugitives came on foot, in disguise, by rail, by boat, by hired carriage, and never failed to find a friend" (Buckmaster 1941, 185).

2. The early activities of the WCTU foreshadowed the well-known Drug Abuse Resistance Education (DARE) program of the last quarter of the twentieth century. DARE was developed jointly by the Los Angeles Police Department and the Los Angeles Unified School District. DARE's goals include teaching school-age children about the nature of tobacco, alcohol, and drugs; how to resist peer pressure; how to build self-esteem; and how to identify and use constructive alternatives. The program is taught by specially trained police officers and is currently offered to millions of students (Senna and Siegel 1998, 126). The DARE program could probably be presented by volunteer police, but the emphasis by post–World War II police unions on paid workers has diminished such opportunities for an expanded role for the public in police activities.

3. In recent times, the most diverse use of the posse is probably in Phoenix, Arizona, under the administration of Joseph M. Arpaio, the sheriff of Maricopa County. His office has established a variety of unique posse programs. For example, one program is entitled the "Deadbeat Parent Posse." On a routine basis, posse members work closely with the Warrants Unit to find and arrest parents who fail to pay court-ordered child support. In "Operation Butt-Out," posse members conduct undercover work along with teenage volunteers to determine the extent of tobacco sales to minors. After sufficient training, members of the antiprostitution posse use highly visible patrols at various locations in order to deter prostitutes from streetwalking. The antigraffiti posse is deployed to arrest persons by observing them at work. Graffiti removal is often expensive, and its use has been associated with gang activities. Finally, posse members are also used to provide additional security at shopping malls during holiday periods (information received from Lt. Thomas K. Tyo, Maricopa County Sheriff's Office, July 2000).

4. At the beginning of the year 2000, it was estimated that one hundred thousand people (mostly women) were being forced to work in U.S. factories, small businesses, prostitution rings, farms, and private homes. Many of these workers are lured to the United States with the promise of well-paying jobs. Upon arrival, however, they are taken to a communal living area and have their identity papers confiscated (Gordy 2000). One notorious case involved the use of fifty illegally admitted deaf Mexicans

to peddle trinkets within the New York City subway system for a period in excess of five years. According to Thomas Perez, a former U.S. deputy assistant attorney general, more than one hundred cases involving victims of involuntary servitude are processed yearly. The U.S. Department of Justice currently defines involuntary servitude as "using physical force, threats of force or legal coercion (such as threats of arrest or incarceration) to keep someone working" (Gordy 2000, 4). See chapter 7 for further discussion.

Chapter 4 | The Spy Era

1. The major American figures in the field of eugenics included Charles Davenport, Alexander Graham Bell, and Henry H. Goddard. These individuals believed that many of the nation's social problems could be alleviated by preventing the unfit from having children. To achieve this, they advocated either long-term custodial care or sterilization. The enactment of laws restricting marriage among the "feebleminded," whites and blacks, and the insane were precursors of more drastic measures. In 1931, twenty-seven states had laws permitting the sterilization of persons deemed unfit because of hereditary conditions (Haller 1963, 137). By the end of 1931, over twelve thousand sterilizations had taken place in the United States; by 1958, the number exceeded sixty thousand. A third of all sterilizations occurred in California. A major boost for advocates of sterilization came in 1927 when Justice Oliver Wendell Holmes declared on behalf of the U.S. Supreme Court (*Buck v. Bell*) that "three generations of imbeciles are enough" (qtd. in Haller 1963, 139). The case, with just one dissent, gave the Court's approval to the Virginia sterilization law.

2. The home guard has been defined as "an organized militia of a town, city, county, or state, without a federal obligation. These units are usually liable for service within the jurisdiction of the government that recruited them" (Stentiford 2002, xi). Units of the state guard, on the other hand, were usually forces that "had a statewide obligation and depended on the local and state resources rather than federal. Since World War II, the term has meant organized militia forces of the states without a federal mission. It has been used in the official names of the wartime militia of most states and as a generic term for such exclusively state forces" (Stentiford 2002, xi–xii). Stentiford notes that such terms may have a slightly different meaning depending on context and year.

Chapter 5 | The Transformation Era

1. Ray also discusses how the controversy over creating state-level police in the United States in the early twentieth century involved familiar assumptions regarding racial and gender issues. For example, proponents of the new state-level police forces argued that they were needed to protect white women from the depredations of immigrants and African Americans. On the other hand, opponents of the new forces (a combination of trade unionists, socialists, and rural householders) con-

tended that they were intended to serve as strikebreakers to defeat the "manliness" of honest workmen (see Ray 1995a).

2. Raymond Blaine Fosdick (1883–1972) was a well-known lawyer, police scholar, administrator, and writer. From 1910 to 1913, he served as commissioner of accounts for the city of New York, investigating city and county government in an effort to root out corruption. Thereafter, he was employed by the Bureau of Social Hygiene, funded by John D. Rockefeller Sr., and assigned to prepare a comprehensive study of police work in Europe. Subsequently, he completed a book entitled *European Police Systems* (1915). During America's participation in World War I, Fosdick chaired the Commission on Training Camp Activities of the Army and Navy Department, working to keep morale high among the troops at home and abroad. He also served as a special representative of the War Department in France and as a civilian assistant to Gen. John Joseph Pershing during the Paris Peace Conference. In 1919 and 1920, Fosdick served as undersecretary general for the League of Nations. He became a close associate and legal advisor of John D. Rockefeller Jr. and in 1936 was selected to be the president of the Rockefeller Foundation. Fosdick worked at the Rockefeller Foundation until his retirement in 1948. An important aspect of Fosdick's work for the foundation was the 1933 publication of *Toward Liquor Control:* "Because of Rockefeller's prestige, financial clout, and skillful public relations, [Fosdick's] recommendations were adopted, sometimes verbatim, by many state legislatures, and in modified form by nearly all others. This detailed system of controls and regulatory mechanisms, first put in place, in 1934, remains to this day as the effective and virtually unnoticed system governing the sale of all alcoholic beverages in the United States" (Levine 1994). For further information on Fosdick, see Fosdick 1915, 1958; Fosdick and Scott 1933; Levine 1994; and the Raymond Blaine Fosdick Papers, held by the Princeton University Library and available online at http://infoshare1 .princeton.edu/libraries/firestone/rbsc/finding_aids/fosdick.html#bio.

3. Today, graduates of its successor institution, the New York City Police Academy, may receive thirty college credits when enrolling at the John Jay College of Criminal Justice, a branch of the City University of New York. However, there exists a long-standing controversy within the academic community regarding the advisability of awarding a year of academic credit for attending a police academy for only six months.

4. A notable exception was a period during 1922 when Commissioner Enright ordered the police reserve to serve on regular patrols to cope with a serious crime wave. Upon being mobilized in this manner, the members had all the powers of regular police.

5. For examples, see Reppetto 1978: "One [of these] was Captain Cornelius Willemse. . . . After he retired in 1924, he wrote two books in which he freely admitted using the rubber hose and blackjack as casually as others employed the knife and fork" (176).

Chapter 6 | The Assimilation Era

1. For example, see the following representative Web sites: http://www.topeka
.org/policedepartment/reserve_program.shtml;http://www.lapdonline.org/get_
involved/reserve_program/reserve_program_main.htm; and http://mpdc.dc.gov/
serv/programs/services_PRC.shtm.

2. The birth of the atomic age and the Manhattan Project are well chronicled (see,
e.g., P. S. Boyer 1985; A. C. Brown and Macdonald 1977; Giovannitti and Freed 1965;
Goodchild 1980; Lifton and Mitchell 1995; Rhodes 1986). The atomic bombs that
devastated the Japanese cities of Hiroshima and Nagasaki shortened the war with
Japan, but the toll in human life and suffering was staggering. Only two days after the
first use of the weapon, over Hiroshima, Lewis Mumford declared that the atomic
bomb was so awesome it should never have been deployed (Lifton and Mitchell
1995, 9).

3. La Guardia's office was a precursor of Tom Ridge's Office of Homeland Security,
established in 2001. It took another two years for the U.S. Department of Homeland
Security to be formed, in 2003.

4. It has nevertheless been pointed out that state guard units can be federalized
because nothing in the Constitution prohibits a federal role for state militia, except
that such militias cannot be "drafted en masse into the federal military" (Stentiford
2002, 219).

5. The first reported death of a New York City volunteer police officer took place
during riots on election night in November 1917. Adam Mang, a member of the
Home Defense League of the Twenty-sixth Precinct, was killed by a blow from a brick
thrown while he was assisting police in extinguishing bonfires in the streets of Manhattan. Mang was survived by his wife and three children (two sons, ages fourteen
and twelve, and a daughter, age five). Special Deputy Police Commissioner A. M.
White, head of the Home Defense League, sent out an appeal for funds to assist the
family to league officers throughout the city ("Aid for Rioters' Victim" 1917).

6. NPS volunteers come from all over the United States and the world and serve in
roles related to park interpretation, resource management, visitor orientation and information, maintenance, administration, and protection. In particular, volunteers assist with landscaping and revegetation, gardening, trail maintenance, archaeological
surveys, oral-history and living-history projects and programs, digital photography,
and school-outreach programs. Some volunteers may also participate in safety patrols, search-and-rescue operations, and wilderness firefighting (NPS 2002, 5, 9–10).

Chapter 7 | Potential Roles for Volunteer Police Service

1. Berkley believed that if police were properly oriented, they could invigorate
rather than detract from American democracy. In his classic study *The Democratic
Policeman* (1969), Berkley, having observed police organizations throughout Europe

and the United States, strongly endorsed the value of volunteer police work, linking it to the promotion of democratic values and institutions.

2. In New York City, the practice of holding officers in reserve lasted until the late summer of 1929. At that time, reserve duty required police officers to serve eight additional hours every fifth day by passing time in the station house until something unexpected required their attention. The officers were eventually replaced by emergency service vehicles with crews of six to ten men. The first police emergency trucks, painted red and resembling big fire wagons, were equipped with machine guns, tear gas, riot guns, ropes, and tools of all kinds. The trucks and their crews were housed at convenient locations throughout the city ("Add Five Emergency Trucks" 1929; "Police Rank and File" 1929).

3. Of course, there is no guarantee that every volunteer police officer will turn out to be an asset. Since 2002, auxiliary and reserve police have been arrested for a variety of crimes, including assault, drug trafficking, theft, disorderly conduct, and possession of child pornography. These arrests took place in South Carolina, Texas, New York, Massachusetts, Indiana, Tennessee, and Florida (see "Auxiliary Cop Busted" 2002; "New England in Brief" 2002; "North Texas Fire" 2003; "Cop Busted" 2004; Bandler 2004; "Shelby County Sheriff's Office" 2004; Pring 2004; Great Falls 2004). Perhaps the most infamous former auxiliary officer is David Berkowtiz, whose birth name was Richard David Falco. Shortly after his birth in 1953, he was adopted by Nathan and Pearl Berkowtiz, a childless couple from the Bronx, New York. Prior to 1971 and his enlistment in the U.S. Army, Berkowitz was an auxiliary fireman and also did some training as an auxiliary police officer at the local Forty-fifth Precinct. In the mid-1970s, he killed six people, mostly in parked cars in "lovers' lanes." He came to be known as "Son of Sam" as a result of a name he used in a letter that he left at one of his crime scenes ("Infamous Serial Killers" 2004; "David's Life" 2004). Berkowitz was sentenced to six life terms. Later, the "Son of Sam Law" was passed in New York and other states to restrict the ability of convicted criminals to profit from the sale of books or other accounts relating to their crimes (Oats 1998).

Chapter 8 | The Role of Volunteer Police in Terrorism Prevention

1. The Molly Maguires (a secret organization of Irish miners), and later the Western Federation of Mineworkers, had engaged in the commission of violent acts in the name of exploited members of the working class. During the 1870s, the Molly Maguires used terror tactics in the hard-coal region of eastern Pennsylvania to oppose the abuses of mine owners and their private police (Broehl 1964).

2. The U.S. Commission on National Security/Twenty-first Century was initiated out of the conviction that the entire range of U.S. national security policies and processes required examination in light of new circumstances. The panel was led by former U.S. senators Warren B. Rudman and Gary Hart. It called for a major overhaul of the security apparatus of the nation. The work of the commission was conducted

in three phases. In July 1998, the first phase produced a report describing the future security environment of the United States. The second phase produced a strategy to address the future, and the third focused on changes to the structures and processes of national security. Copies of the reports produced as a result of each phase are available at http://www.au.af.mil/au/awc/awcgate/nssg/. These documents provide a detailed analysis of the national security system and the commission's recommendations for change.

3. Photo images of the World Trade Center site were posted at http://www.capnhq.gov.

4. The federal law contains a variety of provisions related to child protection. For example, it provides for a mandatory life sentence for twice-convicted sexual offenders; denies pretrial release for alleged child abductors; expands federal prosecutors' ability to obtain wiretaps for monitoring suspected sex crimes, including pornography, kidnapping, prostitution, and sex trafficking; and extends the statute of limitations for child abductions and sex crimes. Included in the bill is a section known as "Suzanne's Law." This measure requires law enforcement agencies to notify the National Crime Information Center of missing persons younger than twenty-one years. Under previous rules, the age was eighteen. The measure is named for Suzanne Lyall, who disappeared in 1998 from the University at Albany's New York campus, when she was nineteen years old (Eilperin and Dewar 2003).

5. Of course, such technology is also available to the general public. Ranchers belonging to the "American Border Patrol," a private group in southern Arizona, along the border with Mexico, are using the latest computer technology to catch and detain illegal immigrants. Prior to the beginning of a patrol, a briefing is usually held using 3-D animated maps projected onto a big screen. In this way, members can become familiar with the exact locations to which they will be assigned. In addition, once in the field, members set up mobile microwave and satellite links and communicate with each other using Rino GPS-equipped radios. While members are on patrol, everything is videotaped so that it can be quickly posted on the group's Web site. According to Roger Barnett, a patrol member, the group detained and turned over to the U.S. Border Patrol nearly ten thousand illegal immigrants during the last four or five years (see Goldman 2003).

6. For the latest information on state programs, visit the official site of the ATA at http://www.highwaywatch.com/index.html.

7. The AOPA's toll-free hotline is 1-866-GA-SECURE. A recommended list of security precautions for the airport watch program, and related information, can be found at AOPA's official Web site: http://www.aopa.org/asn/watchindex.shtml.

8. The numbers in parentheses refer to the page numbers in the report where the commission's original recommendations can be found (9/11 Commission 2004).

REFERENCES

Abadinsky, H. 1997. *Drug abuse: An introduction.* Chicago: Nelson-Hall.

Abrahamson, J. 1983. *The American home front.* Washington, D.C.: National Defense University Press.

Add five emergency trucks. 1929. *New York Times,* August 6.

Aid for rioters' victim. 1917. *New York Times,* November 16.

Albanese, J. S. 1999. *Criminal justice.* Boston: Allyn and Bacon.

Allen, E. 1979. *The black ships: Rumrunners of Prohibition.* Boston: Little, Brown.

Allen, S. 2001. Making a difference: Volunteers float riverkeepers' boat. *Oregonian,* September 27.

Alpert, G. P., and R. G. Dunham. 1992. *Policing urban America.* 2d ed. Prospect Heights, Ill.: Waveland Press.

Alter, J. 1997. Powell's new war. *Newsweek,* April 28, 28–34.

Anderson, C. 1989. Auxiliary police not immune from suit under old state law. *New York Law Journal* 201 (101): 1–2.

Andrews, C. S. 1904. Private societies and the enforcement of the criminal law. *Forum* 36 (October): 280–88.

Andrist, R. 1973. Paladin of purity. *American Heritage* 24 (6): 4–7, 84–89.

Archibold, R. C. 2000. Celebrating a milestone for freedom. *New York Times,* January 1.

Arpaio, J., and L. Sherman. 1996. *America's toughest sheriff: How to win the war against crime.* Arlington: Summit Publishing.

Asbury, H. 1968. *The great illusion: An informal history of Prohibition.* Westport, Conn.: Greenwood Press.

Austin, D., and J. Braaten. 1991. Turning lives around: Portland youth find a new PAL. *Police Chief* 58 (5): 36–38.

Auxiliary cop busted in attack. 2002. *New York Post,* April 3.

Auxiliary police union praises members after 9-11 attack. 2001. *Civil Service Sentinel,* November 5, 3.

Bailey, F., and A. Green. 1999. *"Law never here": A social history of African American responses to issues of crime and justice.* Westport, Conn.: Praeger.

Bales, K. 1999. *Disposable people: New slavery in the global economy.* Berkeley: University of California Press.

Ball, L. 1978. *The United States marshals of New Mexico and Arizona territories.* Albuquerque: University of New Mexico Press.

Baltimore County Police Auxiliary Unit. 2003. Volunteers in service to Baltimore County. http://www.co.ba.md.us/Agencies/police/auxil.html (accessed January 5, 2005).

Bandler, J. 2004. Two $1M theft suspects auxiliary police. *New York Journal News,* June 18. http://www.nyjournalnews.com/newsroom/061804/a0118armored. html (accessed July 20, 2004).

Bannach, H. E. 1941. Police cadet organization. *School Activities* 12 (9): 353–54.

Bard, M., and R. Shellow. 1976. *Issues in law enforcement: Essays and case studies.* Reston, Va.: Reston Publishing.

Barker, M. L. 1994. American Indian tribal police: An overview and case study. Ph.D. diss., State University of New York at Albany.

Barker, S. 2002. CAP chief ready for stepped-up role. *Knoxville News-Sentinel,* December 30.

Bayley, D. H. 1985. *Patterns of policing: A comparative international analysis.* New Brunswick, N.J.: Rutgers University Press.

———. 1994. *Police for the future.* New York: Oxford University Press.

Beisel, N. 1997. *Imperiled innocents: Anthony Comstock and family reproduction in Victorian America.* Princeton: Princeton University Press.

Benjamin, D. 2003. The portable threat. *Pittsburgh Post-Gazette,* November 16.

Bennett, C. E. 1981. Let the military join the anti-drug posse. *New York Times,* July 7.

Bennett, D. R. 1971. *Anthony Comstock: His career of cruelty and crime.* New York: Da Capo Press. (Orig. pub. 1878.)

Bennett-Sandler, G. 1979. Citizen participation in policing: Issues in the social control of a social control agency. In *Critical issues in criminal justice,* ed. R. G. Iacovetta and D. H. Chang. Durham: Carolina Academic Press. 246–65.

Berg, B., and W. Doerner. 1988. Volunteer police officers: An unexamined personnel dimension in law enforcement. *American Journal of Police* 7 (1): 81–89.

Berg, G. 2000. Blessed by the unsung heroes. *Reserve News* 17 (7–8): 6.

Berkley, G. 1969. *The democratic policeman.* Boston: Beacon Press.

Berne, E. 1964. *Games people play: The psychology of human relationships.* New York: Grove.

Bertelsen V. C., Jr. 2001. Thanks from the commandant. October 2. http://www .cgaux.org/cgauxweb/tbbridge.shtml (accessed January 1, 2002).

Beth, L. P. 1971. *The development of the American Constitution, 1877–1917.* New York: Harper and Row.

Beukema, H. 1982. The social and political aspects of conscription: Europe's experience. In *The military draft: Selected readings in conscription,* ed. M. Anderson and B. Honegger. Stanford, Calif.: Hoover Institute. 479–91.

Bigham, W. 2001. Lake Wylie's new keeper to lead watery neighborhood watch program. *Rock Hill (S.C.) Herald,* December 11.

Bill Brogan's boys. 1945. *Time,* January 1, 48.

Blacksburg Police Department. 1949. Boys do police work. http://spec.lib.vt.edu/bicent/timeline/police/boycops.htm (accessed July 30, 2000).

Blocker J. S., Jr. 1976. *Retreat from reform: The Prohibition movement in the United States, 1890–1913.* Westport, Conn.: Greenwood Press.

———. 1989. *American temperance movements: Cycles of reform.* Boston: Twayne Publishers.

Bocklet, R. 1988. Volunteers aid to better policing. *Law and Order* 36 (1): 180–84.

Bodenhamer, D. J. 1992. *Fair trial: Rights of the accused in American history.* New York: Oxford University Press.

Bohardt, P. 1977. A viable police reserve. *FBI Law Enforcement Journal* 46 (February): 9–15.

Bohm, R. M. 1986. Crime, criminal, and crime control policy myths. *Justice Quarterly* 3 (2): 193–214.

Boney, F. N. 1972. *Slave life in Georgia.* Savannah: Beehive Press. (Orig. pub. 1855.)

Bonsall, D. M. 1993. Volunteers in law enforcement: The coproduction of police services in the community. Master's thesis, University of South Florida.

Bopp, W. J., and D. O. Schultz. 1972. *A short history of American law enforcement.* Springfield, Ill.: Charles C. Thomas.

Boston Police Department. 2004. Positive messages help BPD's junior police academy program to develop youth citizenship. http://www.cityofboston.gov/police/jr_police.asp (accessed January 5, 2005).

Bouza, A. 1993. *How to stop crime.* New York: Plenum Press.

Bowen, C. D. 1986. *Miracle at Philadelphia: The story of the Constitutional Convention, May to September 1787.* Rev. ed. Boston: Little, Brown.

Boyer, P. 1968. *Purity in print: The vice society movement and book censorship in America.* New York: Scribner's.

———. 1978. *Urban masses and moral order in America, 1820–1920.* Cambridge: Harvard University Press.

———. 1985. *By the bomb's early light: American thought and culture at the dawn of the atomic age.* New York: Pantheon.

Boy police of New York. 1915. *Outlook,* July 28, 706–8.

Boy police of New York. 1917. *Literary Digest,* April 28, 1258–59.

Braga, A., D. Kennedy, A. Piehl, and E. Waring. 2001. *Reducing gun violence: The Boston gun project's Operation Ceasefire.* Washington, D.C.: National Institute of Justice, U.S. Department of Justice.

Brantingham, P., and F. Faust. 1976. A conceptual model of crime prevention. *Crime and Delinquency* 22 (3): 284–96.

Bristow, A. P. 1969. *Effective police manpower utilization.* Chicago: Bannerstone House.

Broehl, W. E., Jr. 1964. *The Molly Maguires.* Cambridge: Harvard University Press.

Broun, H., and M. Leech. 1927. *Anthony Comstock: Roundsman of the Lord.* New York: Literary Guild of America.

Brown, A. C., and C. B. Macdonald, eds. 1977. *The secret history of the atomic bomb.* New York: Delta.

Brown, E. 1976. The police reserve officer in Dallas, Texas. *Texas Police Journal* 24 (June): 5–8, 15.

Brown, L. P. 1988. Strategies for dealing with crack houses. *FBI Law Enforcement Bulletin* 57 (6): 4–7.

Brown, R. M. 1969. The American vigilante tradition. In *The history of violence in America: Historical and comparative perspectives,* ed. H. D. Graham and T. R. Gurr. New York: Praeger. 154–226.

———. 1971. Legal and behavioral perspectives on American vigilantism. In *Perspectives in American history.* Cambridge, Mass.: Charles Warren Center for Studies in American History at Harvard University. 5: 95–144.

———. 1975. *Strain of violence: Historical studies of American violence and vigilantism.* New York: Oxford University Press.

Browne, R. B., and L. A. Kreiser, Jr. 2003. *The Civil War and Reconstruction.* Westport, Conn.: Greenwood Press.

Buckmaster, H. 1941. *Let my people go: The story of the Underground Railroad and the growth of the abolition movement.* New York: Harper and Brothers.

Bunker, T. 2002. Seeking evildoers, and committing evils. *Boston Herald,* August 5.

Burden, O. 1988. Volunteers: The wave of the future? *Police Chief* 55 (7): 25–29.

Bureau of Justice Statistics. 1999. Local police departments, 1997. Washington, D.C.: U.S. Department of Justice, Office of Justice Programs.

Burnham, F. A. 1974. *Hero next door.* Fallbrook, Calif.: Areo Publishers.

Burrows, E., and M. Wallace. 1999. *A history of New York City to 1898.* New York: Oxford University Press.

Burstein, H. 1994. *Introduction to security.* Englewood Cliffs, N.J.: Prentice-Hall.

Bush, G. H. W. 1989. Remarks at the *Commercial Appeal*'s Thanksgiving celebration in Memphis, Tennessee, November 22, 1989. http://bushlibrary.tamu.edu/research/papers/1989/89112200.html (accessed January 1, 2005).

Cagin, S., and P. Dray. 1991. *We are not afraid: The story of Goodman, Schwerner, and Chaney and the civil rights campaign for Mississippi.* New York: Bantam Books.

Call City Patrol Corps to meet crime crisis. 1945. *Brooklyn Eagle,* November 21.

Canada, G. 1995. *Fist stick knife gun: A personal history of violence in America.* Boston: Beacon Press.

CAP history. 2002. http://www.capnhq.gov/nhq/pa/50-2/history.html (accessed February 3, 2002).

CAP news. 2001. http://www.capnhq.gov/nhq/capnews/01-09/news.htm (accessed January 8, 2002).

CAP organization. 2002. http://www.capnhq.gov/nhq/pa/50-2/organization.html (accessed January 8, 2002).

CAP support to LEA. 2002. http://www.capnhq.gov/nhq/do/cd/leaspt.htm (accessed January 8, 2002).

Carnes, M., J. Garraty, and P. Williams. 1996. *Mapping America's past: A historical atlas.* New York: Henry Holt.

Carte, G., and E. Carte. 1975. *Police reform in the United States: The era of August Vollmer, 1905–1932.* Berkeley: University of California Press.

Carter, J. 1975. *Why not the best?* Nashville: Broadman Press.

Cashman, S. D. 1981. *Prohibition: The lie of the land.* New York: Free Press.

Caudry, R. D. 1981. *Department of Defense Civilian/Military Review Board recommendation on the Auxiliary Military Police in World War II.* Washington, D.C.: Office of the Assistant Secretary, Department of the Air Force.

Champion, D., and G. Rush. 1997. *Policing in the community.* Upper Saddle River, N.J.: Prentice-Hall.

Chanen, J. S. 1994. Above and beyond. *ABA Journal* 80 (December): 104.

Chapin, B. 1983. *Criminal justice in colonial America, 1606–1660.* Athens: University of Georgia Press.

Cherrington, E. H. 1969. *The evolution of Prohibition in the United States of America.* Montclair, N.J.: Patterson Smith. (Orig. pub. 1920.)

Chivers, C. J. 2000. Poaching adds new hurdle to police recruiting efforts. *New York Times,* April 6.

Cilluffo, F. J. 2001. Critical infrastructure protection: Who's in charge. Statement to the U.S. Senate Committee on Government Reform, October 4. http://www.iwar.org.uk/cip/resources/senate-oct-04-01/100401cilluffo.htm (accessed January 20, 2005).

The Civil Air Patrol story. 2003. http://www.capnhq.gov/nhq/dpldpm/capstory. PDF (accessed February 17, 2003).

Claiborne, W. 1994. Volunteer police. *Washington Post,* April 14. http://web.wt.net/~tat/wpost.htm (accessed January 2, 2005).

Clark, J. R. 1993. Pulling back the blue curtain. *Law Enforcement News* 19 (388): 1, 6.

Clark, N. 1965. *The dry years: Prohibition and social change in Washington.* Seattle: University of Washington Press.

Classes don't make drivers safer: Study. 1998. *Schenectady Daily Gazette,* January 6.

Coffey, T. 1975. *The long thirst: Prohibition in America, 1920–1933.* New York: W. W. Norton.

Colorado Historical Society. 1994. *An inventory of the records of the Denver Auxiliary*

Police for Civil Defense. Collection No. 198. Library of the Colorado Historical Society, Denver.

Columbus Police Reserve. 2000. http://www.cpdresv.com/cpd/history/1950s.html (accessed August 2, 2000).

Comstock, A. 1967. *Traps for the young.* Cambridge: Harvard University Press. (Orig. pub. 1883.)

Conference on Special Constables. 1987. *Report of the conference on special constables.* London: N.p.

Conley, J. 2003. New Bedford program to help the elderly. *Roanoke Times and World News,* January 22.

Cook, F. J. 1974. Who rules New Jersey? In *Theft of the city,* ed. J. A. Gardiner and D. J. Olson. Bloomington: Indiana University Press. 73–85.

Cop busted in fed narc sting. 2004. http://www.bikernews.net/getnews.cfm?article= 61&drugbust=true (accessed July 19, 2004).

Corbett, B. I. 1931. Junior safety cadets make fine record. *American City,* April, 138.

Cox, B. E. 1972. The role of a police reserve. *Utah Peace Officer* 49 (4): 19–55.

Crelinsten, R. D., D. Laberge-Altmejd, and D. Szabo. 1978. *Terrorism and criminal justice: An international perspective.* Lexington, Mass.: Lexington Books.

Cress, L. D. 1982. *Citizens in arms: The army and the militia in American society to the War of 1812.* Chapel Hill: University of North Carolina Press.

CrimeWeb alert system quickly outgrows its humble Texas roots. 2003. *Law Enforcement News* 29 (599–600): 1, 10.

Critchley, T. 1967. *A history of police in England and Wales.* London: Constable and Co.

Crowe, C. 2001. CAP delivers listening devices, takes more aerial photos. http://www .aetc.randolph.af.mil/pa/AETCNS/Sep2001/01-206.htm (accessed December 12, 2002).

Crump, I. 1917. *The boys' book of policemen.* New York: Dodd, Mead, and Co.

Curriden, M., and L. Phillips. 1999. *Contempt of court: The turn-of-the-century lynching that launched one hundred years of federalism.* New York: Faber and Faber.

Currie, E. 1994. *Reckoning: Drugs, the cities, and the American future.* New York: Hill and Wang.

Cuvillier, L. 1926. Arms for reserve officers. Letter. *New York Times,* August 19.

David's life. 2004. http://www.angelfire.com/oh/yodaspage3/life.html (accessed July 20, 2004).

Debnam, B. 2003. Minutemen and the Declaration: Citizen soldiers. *TV Plus—The Sunday Gazette Supplement,* June 29, 21–24.

Deitch, L., and L. Thompson. 1985. The reserve police officer: One alternative to the need for manpower. *Police Chief* 52 (5): 59–61.

De La Cruz, D. 1999. Residents, officials applaud NYC's plummeting crime rate. *Schenectady Daily Gazette,* January 2.

Deloria, V., Jr., and C. Lytle. 1983. *American Indian, American justice*. Austin: University of Texas Press.

Demaroff, R. C. 1930. Safety instruction and junior patrols. *American City*, April, 156.

De Tocqueville, A. 1957. *Democracy in America*. 2 vols. New York: Vintage Books. (Orig. pub. 1835, 1840.)

Deusch, F. H. 1997. The Providence junior police corps. http://seniortimes.com/nov97/jrpolice.html (accessed August 13, 2000).

DeWitt, D. 2002. Bush touts volunteers as the guardians of America. *St. Petersburg Times*, February 1.

Dionne, E. J. 2003. Mayors see red in orange alerts. *Schenectady Daily Gazette*, June 14.

Dorchester Association for the Detection and Prosecution of Trespassers. 1829. *Regulations of the Dorchester association for the detection and prosecution of trespassers on gardens, fields, in the Town of Dorchester and vicinity*. Boston: Press of Isaac R. Butts.

Douglass, Frederick. 1985. The significance of emancipation in the West Indies. In *The Frederick Douglass papers*, ed. John W. Blassingame. New Haven: Yale University Press. 3: 204. (Orig. pub. 1857.)

Driscoll, G. 1925. Untitled. *McHaught's Magazine*, December, 170.

Driver, H. 1975. *Indians of North America*. 2d ed. Chicago: University of Chicago Press.

Dulaney, W. M. 1996. *Black police in America*. Bloomington: Indiana University Press.

Du Priest, G. H. 1932. The Waseca County horse thief detectives. *Minnesota History* 13 (June): 153–57.

Eckhardt, A. 2001. One thing the public can do. *Times News Weekly*, October 18. http://www.timesnewsweekly.com/OldSite/101801/NewFiles/LETTERS.html (accessed January 1, 2002).

Edinburg C.I.S.D. Police Department. 2000. What is a school Law Enforcement Explorer? http://wysiwyg://fl.216/http://ecisdexplorers.homestead.com/SchoolExplorer~main.html (accessed July 30, 2000).

Eggen, D. 2002. Proposal to enlist citizen spies was doomed from start. *Washington Post*, November 24.

Eilperin, J., and H. Dewar. 2003. Congress establishes nationwide Amber Alert system. *Schenectady Daily Gazette*, April 11.

Elder rights and resources. 2004. http://www.aoa.gov/eldfam/Elder_Rights/LTC/LTC_pf.asp (accessed July 31, 2004).

Engelmann, L. 1979. *Intemperance: The lost war against liquor*. New York: Free Press.

Esbensen, F., and D. Osgood. 1997. *Research in brief: National evaluation of GREAT*. Washington, D.C.: National Institute of Justice, U.S. Department of Justice.

Evans, C. 1998. History: Guarding our assets. http://www.h2oweek.com/history/19981119/hist/hist.html (accessed December 12, 2002).

FBI. 2005. History of the FBI. http://www.fbi.gov//libref/historic/history/historymain .htm (accessed January 18, 2005).

Federal Motor Carrier Safety Administration. 2002. U.S. Transportation Secretary Mineta applauds contributions of truck drivers. Press release. August 16. http://www.fmcsa.dot.gov/contactus/press/2002/081602.htm (accessed October 2, 2002).

FEMA/CERT. 2001. Use of CERT skills in emergency situations. June 15. http://www .fema.gov/emi/cert/examp.htm (accessed January 7, 2002).

FEMA/EMI. 1997a. Community Emergency Response Team (CERT). September 5. http://www.fema.gov/emi/cert/prog.htm (accessed December 17, 2001).

———. 1997b. Community Emergency Response Team program maintenance. September 5. http://www.fem.gov/emi/cert/prgmnt.htm (accessed December 17, 2001).

———. 1999. Community Emergency Response Teams, Arizona. July 22. http://www .fema.gov/emi/cert/c_az.htm (accessed December 17, 2001).

———. 2001. Community Emergency Response Teams, New Jersey. February 22. http://www.fema.gov/emi/cert/c_nj.htm (accessed December 12, 2001).

Fighting the slave trade. 2000. *Washington Post*, April 17.

Fisher, K. L. 1999. Letter to the editor. *New York Times*, February 8.

Flanders, R. B. 1933. *Plantation slavery in Georgia*. Chapel Hill: University of North Carolina Press.

Fogelson, R. 1977. *Big-city police*. Cambridge: Harvard University Press.

Foner, E. 1998. *The story of American freedom*. New York: W. W. Norton.

Fosdick, R. 1915. *European police systems*. New York: Century Company.

———. 1920. *American police systems*. New York: Century Book Company.

———. 1958. *Chronicle of a generation: An autobiography*. New York: Harper

Fosdick, R., and A. Scott. 1933. *Toward liquor control*. New York: Harper.

Franklin, J. H., and I. Starr. 1967. *The Negro in twentieth century America: A reader on the struggle for civil rights*. New York: Vintage Books.

Freeh, L. J. 1996. What can be done about terrorism? *USA Today Magazine*, January 1, 24.

French, L. 1982. *Indians and criminal justice*. Totowa, N.J.: Allanheld, Osmon, and Co.

Friedman, L. M. 1993. *Crime and punishment in American history*. New York: Basic Books.

Friedman, W. 1998. Volunteerism and the decline of violent crime. *Journal of Law and Criminology* 88 (4): 1453–74.

Fuchs, L. H. 1983. *Hawaii pono: A social history*. San Diego: Harcourt Brace Jovanovich.

Gardinier, B. 1998. Guard helps battle narcotics. *Albany Times Union*, May 21.

Garry, E. 1980. *Volunteers in the criminal justice system: A literature review and se-*

lected bibliography. Washington, D.C.: National Institute of Justice, U.S. Department of Justice.

Gaseau, M. 2002. Double duty: Neighborhood watch members groomed as emergency-response volunteers. *Sheriff* 54 (5): 35.

Gertzman, J. A. 1994. John Saxton Sumner of the New York Society for the Suppression of Vice: A chief smut-eradicator of the interwar period. *Journal of American Culture* 17 (2): 41–47.

Gibson, L. 1954. *The coming of the American Revolution, 1763–1776.* New York: Harper and Row.

Gill, M., and R. Mawby 1990. *Special constables: A study of the police reserve.* Aldershot, England: Gower Publishing.

Gilmore, G. J. 2001. Coast guard on guard, to meet terrorism threat. U.S. Department of Defense, American Forces Information Service. November 1. http://www .defenselink.mil/news/Nov2001/n11012001_200111011.html (accessed January 1, 2002).

Giovannitti, L., and F. Freed. 1965. *The decision to drop the bomb.* New York: Howard-McCann.

Gipson, L. H. 1954. *The coming of the Revolution: 1763–1775.* New York: Harper and Brothers.

Goldman, J. 2003. Border vigilance or vigilantism? http://abcnews.go.com (accessed May 28, 2003).

Goldstein, H. 1990. *Problem-oriented policing.* New York: McGraw-Hill.

Goldstein, R. J. 1978. *Political repression in modern America: From 1870 to the present.* Cambridge, Mass.: Schenkman Publishing.

Goodchild, P. 1980. *J. Robert Oppenheimer: Shatterer of worlds.* New York: Houghton-Mifflin.

Gordy, M. 2000. A call to fight forced labor. *Parade,* February 20, 4–5.

Grabosky, P. N. 1992. Law enforcement and the citizen: Non-governmental participants in crime prevention and control. *Policing and Society* 2:249–71.

———. 1997. Junior cops on the city's blocks: Law Enforcement Explorers gain leadership, policing skills. http://detroitnews.com/1997/detroit/9703/19/03130030.htm (accessed August 3, 2000).

———. 1998. *Drug crazy: How we got into this mess and how we can get out.* New York: Random House.

Great Falls officer arrested. 2004. http://www.charlotte.com/mld/charlotte/news/ breaking_news/9099627.htm?1c (accessed July 19, 2004).

Green, E. 1997. Origins of American policing: Slave patrols in South Carolina from colonial times to 1865. Ph.D. diss., Howard University.

Greenberg, D. 1976. *Crime and law enforcement in the colony of New York, 1691–1776.* Ithaca: Cornell University Press.

Greenberg, M. A. 1984. *Auxiliary police: The citizen's role in public safety.* Westport, Conn.: Greenwood Press.

———. 2001. The evolution of volunteer police in America. Ph.D. diss., City University of New York.

———. 2003. Citizen police: A valuable resource for America's homeland security. *Journal of Security Administration* 26 (1): 25–37.

Greenberg, M. A., and K. Cooper. 1996. Unused secret weapon against terrorism. *Law Enforcement News* 22 (455): 12, 14.

Guarding five million children. 1932. *School Life,* September 7, 18.

Gurr, T. R. 1989. Political terrorism: Historical antecedents and contemporary trends. In *Violence in America,* vol. 2, *Protest, rebellion, reform,* ed. T. R. Gurr. Newbury Park, Calif.: Sage. 201–30.

Gurteen, S. H. 1882. *A handbook of charity organization.* Buffalo: Charity Organization Society of the City of Buffalo.

Gusfield, J. R. 1963. *Symbolic crusade: Status politics and the American temperance movement.* Urbana: University of Illinois Press.

Hadden, S. E. 1993. Law enforcement in a new nation: Slave patrols and public authority in the old South, 1700–1865. Ph. D. diss., Harvard University.

———. 2001. *Slave patrols: Law and violence in Virginia and the Carolinas.* Cambridge: Harvard University Press.

Hagan, W. 1966. *Indian police and judges: Experiments in acculturation and control.* New Haven: Yale University Press.

Hageman, M. J. 1985. *Police community relations.* London: Sage.

Hall, K. L. 1989. *The magic mirror: Law in American history.* New York: Oxford University Press.

Haller, M. 1963. *Eugenics: Hereditarian attitudes in American thought.* New Brunswick, N.J.: Rutgers University Press.

Halpern, T., D. Rosenberg, and I. Sual. 1996. Militia movement: Prescription for disaster. *USA Today Magazine,* January 1, 16.

Hamm, R. F. 1994. Administration and prison suasion: Law enforcement in the American temperance movement, 1880–1920. *Contemporary Drug Problems* 21 (3): 375–99.

———. 1995. *Shaping the Eighteenth Amendment: Temperance reform, legal culture, and the polity, 1880–1920.* Chapel Hill: University of North Carolina Press.

Hammond, W. F., Jr. 2001. One hundred and two retired state troopers back on duty. *Schenectady Daily Gazette,* December 19.

Haner, J. 2001. Ships vulnerable due to shaky port security. *Schenectady Daily Gazette,* October 28.

Harmon, C. C. 2000. *Terrorism today.* London: Frank Cass Publishers.

Harring, S. 1983. *Policing a class society: The experience of American cities, 1865–1915.* New Brunswick, N.J.: Rutgers University Press.

Harris, J. 1994. *This drinking nation.* New York: Macmillan.

Hartmann, F. X., ed. 1988. *Debating the evolution of American policing: An edited transcript to accompany "The evolving strategy of policing."* Perspectives on Policing 5. Washington, D.C.: National Institute of Justice, U.S. Department of Justice, and Harvard University.

Hashagan, P. 1998. Firefighting in colonial America. http://www.firehouse.com/magazine/american/colonial.html (accessed July 5, 2003).

Hassrick, R. 1964. *The Sioux: Life and customs of a warrior society.* Norman: University of Oklahoma Press.

Hastie, W. H. 1973. Toward an equalitarian legal order, 1930–1950. *Annals* 407 (May): 18–31.

Hayeslip, D. 1989. Local level drug health, enforcement: New strategies. *NIJ Reports* 213 (March–April): 2–7.

Healy, G. 2002. Beware of amateur spies. *Milwaukee Journal Sentinel,* July 25.

Hebert, E. 1993. NIJ's drug market analysis program. *NIJ Journal* 226 (April): 2–7.

Henderson, D. F. 1985. *Congress, courts, and criminals: The development of federal criminal law, 1801–1829.* Westport, Conn.: Greenwood Press.

Henderson, W. C. 1976. The slave court system in Spartanburg County. In *The Proceedings of the South Carolina Historical Association.* Columbia, S.C.: N.p. 24–38.

Henry, M. A. 1968. *The police control of the slave in South Carolina.* New York: Negro Universities Press.

Henry, V. F. 2002. *The COMPSTAT paradigm: Management accountability in policing, business, and the public sector.* Flushing, N.Y.: Looseleaf Law Publications.

Hentoff, N. 2002. Joe Lieberman joins big brother. *Village Voice,* August 20, 28.

Hess, K., and H. Wrobleski. 1996. *Introduction to private security.* 4th ed. St. Paul: West Publishing.

Hewitt, B., and W. Siew. 1998. In the trenches. *People Weekly,* November 23, 143–44.

Hill-Holtzman, N. 1992. Williams hails role of reservists. *Los Angeles Times,* August 13.

Hipp, M. 2000. Glenville firefighter recruitment falls short; problem longstanding. *Sunday Gazette,* April 30.

History: 1998. 2002. http://www.hagerstownmd.org/Police/history.asp (accessed January 18, 2005).

Hodges, G. R. 1998. *Security, freedom and culture among early American workers.* Armonk, N.Y.: M. E. Sharpe.

Hoebel, E. A. 1954. *The law of primitive man.* Cambridge: Harvard University Press.

———. 1968. *The law of primitive man: A study in comparative legal dynamics.* New York: Atheneum.

Hoffman, B. 1998. *Inside terrorism.* New York: Columbia University Press.

Hofstadter, R. 1955. *The age of reform: From Bryan to F.D.R.* New York: Vintage Books.

———. 1968. *The Progressive historians: Turner, Beard, Parrington.* New York: Knopf.

Hofstadter, R., W. Miller, and D. Aaron. 1972. *The United States.* 3d ed. Englewood Cliffs, N.J.: Prentice-Hall.

Honolulu Police Department. 2000a. HPD reserve officer program. http://www .honolulupd.org/main/reserves.htm (accessed July 30, 2000).

———. 2000b. Junior police officers. http://www.honolulupd.org/history/museum/ mu15.htm (accessed July 30, 2000).

Horan, J. D. 1967. *The Pinkertons: The detective dynasty that made history.* New York: Crown Publishers.

Hough, E. 1919. *The web.* Chicago: Reilly and Lee.

Hovey, E. B. 1998. Stamping out smut: The enforcement of obscenity laws, 1872–1915. Ph.D. diss., Columbia University.

Howell, J. 1998. *Youth gangs: An overview.* Washington, D.C.: Office of Juvenile Justice and Delinquency Prevention, U.S. Department of Justice.

Hoxie, F. 1986. Towards a new North American Indian legal history. *American Journal of Legal History* 30 (October): 351–52.

Humeyumptewa, A. 1994. *An inventory of the records of the Denver Auxiliary Police for Civil Defense.* Denver: Colorado Historical Society.

Humphrey, N. 1942. Police and tribal welfare in plains and Indian culture. *Journal of Criminal Law and Criminology* 33:147–61.

Huppke, R. 1999. Drug smuggling on interstates a challenge for cops. *Albany Sunday Times Union,* January 17.

Infamous serial killers: Son of Sam. 2004. http://faculty.ncwc.edu/toconnor/428/ case01.htm (accessed July 20, 2004).

Jacobs, J. 1961. *The death and life of great American cities.* New York: Vintage Books.

Janofsky, M. 1998. Delaware driver's licenses to note sex offenders. *New York Times,* April 21.

Jenkins, B. M. 1980. International terrorism: Trends and potentialities. In *International terrorism: Current research and future directions,* ed. A. D. Buckley and D. O. Olson. Wayne, N.J.: Avery Publishing Group. 101–7.

Jennings, J. 1974. *Prehistory of North America.* New York: McGraw-Hill.

Jensen, J. M. 1968. *The price of vigilance.* Chicago: Rand McNally and Co.

Jensen, M. 1998. Volunteers can make a difference. *Law and Order* 46 (9): 102–5.

Johnson, D. 1981. *American law enforcement: A history.* St. Louis: Forum Press.

Johnson, G. G. 1937. *Ante-bellum North Carolina: A social history.* Chapel Hill: University of North Carolina Press.

Johnson, H. A., and N. T. Wolfe. 1996. *History of criminal justice.* Rev. ed. Cincinnati: Anderson.

Johnson, R. C. 1973. Anthony Comstock: Reform, vice, and the American way. Ph.D. diss., University of Wisconsin, Madison.

Jordan, W. T. 1998. Citizens' police academies. Ph.D. diss., Florida State University.

Joseph, M. 1926. Letter to the editor. *New York Times,* August 18.

Junior police. 1922. *Playground,* January, 631.

Juvenile coppettes. 1916. *Literary Digest,* June 10, 1735–36.

Kakalik, J., and S. Wildhorn. 1977. *The private police: Security and danger.* New York: Crane Russak.

Karmen, A. 1990. *Crime victims: An introduction to victimology.* Rev. ed. Pacific Grove, Calif.: Brooks/Cole.

Kars, M. 2002. *Breaking loose together: The Regulator Rebellion in pre-Revolutionary North Carolina.* Chapel Hill: University of North Carolina Press.

Kastberg, S. 1998. Watching the water. *Albany Times Union,* August 2.

Katz, M. B. 1996. *In the shadow of the poorhouse: A social history of welfare in America.* Rev. ed. New York: Basic Books.

Katz, W. L. 1990. *Breaking the chains: African-American slave resistance.* New York: Atheneum.

Kay, M. L., and L. L. Cary. 1995. *Slavery in North Carolina, 1748–1775.* Chapel Hill: University of North Carolina Press.

Kelling, G., and M. Moore. 1988. *The evolving strategy of policing.* Perspectives on Policing 4. Washington, D.C.: National Institute of Justice, U.S. Department of Justice, and Harvard University.

Kelling, G., and J. Stewart. 1989. *Neighborhoods and police: The maintenance of civil authority.* Perspectives on Policing 10. Washington, D.C.: National Institute of Justice, U.S. Department of Justice, and Harvard University.

Kerr, K. A. 1985. *Organized for Prohibition: A new history of the Anti-Saloon League.* New Haven: Yale University Press.

Kessler, R. 1993. *The FBI.* New York: Pocket Books.

King, C. 2000. The safety bunch. *Car and Travel* 6 (8): 16–18.

King, E. M. 1960. *The auxiliary police unit.* Springfield, Ill.: Charles C. Thomas.

Klockars, C. 1985. *The idea of police.* Beverly Hills: Sage.

Kowalski, J. 2000. Grant aimed at guns: U.S. attorney gets money to prosecute firearms crimes. *Schenectady Daily Gazette,* June 1.

Krainik, P. W. 2002. Amber alert. *Law and Order* 50 (12): 84–85.

Krebs, A. 1975. Harry J. Anslinger dies at eighty-three: Hard-hitting foe of narcotics. *New York Times,* November 18.

Krueger, G. 2001. Canoochee River gets Georgia's fifth riverkeeper. *Augusta (Ga.) Chronicle,* December 29.

Kyvig, D. 1979. *Repealing national Prohibition.* Chicago: University of Chicago Press.

Lab, S. 1992. *Crime prevention: Approaches, practices and evaluations.* 2d ed. Cincinnati: Anderson.

———. 2000. *Crime prevention: Approaches, practices and evaluation.* 4th ed. Cincinnati: Anderson.

Lake George watchdog to debut. 2003. *Schenectady Daily Gazette,* July 11.

Lane, R. 1967. *Policing the city: Boston, 1822–1885.* Cambridge: Harvard University Press.

Laqueur, W. 1977. *Terrorism.* Boston: Little, Brown, and Co.

Lardner, J., and T. Repetto. 2000. *NYPD: A city and its police.* New York: Henry Holt.

Lenkowsky, L. 2000. Still "bowling alone"? Review of *Bowling alone,* by R. Putnam. *Commentary,* October, 57–60.

Leon, C. K. 1991. Special constables: An historical and contemporary survey. Ph.D. diss., University of Bath.

Lesce, T. 1985. Reserves in small departments. *Law and Order* 33 (6): 33–38.

Levine, H. G. 1994. Drug commissions, the next generation: "To boldly go where no commission has gone before." http://www.hereinstead.com/sys-tmpl/drugcommissionswideforprinting/ (accessed January 19, 2005).

Levy, L. W. 1999. *Origins of the Bill of Rights.* New Haven: Yale University Press.

Lifton, R. J., and G. Mitchell. 1995. *Hiroshima in America: A half century of denial.* New York: Avon Books.

Littlepage, R. L. 2001. Riverkeeper important in protecting the St. Johns. *Florida Times-Union,* September 28.

Litwack, L. F. 1979. *Been in the storm so long: The aftermath of slavery.* New York: Knopf.

Livingstone, N. C., and T. E. Arnold. 1986. Democracy under attack. In *Fighting back: Winning the war against terrorism,* ed. N. C. Livingstone and T. E. Arnold. Lexington, Mass.: Lexington Books, D. C. Heath and Co. 1–10.

Lorant, S. 1975. *Pittsburgh: The story of an American city.* Lenox, Mass.: N.p.

Los Angeles County Sheriff's Department. 2000. LASD reserve strength. *Reserve News* 17 (7–8): 2.

Lovins, A., and L. Hunter. 1995. Reinventing the wheels. *Atlantic Monthly,* January, 75–86.

Lowry, F. 1981. Civil Air Patrol: Three who were there. *Aerospace Historian* 28 (4): 268–74.

Lubove, R. 1962. *The Progressives and the slums: Tenement house reform in New York City, 1890–1917.* Pittsburgh: University of Pittsburgh Press.

Lundy, M. 1952. A real copper's badge for junior. *Reader's Digest,* June, 127–30.

LVMPD. 2001–5. About us. http://www.lvmpdsar.com/team.html (accessed January 17, 2005).

Mails, T. 1972. *The mystic warriors of the plains.* New York: Doubleday.

———. 1973. *Dog soldiers, bear men and buffalo women: A study of the societies and cults of the Plains Indians.* Upper Saddle River, N.J.: Prentice-Hall.

Maller, P. 2003. Civil Air Patrol taking on terror. *Milwaukee Journal-Sentinel,* February 17.

Manchester, W. 1974. *The glory and the dream: A narrative history of America.* 2 vols. Boston: Little, Brown, and Co.

Manning, P. K. 1977. *Police work: The social organization of policing.* Cambridge: MIT Press.

Marx, G. T., and A. Dane. 1976. Community police patrols and vigilantism. In *Vigilante politics,* ed. H. J. Rosenbaum and P. G. Sederberg. Philadelphia: University of Pennsylvania Press. 129–57.

Mason, D. 1988. Increasing services in spite of shrinking revenues. *Law and Order* 36 (6): 31–32.

Massachusetts Anti-Slavery Society. 1970. *Fifteenth annual report, presented to the Massachusetts Anti-Slavery Society by its board of managers, January 27, 1847.* Westport, Conn.: Negro Universities Press. (Orig. pub. 1847.)

Mastrofski, S., R. Parks, and R. Worden. 1998. *Research in brief: Community policing in action: Lessons from an observational study.* Washington, D.C.: National Institute of Justice, U.S. Department of Justice.

McCoy, R. E. 1956. Banned in Boston: The development of literary censorship in Massachusetts. Ph.D. diss., University of Illinois, Chicago.

McGrath, G. 2002. Auxiliary makes coast guard's job a little easier. *Wilmington (N.C.) Morning Star,* March 30.

Mehren, E. 1981. "Old" Old West posse fights crime in Sun City. *Los Angeles Times,* December 27.

Meis, J. F. 1981. *Decision of the Department of Defense Civilian/Military Service Review Board regarding service of Auxiliary Military Police in World War II.* Washington, D.C.: Office of the Secretary, Department of the Air Force.

Melton, J. 2002. AAA celebrates the safety patrol. http://www.aaasouth.com/previous_issues/sep_oct_02/safetypatrol.asp (accessed January 19, 2005).

Mendon, et. al. 1860. *Constitution of the society for detecting horse thieves in the Towns of Mendon, Bellingham and Milford with the names of the officers and members and the amount of funds.* Rev. ed. Milford, Mass.: Milford Press, G. W. Stacy, Printer.

Methvin, E. 1998. Where crime is on the run. *Reader's Digest,* June, 101–5.

Miller, J., M. Stone, and C. Mitchell. 2002. *The cell: Inside the 9/11 plot, and why the FBI and CIA failed to stop it.* New York: Hyperion.

Mitchell, B. 1984. The role of the public in criminal detection. *Criminal Law Review,* August, 459–66.

Mohr, C. L. 1989. Slavery in Oglethorpe County, Georgia, 1773–1865. In *Southern slavery at the state and local level,* ed. P. Finkelman. New York: Garland Publishing. 102–19.

Morgan, E. 1966. *The Puritan family: Religion and domestic relations in seventeenth-century New England.* Rev. ed. New York: Harper and Row.

Morris, E., and A. Hoe. 1988. *Terrorism: Threat and response.* New York: St. Martin's Press.

Munger, E., Jr. 2003. Youths get hands-on look at law enforcement. *Sunday Gazette,* June 22.

Munson, D. 1988. OJJDP funds twenty-one new projects during fiscal year. *NIJ Reports* 213 (March–April): 8–12.

Murray, R. 1969. *The Harding era.* Minneapolis: University of Minnesota Press.

Musarra, R. 2000. Junior police unit first met at the YMCA. http://ohio.com/bj/news/snap/docs/02578.5.htm (accessed August 13, 2000).

National Advisory Commission on Criminal Justice Standards and Goals. 1973. *Report on police.* Washington, D.C.: Government Printing Office.

———. 1976. *Private security: Report of the task force on private security.* Washington, D.C.: U.S. Government Printing Office.

Nelli, H. S. 1976. *The business of crime: Italians and syndicate crime in the United States.* New York: Oxford University Press.

Nevins, A., and H. S. Commager. 1976. *A short history of the United States.* New York: Knopf.

New England in brief, Hampton, N.H.: Auxiliary officer is arrested. 2002. *Boston Globe,* December 21.

Newman, M. 1992. They volunteer to protect and serve. *New York Times,* April 19.

New York City Police Department. 1918. *Annual report for the year 1918.* New York: New York City Police Department.

———. 1919. *Annual report for the year 1919.* New York: New York City Police Department.

———. 1920. *Annual report for the year 1920.* New York: New York City Police Department.

———. 1943. *Annual report for the year 1943.* New York: New York City Police Department.

New York State Disaster Preparedness Commission. 1991. *Auxiliary police guidance manual.* New York: State Emergency Management Office.

New York State Police. 1967. *The New York State Police: The first fifty years, 1917–1967.* Albany: New York State Police.

Nicolosi, A. S. 1968. The rise and fall of the New Jersey vigilant societies. *New Jersey History* 86 (Spring): 29–53.

9/11 Commission. 2004. *The 9/11 Commission report: Final report of the National Commission on Terrorist Attacks upon the United States.* New York: W. W. Norton.

Nolan, P. B. 1987. *Vigilantes on the middle border: A study of self-appointed law enforcement in the states of the upper Mississippi from 1840 to 1880.* New York: Garland Publishing.

North Texas fire, police official nabbed. 2003. *Laredo Morning Times,* April 29.

Norton Detecting Society. 1859. *Constitution of the Norton Detecting Society, formed for the purpose of detecting horse thieves, stolen from any member of said society. To which are added the names of members.* Taunton, Mass.: C. A. Hack, Book, and Job Printer.

NPS. 2002. *Volunteers-in-Parks: FY02 annual report.* Washington, D.C.: National Park Service, U.S. Department of the Interior.

Nye, J. S., Jr. 2001. Government's challenge: Getting serious about terrorism. In *How did this happen? Terrorism and the new war,* ed. J. F. Hoge Jr. and G. Rose. New York: Public Affairs. 199–209.

Oats, D. 1998. Son of Sam is back. http://www.queenscourier.com/archives/1998/lead081298b.htm (accessed July 20, 2004).

Odegard, P. 1966. *Pressure politics: The story of the Anti-Saloon League.* New York: Octagon Books. (Orig. pub. 1928.)

Odem, M. E. 1995. *Delinquent daughters: Protecting and policing adolescent female sexuality in the United States, 1885–1920.* Chapel Hill: University of North Carolina Press.

Off-beat teacher. 1996. *NEA Today* 15 (3): 36.

Office of National Drug Control Policy. 1998. *National drug control strategy, 1998.* Washington, D.C.: Office of National Drug Control Policy.

Olin, C. 2001. An approximate synopsis of multi-mission and overall volunteer effort as of 12/7/02. http://www.cgaux.org/cgauxweb/memtable.shtml (accessed January 1, 2002).

Operation Golden Eagle tops 150,000 hours. 2002. http://www.cgaux.org/cgauxweb/memtable.shtml (accessed January 7, 2002).

Operation TIPS. 2002. Editorial. *Winston-Salem Journal,* August 15, 12.

OSHP Auxiliary. 1992. OSHP Auxiliary reaches fifty-year milestone. *Flying Wheel* 28 (1): 12–13.

Paludan, P.S. 1981. *Victims: A true story of the Civil War.* Knoxville: University of Tennessee Press.

Paramus reserve loses six to full-time positions. 1995. *Shield: N.J.'s Association for Auxiliary and Special Law Enforcement* 4 (1): 30.

Parrish, M. 1992. *Anxious decades: America in prosperity and depression, 1920–1941.* New York: W. W. Norton.

Parsavand, S. 2003. Schumer urges security for trucks be increased. *Schenectady Daily Gazette,* June 24.

Peak, K. J. 1997. *Policing America: Methods, issues, challenges.* 2d ed. Upper Saddle River, N.J.: Prentice-Hall.

Pepinsky, H. 1989. Issues of citizen involvement in policing. *Crime and Delinquency* 35 (3): 458–70.

Percy, S. L. 1979. Citizen coproduction of community safety. In *Evaluating alternative law enforcement policies,* ed. R. Baker and F. Meyer. Lexington, Mass.: Lexington Books. 125–34.

Perloff, R. 2000. The horror that was lynching. *New York Sunday Times,* January 16.

Perrett, G. 1982. *America in the twenties: A history.* New York: Simon and Schuster.

Pickett, D. 2002. Cable guys aren't meant to be U.S. spies. *Chicago Sun-Times,* July 19.

Police rank and file like emergency plan. 1929. *New York Times,* August 20.

Poll: Most Americans would help drug war. 1990. *Cortland (N.Y.) Standard,* January 26.

Pool, B. 1993. Ex–teen idol Bobby Sherman crusades for better first aid. *Los Angeles Times,* January 28.

Pound, R. 1930. *Criminal justice in America.* New York: Henry Holt.

Powers, R. 1987. *Secrecy and power: The life of J. Edgar Hoover.* New York: Free Press.

Prassel, F. 1972. *The western peace officer.* Norman: University of Oklahoma Press.

Pring, D. 2004. Reserve R.B. officer arrested. *Beach Reporter,* May 13. http://tbrnews .nminews.com/articles/2004/05/13/redondo_beach_news/news03.txt (accessed July 20, 2004).

Profile of the auxiliary: Who are these people? 1999. *Spare Wheel,* December, 1–2.

Putnam, R. 2000. *Bowling alone: The collapse and revival of American community.* New York: Simon and Schuster.

Pyszczynski, T., S. Solomon, and J. Greenberg. 2003. *In the wake of 9/11: The psychology of terror.* Washington, D.C.: American Psychological Association.

Quincy auxiliary unit more welcome in Braintree. 1987. *New York Times,* September 13.

Quinn, S. 1991. Hands up! Who wants to volunteer? *Sydney Sunday Telegraph,* August 25.

Quinney, R. 1973. *The problem of crime.* New York: Dodd, Mead, and Co.

Radzinowicz, L. 1956. *A history of English criminal law,* vol. 2, *The enforcement of the law.* London: Stevens and Sons.

Rand Corporation. 1972. *Special purpose public police,* vol. 5. Washington, D.C.: U.S. Government Printing Office.

Raspberry, W. 2000. Colin Powell's strategy for saving kids. *Schenectady Daily Gazette,* April 17.

Ray, G. 1990. Contested legitimacy: Creation of the State Police of New York, 1890–1930. Ph.D. diss., University of California, Berkeley.

———. 1995a. From Cossack to trooper: Manliness, police reform, and the state. *Journal of Social History* 28 (3): 565–86.

———. 1995b. We can stay until hell freezes over: Strike control and the state police in New York, 1919–1923. *Labor History* 36 (3): 403–25.

Reilly, T. 1998. Florida's flying minute men: The Civil Air Patrol, 1941–1943. *Florida Historical Quarterly* 76 (4): 417–38.

Renyhart, J. 1975. Law Enforcement Explorers get involved. *Police Chief* 42 (12): 54.

Reppetto, T. 1978. *The blue parade.* New York: Free Press.

Reserve park ranger (volunteer). 2002. http://www.ci.glendale.ca.us/job.asp?JobID =143 (accessed July 15, 2003).

Rhodes, R. 1986. *The making of the atomic bomb.* New York: Simon and Schuster.

Richardson, J. F. 1970. *The New York police.* New York: Oxford University Press.

———. 1974. *Urban police in the United States.* Port Washington, N.Y.: Kennikat Press.

———. 1979. *The New York police: Colonial times to 1901.* New York: Oxford University Press.

Ricks, T. A., B. G. Tillett., and C. W. Van Meter. 1994. *Principles of security.* 3rd ed. Cincinnati: Anderson.

Roberg, R., J. Crank, and J. Kuykendall. 2000. *Police and society.* 2d ed. Los Angeles: Roxbury.

Roberts, S. 1979. *Order and dispute.* New York: St. Martin's Press.

Robin, G. 1984. *Introduction to the criminal justice system: Principles, procedures, practice.* Rev. ed. New York: Harper and Row.

Rohde, D. 1998. Calling system like "torture" grand jurors urge changes. *New York Times,* October 9.

Rosen, R. 1982. *The lost sisterhood. Prostitution in America, 1900–1918.* Baltimore: Johns Hopkins University Press.

Rosenbaum, D. 1987. The theory and research behind neighborhood watch: Is it a sound fear and reduction strategy? *Crime and Delinquency* 33 (1): 103–34.

———. 1989. Community crime prevention: A review of what is known. In *Police and policing: Contemporary issues,* ed. D. J. Kenney. New York: Praeger. 203–38.

Rosseland, F. M. 1926. Nine years without an injury to children on their way to or from school. *American City,* November, 684.

Rothman, D. 1971. *The discovery of the asylum: Social order and disorder in the new republic.* New York: Little, Brown, and Co.

———. 1980. *Conscience and convenience: The asylum and its alternatives in Progressive America.* New York: Little, Brown, and Co.

Rousey, D. C. 1996. *Policing the southern city: New Orleans, 1805–1889.* Baton Rouge: Louisiana State University Press.

Rumbarger, J. J. 1968. The social origins and function of the political temperance movement in the reconstruction of American society, 1825–1917. Ph.D. diss., University of Pennsylvania.

Runyon, H. L., and R. J. Falzarano. 1983. Establishing an Explorers post. *Police Chief* 50 (9): 18–20.

Safir, H., and E. Whitman. 2003. *Security: Policing your homeland, your state, your city.* New York: St. Martin's Press.

Sann, P. 1957. *The lawless decade: A political history of a great American transition from the World War I armistice and Prohibition repeal and the New Deal.* New York: Bonanza Books.

Schiff, A. 2001a. Aviation security legislation includes modified Schiff provision permitting armed police officers to assist sky marshals. Press release. November 16. http://www.house.gov/apps/list/press/ca27_schiff/111601aviationleg.html (accessed January 1, 2002).

———. 2001b. Congressman Schiff introduces legislation to permit police officers to serve as auxiliary sky marshals. Press release. October 31. http://www.house .gov/apps/list/press/ca27_schiff/103101SkyMarchIntro.html (accessed January 1, 2002).

Schmalleger, F. 1997. *Criminal justice: A brief introduction.* 2d ed. Upper Saddle River, N.J.: Prentice-Hall.

Schmidt, R. J. 1994. Emergency services Explorers. *Law and Order* 42 (12): 37–39.

Schoolboy patrols approved by the president. 1933. *American City,* October, 70.

Schrecker, E. 1998. *Many are the crimes: McCarthyism in America.* Boston: Little, Brown, and Co.

Schulz, D. M. 1995. *From social worker to crime fighter: Women in United States municipal policing.* Westport, Conn.: Praeger.

Schwartz, P. 2003. Sheriff eyes tiny camera for cars. *Schenectady Daily Gazette,* July 4.

Segrave, K. 1995. *Policewomen: A history.* Jefferson, N.C.: McFarland and Co.

Sellinger, M. K. 1983. Explorers focus on crime. *Police Chief* 50 (9): 26–27.

Semmes, R. 1966. *Crime and punishment in early Maryland.* Montclair, N.J.: Patterson Smith. (Orig. pub. 1938.)

Senna, J., and L. Siegel. 1998. *Essentials of criminal justice.* 2d ed. Belmont, Calif.: West/Wadsworth.

Sessions, W. S. 1990. Director's message: Police and citizens working together. *FBI Law Enforcement Bulletin* 59 (10): 1.

Seth, R. 1961. *The specials: The story of the special constabulary in England, Wales and Scotland.* London: Victor Gollancz.

Severn, B. 1969. *The end of the Roaring Twenties: Prohibition and repeal.* New York: Julian Messner.

Shearing, C. D., and P. C. Stenning. 1987. Say "cheese"!: The Disney order that is not so Mickey Mouse. In *Private Policing,* ed. C. D. Shearing and P. C. Stenning. Newbury Park, Calif.: Sage. 317–23.

Shelby County sheriff's office reserve deputy arrested after traffic accident. 2004. http://shelby-sheriff.org/media_releases/reservearrest.htm (accessed July 20, 2004).

Shenon, P. 2003. Homeland security: Senate panel quickly backs Ridge for new antiterror post. *New York Times,* January 18.

Shepnick, P. 2002. T.O.'s VIPs give police break from the routine. *Ventura County Star,* March 18.

Sherman, L. N.d. *Crime file study guide: Neighborhood safety.* Washington, D.C.: National Institute of Justice, U.S. Department of Justice.

Sherman, L., P. Gartin, and M. Buerger. 1989. Hot spots of predatory crime: Routine activities and the criminology of place. *Criminology* 27 (1): 27–55.

Siena Research Institute. 2000. Majority of New Yorkers believe police engage in racial profiling. http://www.siena.edu/sri/results/2000/00%20May%20Justice.htm (accessed January 2, 2005).

Sinclair, A. 1964. *Era of excess: A social history of the Prohibition movement.* New York: Harper Colophon Books.

Slosson, P. 1958. *The great crusade and after: 1914–1928.* Chicago: Quadrangle Books. (Orig. pub. 1930.)

Smith, B. 1949. *Police systems in the United States.* New York: Harper Brothers.

———. 1960. *Police systems in the United States.* 2d ed. New York: Harper and Row.

Smith, D. 1978. *History of firefighting in America: Three hundred years of courage.* New York: Dial Press.

Solomon, J. 2001. Bush order sets line of succession at agencies. *Schenectady Daily Gazette,* December 25.

Sparrow, M. K. 1988. *Implementing community policing.* Perspectives on Policing 9. Washington, D.C.: National Institute of Justice, U.S. Department of Justice, and Harvard University.

Stampp, K. M. 1972. *The peculiar institution.* New York: Knopf.

Steinberg, A. 1989. *The transformation of criminal justice: Philadelphia, 1800–1880.* Chapel Hill: University of North Carolina Press.

Stentiford, B. M. 2002. *The American home guard: The state militia in the twentieth century.* College Station: Texas A&M University Press.

Stevenson, F. 1918. Backing up the police in guarding New York. *Brooklyn Daily Eagle,* August 25.

Stich, P., S. Pingel, and J. Farrell. 1988. *American history and government,* Middletown, N.Y.: N & N Publishing.

Stinchcombe, A. 1990. *Information and organization.* Berkeley: University of California Press.

Stop-and-go kids. 1946. *American Magazine,* November, 164.

Sullivan, M. 1939. *Our times, 1900–1925.* New York: Charles Scribner's Sons.

Sundeen, R., and G. Siegel. 1986. The uses of volunteers by police. *Journal of Police Science and Administration* 14 (1): 449–61.

Swansburg, J. 2002. On the homefront: The Civil Air Patrol. *New York Times,* January 20.

Sweeping ruling cites racial profiling memo. 1999. *New York Times,* December 18.

Sweet, K. 2002. *Terrorism and airport security.* Lewiston, N.Y.: Edwin Mellon Press.

Sydnor, C. M. 1965. *Slavery in Mississippi.* Gloucester, Mass.: Peter Smith.

Tanji, M. 2003. Secret organization is air force auxiliary. http://www.maui.net/~mauinews/aynews2c.htm (accessed July 14, 2003).

Theoharis, A., and J. Cox. 1988. *The boss: J. Edgar Hoover and the great American inquisition.* Philadelphia: Temple University Press.

Thibault, E., L. Lynch, and R. B. McBride 1998. *Proactive police management.* 4th ed. Upper Saddle River, N.J.: Prentice-Hall.

Thompson, T. 1986. *Sex in Middlesex: Popular mores in a Massachusetts County, 1649–1699.* Amherst: University of Massachusetts Press.

Thornton, R. 1987. *American Indians, holocaust and survival.* Norman: University of Oklahoma Press.

Tilley, J. 2003. History of the U.S. Coast Guard Auxiliary. http://www.cgaux.org/cgauxweb/news/auxhist.html (accessed July 1, 2003).

Timberlake, J. H. 1963. *Prohibition and the Progressive movement, 1900–1920.* Cambridge: Harvard University Press.

Timiltry, J. F. 1939. Boston's junior police corps. *Reader's Digest,* June, 132–33.

Timoney, J. 1993. *Neighborhood resource centers.* New York: New York City Police Department.

Traisman, K. 1983. Native law: Law and order among eighteenth century Cherokee, Great Plains, Central Prairie, and Woodland Indians. *American Indian Law Review* 9 (Fall): 273–87.

Trattner, W. I. 1989. *From poor law to welfare state: A history of social welfare in America.* 4th ed. New York: Free Press.

Travis, L. F. 1995. *Introduction to criminal justice.* 2d ed. Cincinnati: Anderson.

Turner, W. 1968. *The police establishment.* New York: Putnam.

United Nations High Commissioner for Human Rights. 1998. Fact Sheet No. 14: Contemporary forms of slavery. http://www.unhchr.ch/htlm/menu6/2/fs14.htm (accessed November 1, 1999).

U.S. Department of Transportation. N.d. *Volunteer to make a difference.* Recruiting brochure. St. Louis: Auxiliary Center, U.S. Coast Guard.

U.S. President's Commission on Law Enforcement and Administration of Justice. 1967. *The challenge of crime in a free society: A report.* Washington, D.C.: U.S. Government Printing Office.

von Kampen, T. 2003. Civil Air Patrol motivates youths to help serve nation. *Omaha World Herald,* March 9.

Ward, R. H. 1990. The multinational investigative task force as a model for counterterrorism. In *International responses to terrorism: New initiatives,* ed. R. H. Ward and A. G. Ezeldin. Chicago: Office of International Criminal Justice, University of Illinois at Chicago. 65–70.

Whalen, G. 1930. *The New York Police College.* New York: New York City Police Department.

Walker, M. 2000. *America reborn: A twentieth-century narrative in twenty-six lives.* New York: Knopf.

Walker, S. 1933. *The night club era.* New York: Blue Ribbon Books.

Walker, S. S. 1976. The urban police in American history: A review of the literature. *Journal of Police Science and Administration* 4 (3): 252.

———. 1977. *A critical history of police reform: The emergence of professionalism.* Lexington, Mass.: D. C. Heath and Co.

———. 1980. *Popular justice: A history of American criminal justice.* New York: Oxford University Press.

———. 1998. *Popular justice: A history of American criminal justice.* Rev. ed. New York: Oxford University Press.

Watkins, C. 1979. An auxiliary force that functions effectively. *Police Chief* 46 (9): 18.

WBFD fire police history. 2002. http://www.panix.com/~keneet/firepolice.htm (accessed January 11, 2002).

Weed, F. J. 1987. Grass-roots activism and the drunk driving issue: A survey of MADD chapters. *Law and Policy* 9 (3): 259–78.

Weinblatt, R. 1993. *Reserve law enforcement in the United States: A national study of state, county and city standards concerning the training and numbers of non-full-time police and sheriff's personnel.* Monmouth Junction, N.J.: New Jersey Auxiliary Police Officers Association and the Center for Reserve Law Enforcement.

———. 2001. Reserves aid rural counties. *Law and Order* 49 (1): 30–32.

Weinstein, N. 2004. Ombudsman volunteers play key role as advocate for elderly in nursing homes. *Senior Lifestyles: Supplement to the Daily Gazette,* July 31.

Weinstein, S. 1995. *The encyclopedia of New York City.* New Haven: Yale University Press.

Wernick, R. 1989. Montesquieu: Architect of American liberty. *Smithsonian* 20 (6): 183–96.

Whipple, L. 1970. *The story of civil liberty in the United States.* New York: Da Capo Press. (Orig. pub. 1927.)

Whisenand, P. 1977. *Crime prevention.* Boston: Holbrook Press.

Wichita Police Department. 2000. Wichita Police Department reserve section. http://www.wichitapolice.com/reserve.htm (accessed July 30, 2000).

Wilkinson, P. 1986. Terrorism versus liberal democracy: The problems of response. In *The new terrorism,* ed. W. Gutteridge. London: Mansell Publishing. 3–28.

Will, G. 1999. Decline in crime rate spasmodic. *Albany Times Union,* August 22.

Williams, H., and P. Murphy. 1990. *The evolving strategy of police: A minority view.* Perspectives on Policing 13. Washington, D.C.: National Institute of Justice, U.S. Department of Justice, and Harvard University.

Wills, G. 2000. Bowling alone: The collapse and revival of American community. Review of *Bowling alone,* by R. Putnam. *American Prospect,* July 17, 34.

Wilson, J. Q. 1975. *Thinking about crime.* New York: Basic Books.

Winright, T. 2001. Bowling alone but not patrolling alone. *FBI Law Enforcement Bulletin* 70 (4): 11–12.

Wood, P. H. 1974. *Black majority: Negroes in colonial South Carolina from 1670 through the Stono Rebellion.* New York: Knopf.

Woodward, C. 1969. On believing what one reads: The dangers of popular revisionism. In *The historian as detective: Essays on evidence,* ed. R. Winks. New York: Harper and Row. 24–38.

Woodward, F. 1986. Use of police auxiliary officers in crowd control situations. *FBI Law Enforcement Bulletin* 55 (2): 19–22.

Wrentham, et. al. 1837. *Constitution of a society in the Towns of Wrentham, Franklin, Medway, Medford, Walpole, Foxborough, Mansfield, and Attleborough, for detecting horse thieves and recovering stolen horses to which are added the names of the officers and members.* Rev. ed. Dedham, Mass.: Mann's Book and Job Office.

Wrobleski, H., and K. Hess. 1997. *Introduction to law enforcement and criminal justice.* 5th ed. St. Paul: West Publishing.

Yanochik, M. A. 1997. Essays on the economics of slavery. Ph.D. diss., Auburn University.

Yellin, E. 2000. Group seeks to overhaul foster care in Tennessee. *New York Times,* May 11.

Zinn, H. 1990. *A people's history of the United States.* New York: Harper Perennial.

INDEX

Adams, Samuel, xvi
Administration on Aging (AoA), 11, 203
African American. *See* black codes; mi-
    norities; racism; slave patrols; slavery
Aircraft Owners and Pilots Association
    (AOPA), 225, 246n7
air safety, 210
Akron, OH, 139–40
al-Qaida, xv, 210
Amber Alert, 219–20
ambulance squads, xvii, 20, 121–22
American Automobile Association (AAA),
    xvi, 10, 133, 136–39, 143
American Bankers Association (ABA),
    143–44
"American Border Patrol," 246n5
American Civil Liberties Union (ACLU),
    63
American Protective League (APL), 6, 13,
    73, 95–104, 107, 144
American Truckers Association (ATA),
    224–25
Anslinger, Harry, 115
Anti–Horse Thief and Detective Societies,
    53–58, 67–69
Anti-Saloon League (ASL), 11, 13–14,
    89–95, 102–4, 107, 144
Arpaio, Joseph, xix–xx, 241n3
Association Against the Prohibition
    Amendment (AAPA), 130–32
Auxier, Anne, 227

Auxiliary Military Police (AMP), 102,
    162–66
auxiliary police: arrested, 245n3; Balti-
    more County, MD, 169; Columbus,
    OH, 155, 172; definitions, 14–16; Den-
    ver, 159–60; New York City, vi, 8, 158–
    59, 167–68, 223; Ohio State Highway
    Patrol, 160–61, 168; Quincy, MA, 11; in
    schools, 188; types, 181; Washington,
    DC, 228; Wichita, KS, 8, 155; World War
    II, 154–66. *See also* Auxiliary Military
    Police; reserve police; volunteer police

Berkley, George, 188, 244n1
Berkowitz, David, 245n3
Bertelsen, Viggo, Jr., 215
black codes, 50–51
Blacksburgh, VA, 8
Block, Sherman, 207
Bogart, Humphrey, xvi, 158
Borman, Frank, xvi
Boston, 10–11, 120–21, 138–39, 222
Boston Gun Control Project, 179, 194–95
Boylan, Malcolm, 156
Boy Scouts of America (BSA), 7, 120, 135;
    Law Enforcement Explorers, 10, 141–
    43, 145
Briggs, Albert M., 96–97
Brogan, William, 140
Brown, Lee P., 193–94
Bush, George H. W., 20, 191